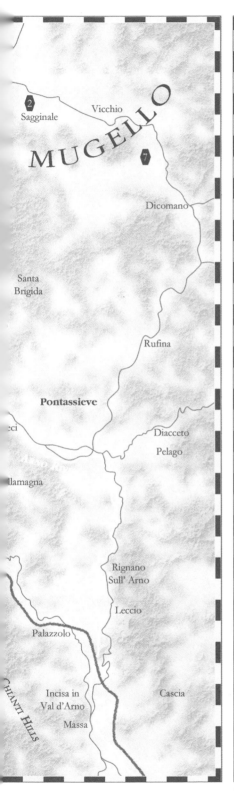

1
BARBARA LOCCI & ANTONIO LO BIANCO
AUGUST 1968
Sardinian Trail Murders

2
STEFANIA PETTINI & PASQUALE GENTILCORE
SEPTEMBER 1974
BORGO SAN LORENZO

3
CARMELA DE NUCCIO & GIOVANNI FOGGI
JUNE 1981
VIA DELL'ARRIGO

4
SUSANNA CAMBI & STEFANO BALDI
OCTOBER 1981
BARTOLINE FIELDS

5
ANTONELLA MIGLIORINI & PAOLO MAINARDI
JULY 1982
MONTESPERTOLI

6
HORST MEYER & UWE RÜSCH
SEPTEMBER 1983
GIOGOLI

7
PIA RONTINI & CLAUDIO STEFANACCI
JULY 1984
VICCHIO

8
NADINE MAURIOT & JEAN-MICHEL KRAVEICHVILI
SEPTEMBER 1985
SCOPETI

BY DOUGLAS PRESTON
Blasphemy
Dolci Colline di Sangue (with Mario Spezi)
Tyrannosaur Canyon
The Codex
The Royal Road
Talking to the Ground
Jennie
Cities of Gold
Dinosaurs in the Attic

BY DOUGLAS PRESTON AND LINCOLN CHILD
The Wheel of Darkness*
The Book of the Dead*
Dance of Death*
Brimstone*
Still Life with Crows*
The Cabinet of Curiosities*
The Ice Limit*
Thunderhead*
Riptide*
Reliquary
Mount Dragon
Relic

BY MARIO SPEZI
Inviato in Galera
Dolci Colline di Sangue (with Douglas Preston)
Le Sette di Satana
Il Passo dell'Orco
Toscana Nera
Il Violinista Verde
Il Mostro di Firenze

*Available from Grand Central Publishing

The
MONSTER
of
FLORENCE

DOUGLAS PRESTON
with MARIO SPEZI

GC

GRAND CENTRAL
PUBLISHING

LARGE PRINT

Grand Central Publishing
Hachette Book Group USA
237 Park Avenue
New York, NY 10017

Visit our website at www.HachetteBookGroupUSA.com.

Printed in the United States of America
First Edition: June 2008
10 9 8 7 6 5 4 3 2 1

Parts of this book first appeared in *Dolci Colline di Sangue*
(Sonzogno, 2006) as well as in the *Atlantic Monthly* and *The New
Yorker*.

Grand Central Publishing is a division of Hachette Book Group USA, Inc.
The Grand Central Publishing name and logo is a trademark of
Hachette Book Group USA, Inc.

Library of Congress Cataloging-in-Publication Data

Preston, Douglas J.
   The monster of Florence / Douglas Preston, with Mario Spezi.
      p. cm.
   ISBN-13: 978-0-446-58119-6 (regular edition)
   ISBN-13: 978-0-446-50534-5 (large print edition)
   ISBN-10: 0-446-58119-4 (regular edition)
   ISBN-10: 446-50534-X (large print edition) 1. Serial murders—
Italy—Florence—Case studies. I. Spezi, Mario II. Title.
   HV6536.183F5666 2008   40379
   363.152'3—dc22   200800771
   27.99 6/08 Ingram
The Large Print edition published in accord with the standards of the
N.A.V.H

To my partners in our Italian adventure: my wife, Christine, and my children Aletheia and Isaac. And to my daughter Selene, who wisely kept her feet planted firmly in America.
—Douglas Preston

A mia moglie Myriam e a mia figlia Eleonora, che hanno scusato la mia ossessione.
—Mario Spezi

The
MONSTER
of
FLORENCE

TIMELINE

1951   Pietro Pacciani murders his fiancée's
            seducer

1961   January 14. Salvatore Vinci's wife,
            Barbarina, found dead

1968   August 21. Barbara Locci and Antonio
            Lo Bianco murdered

1974   September 14. Borgo San Lorenzo
            killings

1981   June 6. Via dell'Arrigo killings

            October 22. Bartoline Fields killings

1982   June 19. Montespertoli killings
            August 17. Francesco Vinci arrested for
            being the Monster

1983   September 10. Giogoli killings

            September 19. Antonio Vinci arrested
            for illegal possession of firearms

1984	January 24. Piero Mucciarini and Giovanni Mele arrested for being the Monster
	July 29. Vicchio killings
	August 19. Prince Roberto Corsini murdered
	September 22. Mucciarini and Mele released from prison
	November 10. Francesco Vinci released from prison
1985	September 7. Scopeti killings
	October 8. Francesco Narducci drowns in Lake Trasimeno
1986	June 11. Salvatore Vinci arrested for the murder of his wife, Barbarina, in 1961
1988	April 12. Trial of Salvatore Vinci begins
	April 19. Salvatore Vinci acquitted, disappears
1989	August 2. Date of FBI psychological profile of the Monster of Florence
1992	April 27–May 8. Search of Pacciani's house and grounds

1993	January 16. Pacciani arrested as the Monster of Florence
1994	April 14. Pacciani's trial begins November 1. Pacciani convicted
1995	October. Chief Inspector Michele Giuttari takes over the Monster investigation
1996	February 12. Pacciani acquitted on appeal February 13. Vanni arrested for being Pacciani's accomplice
1997	May 20. Trial begins for Lotti and Vanni, accused as the Monster's accomplices
1998	March 24. Lotti and Vanni convicted
2000	August 1. Douglas Preston arrives in Florence
2002	April 6. Narducci's body exhumed
2004	May 14. *Chi L'ha Visto?* program aired on Italian television June 25. Preston leaves Florence November 18. Spezi's home searched by police

2005   January 24. Second police search of
Spezi's home

2006   February 22. Interrogation of Preston
April 7. Spezi arrested
April 19. Publication date of *Dolci
Colline di Sangue*
April 29. Spezi released from prison
September/October. Preston returns to
Italy with *Dateline NBC*

2007   June 20. *Dateline NBC* program on the
Monster of Florence
September 27. Trial of Francesco
Calamandrei as the Monster of
Florence begins

2008   January 16. First hearing in trial of
Giuttari and Mignini for abuse of office

CAST OF SECONDARY CHARACTERS,

IN APPROXIMATE ORDER OF APPEARANCE

❖

Chief Inspector Maurizio Cimmino, head of the Florentine police's mobile squad.

Chief Inspector Sandro Federico, police homicide detective.

Adolfo Izzo, prosecutor.

Carmela De Nuccio and **Giovanni Foggi**, killed on Via dell'Arrigo, June 6, 1981.

Dr. Mauro Maurri, chief medical examiner.

Fosco, his assistant.

Stefania Pettini and **Pasquale Gentilcore**, killed near Borgo San Lorenzo, September 13, 1974.

Enzo Spalletti, Peeping Tom arrested as the Monster, released when the Monster struck again while he was in jail.

Fabbri, another Peeping Tom questioned in the case.

Stefano Baldi and **Susanna Cambi**, killed in the Bartoline Fields, October 22, 1981.

Prof. Garimeta Gentile, gynecologist rumored to be the Monster.

"Dr." Carlo Santangelo, phony medical examiner who haunted cemeteries at night.

Brother Galileo Babbini, Franciscan monk and psychoanalyst who helped Spezi deal with the horror of the case.

Antonella Migliorini and **Paolo Mainardi**, killed in Montespertoli near Poppiano Castle on June 19, 1982.

Silvia Della Monica, prosecutor in the case, who received in the mail a piece of the Monster's last victim.

Stefano Mele, immigrant from Sardinia, who confessed to murdering his wife and her lover on August 21, 1968, and was sentenced to fourteen years in prison.

Barbara Locci, wife of Stefano Mele, murdered near Signa with her lover on August 21, 1968.

Antonio Lo Bianco, Sicilian bricklayer, murdered with Barbara Locci.

Natalino Mele, son of Stefano Mele and Barbara Locci, who was sleeping in the backseat of the car and who witnessed his mother's murder at age six.

Barbarina Vinci, wife of Salvatore Vinci back in Sardinia, probably murdered by him on January 14, 1961.

Giovanni Vinci, one of the Vinci brothers, who raped his sister back in Sardinia, and was a lover of Barbara Locci.

Salvatore Vinci, the ringleader of the 1968 double homicide, lover of Barbara Locci, who probably owned the Monster's gun and bullets, which may have been stolen from him in 1974, four months before the Monster's murders began. Arrested for being the Monster.

Francesco Vinci, youngest of the Vinci clan, lover of Barbara Locci, uncle of Antonio Vinci. Arrested for being the Monster.

Antonio Vinci, son of Salvatore Vinci, nephew of Francesco Vinci, arrested for illegal possession of firearms after the Monster's killings in Giogoli.

Cinzia Torrini, filmmaker who produced a film on the Monster of Florence case.

Horst Meyer and **Uwe Rüsch**, both twenty-four years old, killed in Giogoli, September 10, 1983.

Piero Luigi Vigna, lead prosecutor in the Monster case in the 1980s, responsible for the arrest of Pacciani. Vigna went on to head Italy's powerful antimafia unit.

Mario Rotella, examining magistrate in the Monster case in the 1980s, who was convinced the Monster was a member of a clan of Sardinians—the so-called "Sardinian Trail" leg of the investigation.

Giovanni Mele and **Piero Mucciarini**, the brother and brother-in-law of Stefano Mele, arrested for being the two Monsters of Florence.

Paolo Canessa, prosecutor in the Monster case in the 1980s, who is today the public minister (equivalent to a U.S. attorney) of Florence.

Pia Rontini and **Claudio Stefanacci**, killed at La Boschetta, near Vicchio, July 29, 1984.

Prince Roberto Corsini, murdered on his estate by a poacher, August 19, 1984, the subject of rumors that he was the Monster.

Nadine Mauriot, thirty-six years old, and **Jean-Michel Kraveichvili**, twenty-five years old, killed by the Monster in the Scopeti clearing, Saturday, September 7, 1985.

Sabrina Carmignani, who came across the Scopeti clearing on Sunday, September 8, 1985, the day of her nineteenth birthday, and encountered the aftermath of the murder of the French tourists.

Ruggero Perugini, the chief inspector who took over the Squadra Anti-Mostro and prosecuted Pietro Pacciani. He was the model for **Rinaldo Pazzi**, the fictional chief inspector in Thomas Harris's book (and movie) *Hannibal*.

Pietro Pacciani, Tuscan farmer who was convicted of being the Monster, acquitted on appeal, and then ordered to restand trial. He was the alleged leader of the so-called *compagni di merende*, the "picnicking friends."

Aldo Fezzi, the last *cantastorie*, or story singer, in Tuscany, who composed a song about Pietro Pacciani.

Arturo Minoliti, carabinieri marshal, who believed that the bullet found in Pacciani's garden, used to convict Pacciani as the Monster, might have been planted by investigators.

Mario Vanni, nicknamed il Torsolo (Apple Core), the former postman of San Casciano, convicted of being Pacciani's accomplice in the Monster killings. During Pacciani's trial, Vanni uttered the phrase that became immortalized in Italian, "We were picnicking friends."

Michele Giuttari, who took over the Monster investigation after Chief Inspector Perugini was promoted to Washington. He formed the Gruppo Investigativo Delitti Seriali, the Serial Killings Investigative Group, also known as GIDES. He engineered Spezi's arrest and Preston's interrogation.

Alpha, the first "secret witness," whose name was actually **Pucci**, a mentally retarded man who falsely confessed to having witnessed Pacciani commit one of the Monster's killings.

Beta, the second secret witness, **Giancarlo Lotti**, who was nicknamed **Katanga** (Jungle Bunny). Lotti falsely confessed having helped Pacciani with several of the Monster's killings.

Gamma, the third secret witness, named **Ghiribelli**, an aging prostitute and alcoholic who allegedly would turn a trick for a twenty-five-cent glass of wine.

Delta, the fourth secret witness, named **Galli**, a pimp by profession.

Lorenzo Nesi, the "serial witness" who suddenly and repeatedly remembered events going back decades, the star witness in the first trial against Pacciani.

Francesco Ferri, president of the Court of Appeals, who presided over Pacciani's appeals trial and declared him innocent. He later wrote a book about the case.

Prof. Francesco Introna, the forensic entomologist who examined photographs of the French tourists and stated that it was scientifically impossible for them to have been murdered Sunday night, as investigators insist.

Gabriella Carlizzi, who ran a conspiracy website that identified the Order of the Red Rose as the satanic sect behind the Monster killings (as well as the entity responsible for 9/11) and who accused Mario Spezi of being the Monster of Florence.

Francesco Narducci, the Perugian doctor whose body was found floating in Lake Trasimeno in October 1985, subject to rumors he had been the Monster of Florence. His apparent suicide was later ruled a murder and Spezi was accused of having participated in it.

Ugo Narducci, Francesco's father, a wealthy Perugian and an important member of the Freemasons—cause for official suspicion.

Francesca Narducci, the dead doctor's wife, heir to the Luisa Spagnoli fashion house fortune.

Francesco Calamandrei, ex-pharmacist of San Casciano, accused of being the mastermind behind five of the Monster's double homicides. His trial began on September 27, 2007.

Fernando Zaccaria, ex–police detective who introduced Spezi to Luigi Ruocco and who accompanied Spezi and Preston to the Villa Bibbiani.

Luigi Ruocco, small-time crook and ex-con who told Spezi he knew Antonio Vinci and who gave Spezi directions to Vinci's alleged safe house on the grounds of the Villa Bibbiani.

Ignazio, alleged friend of Ruocco who had supposedly been to Antonio's safe house and seen six iron boxes and possibly a .22 Beretta.

Inspector Castelli, detective with GIDES who served Preston with papers and was present at his interrogation.

Captain Mora, police captain present at the interrogation of Preston.

Giuliano Mignini, the public minister of Perugia, a public prosecutor in Italy analogous to a U.S attorney or a district attorney.

Marina De Robertis, the examining magistrate in the Spezi case, who invoked the antiterrorist law against Spezi, preventing him from meeting with his lawyers following his arrest.

Alessandro Traversi, one of Mario Spezi's lawyers.

Nino Filastò, one of Mario Spezi's lawyers.

Winnie Rontini, mother of Pia Rontini, one of the Monster's victims.

Renzo Rontini, father of Pia Rontini.

The
MONSTER
of
FLORENCE

INTRODUCTION

In 1969, the year men landed on the moon, I spent an unforgettable summer in Italy. I was thirteen. Our family rented a villa on the Tuscan coast, perched on a limestone promontory above the Mediterranean. My two brothers and I spent the summer hanging around an archaeological dig and swimming at a little beach in the shadow of a fifteenth-century castle called Puccini's Tower, where the composer wrote *Turandot*. We cooked octopus on the beach, snorkeled among the reefs, and collected ancient Roman tesserae from the eroding shoreline. In a nearby chicken coop I found the rim of a Roman amphora, two thousand years old, stamped with an "SES" and a picture of a trident, which the archaeologists told me had been manufactured

by the Sestius family, one of the richest mercantile families of the early Roman republic. In
a stinking bar, to the flickering glow of an old
black-and-white television set, we watched Neil
Armstrong set foot on the moon while the place
erupted in pandemonium, the longshoremen
and fishermen hugging and kissing each other,
tears streaming down their rough faces, crying,
"*Viva l'America! Viva l'America!*"

From that summer on, I knew that I wanted
to live in Italy.

I grew up to become a journalist and writer of
murder mysteries. In 1999, I returned to Italy on
assignment for *The New Yorker* magazine, writing an article about the mysterious artist Masaccio, who launched the Renaissance with his
commanding frescoes in the Brancacci Chapel
in Florence and then died at twenty-six, allegedly poisoned. One cold February night, in my
hotel room in Florence overlooking the Arno
River, I called my wife, Christine, and asked her
what she thought of the idea of moving to Florence. She said yes. The next morning I called a
real estate agency and began looking at apartments, and in two days I had rented the top floor
of a fifteenth-century palazzo and put down a

deposit. As a writer, I could live anywhere—why not Florence?

As I wandered around Florence that cold week in February, I started to plot the murder mystery I would write when we moved there. It would be set in Florence and involve a lost painting of Masaccio.

We moved to Italy. We arrived on August 1, 2000, Christine and I, with our two children, Isaac and Aletheia, aged five and six. We first lived in the apartment I had rented overlooking Piazza Santo Spirito and then we moved into the country, to a tiny town called Giogoli in the hills just south of Florence. There we rented a stone farmhouse tucked into the side of a hill at the end of a dirt lane, surrounded by olive groves.

I began researching my novel. Since it was to be a murder mystery, I had to learn all I could about Italian police procedure and murder investigation. An Italian friend gave me the name of a legendary Tuscan crime reporter named Mario Spezi, who for more than twenty years had worked the *cronaca nera* desk ("black story," or crime beat) at *La Nazione*, the daily paper of Tuscany and central Italy. "He knows more about the police than the police themselves," I was told.

And so it was that I found myself in the windowless back room of Caffè Ricchi, on Piazza Santo Spirito, sitting across from Mario Spezi himself.

Spezi was a journalist of the old school, dry, witty, and cynical, with a highly developed sense of the absurd. There was absolutely nothing a human being could do, no matter how depraved, that would surprise him. A shock of thick gray hair surmounted a wry, fine-looking leathery face, with a pair of canny brown eyes lurking behind gold-rimmed spectacles. He went about in a trench coat and a Bogart fedora, like a character out of Raymond Chandler, and he was a great fan of American blues, film noir, and Philip Marlowe.

The waitress brought in a tray with two black espressos and two glasses of mineral water. Spezi exhaled a stream of smoke, held his cigarette to one side, downed the espresso with one sharp movement, ordered another, and placed the cigarette back on his lip.

We began chatting, Spezi speaking slowly for the benefit of my execrable Italian. I described to him the plot of my book. One of the main characters was to be a carabinieri officer, and I asked him to tell me how the carabinieri operated. Spezi described the structure of the carabinieri, how they differed from the police, and how they conducted investigations, while I took notes. He promised to introduce me to a colonel in the carabinieri who was an old friend. Finally we fell to chatting about Italy and he asked me where I lived.

"A tiny town called Giogoli."

Spezi's eyebrows shot up. "Giogoli? I know it well. Where?"

I gave him the address.

"Giogoli . . . a lovely, historic town. It has three famous landmarks. Perhaps you already know of them?"

I did not.

With a faint smile of amusement, he began. The first was Villa Sfacciata, where one of his very own ancestors, Amerigo Vespucci, had lived. Vespucci was the Florentine navigator, mapmaker, and explorer who was the first to realize that his friend Christopher Columbus had discovered a brand-new continent, not some unknown shore of India, and who lent his name Amerigo (Americus in Latin) to this New World. The second landmark, Spezi went on, was another villa, called I Collazzi, with a façade said to be designed by Michelangelo, where Prince Charles stayed with Diana and where the prince painted many of his famous watercolors of the Tuscan landscape.

"And the third landmark?"

Spezi's smile widened. "The most interesting of all. It's just outside your door."

"There's nothing outside our door but an olive grove."

"Precisely. And in that grove one of the most horrific murders in Italian history took place. A double homicide committed by our very own Jack the Ripper."

As a writer of murder mysteries, I was more intrigued than dismayed.

"I named him," Spezi said. "I christened him *il Mostro di Firenze*, the Monster of Florence. I covered the case from the beginning. At *La Nazione* the other reporters called me the paper's 'Monstrologer.'" He laughed, a sudden irreverent cackle, hissing smoke out from between his teeth.

"Tell me about this Monster of Florence."

"You've never heard of him?"

"Never."

"Isn't the story famous in America?"

"It's completely unknown."

"That surprises me. It seems ... an almost *American* story. And your own FBI was involved—that group Thomas Harris made so famous, the Behavioral Science Unit. I saw Thomas Harris at one of the trials, taking notes on a yellow legal pad. They say he based Hannibal Lecter on the Monster of Florence."

Now I was really interested. "Tell me the story."

Spezi downed his second espresso, lit another Gauloise, and began to talk through the smoke. As his story gathered steam, he slipped a notebook and a well-worn gold pencil from his pocket and began to diagram the narrative. The pencil cut and darted across the paper, making arrows and circles and boxes and dotted lines, illustrating the intricate connections among the suspects, the killings, the arrests, the trials, and the many failed lines of investigation. It was a long story, and he spoke quietly, the blank page of his notebook gradually filling.

I listened, amazed at first, then astonished. As a crime novelist, I fancied myself a connoisseur of dark stories. I had certainly heard a lot of them. But as the story of the Monster of Florence unfolded, I realized it was something special. A story in a category all its own. I do not exaggerate when I say the case of the Monster of Florence may be—just *may* be—the most extraordinary story of crime and investigation the world has ever heard.

Between 1974 and 1985, seven couples—fourteen people in all—were murdered while making love in parked cars in the beautiful hills surrounding Florence. The case had become the longest and most expensive criminal investigation in Italian history. Close to a hundred thousand men were investigated and more than a dozen arrested, many of whom had to be released when the Monster struck again. Scores of lives were ruined by rumor and false accusations. The generation of Florentines who came of age during the killings say that it changed the city and their lives. There have been suicides, exhumations, alleged poisonings, body parts sent by post, séances in graveyards, lawsuits, planting of false evidence, and vicious prosecutorial vendettas. The investigation has been like a malignancy, spreading backward in time and outward in space, metastasizing to different cities and swelling into new investigations, with new judges, police, and prosecutors, more suspects, more arrests, and many more lives ruined.

Despite the longest manhunt in modern Italian history, the Monster of Florence has never been found. When I arrived in Italy in the year 2000 the case was still unsolved, the Monster presumably still on the loose.

Spezi and I became fast friends after that first meeting, and I soon shared his fascination with the case. In the spring of 2001, Spezi and I set out to find the truth and track down the real killer. This book is the story of that search and our eventual meeting with the man we believe may be the Monster of Florence.

Along the way, Spezi and I fell into the story. I was accused of being an accessory to murder, planting false evidence, perjury and obstruction of justice, and threatened with arrest if I ever set foot on Italian soil again. Spezi fared worse: he was accused of being the Monster of Florence himself.

This is the story that Spezi told.

PART I

❖

The Story of Mario Spezi

CHAPTER
I

The morning of June 7, 1981, dawned brilliantly clear over Florence, Italy. It was a quiet Sunday with blue skies and a light breeze out of the hills, which carried into the city the fragrance of sun-warmed cypress trees. Mario Spezi was at his desk at *La Nazione*, where he had worked as a reporter for several years, smoking and reading the paper. He was approached by the reporter who usually handled the crime desk, a legend at the paper who had survived twenty years of covering the Mafia.

The man sat on the edge of Spezi's desk. "This morning I have a little appointment," he said. "She's not bad-looking, married ..."

"At your age?" Spezi said. "On a Sunday morning before church? Isn't that a bit much?"

"A bit much? Mario, I'm a Sicilian!" He struck his chest. "I come from the land that gave birth to the gods. Anyway, I was hoping you could cover the crime desk for me this morning, hang around police headquarters in case something comes up. I've already made the calls, nothing's going on. And as we all know"—and then he spoke the phrase that Spezi would never forget—"nothing ever happens in Florence on a Sunday morning."

Spezi bowed and took the man's hand. "If the Godfather orders it, I shall obey. I kiss your hand, Don Rosario."

Spezi hung around the paper doing nothing until noon approached. It was the laziest, deadest day in weeks. Perhaps because of this, a feeling of misgiving that afflicts all crime reporters began to take hold—that something might be happening and he'd be scooped. So Spezi dutifully climbed into his Citroën and drove the half mile to police headquarters, an ancient, crumbling building in the old part of Florence, once an ancient monastery, where police officials had their tiny offices in the monks' former cells. He took the stairs two at a time up to the office of the chief of the mobile squad. The loud, querulous voice of the chief, Maurizio Cimmino, echoed down the hall from his open door, and Spezi was seized with dread.

Something *had* happened.

Spezi found the chief in shirtsleeves behind his desk, soaked with sweat, the telephone jammed between chin and shoulder. The police radio blared in the background and several policemen were there, talking and swearing in dialect.

Cimmino spied Spezi in the door and turned to him fiercely. "Jesus Christ, Mario, you here already? Don't go busting my balls, all I know is there's two of them."

Spezi pretended to know all about whatever it was. "Right. I won't bother you anymore. Just tell me where they are."

"Via dell'Arrigo, wherever the fuck that is . . . somewhere in Scandicci, I think."

Spezi piled down the stairs and called his editor from the pay phone on the first floor. He happened to know exactly where Via dell'Arrigo was: a friend of his owned the Villa dell'Arrigo, a spectacular estate at the top of the tiny, twisting country road of the same name.

"Get out there quick," his editor said. "We'll send a photographer."

Spezi left the police headquarters and tore through the deserted medieval streets of the city and into the Florentine hills. At one o'clock on a Sunday afternoon, the entire population was at home after church, getting ready to sit down to the most sacred meal of the week in a country where eating *in famiglia* is a hallowed activity. Via dell'Arrigo climbed up a steep hill through vineyards, cypresses, and groves of ancient olive trees. As the road mounted toward the steep, forested summits of the Valicaia hills, the views became expansive, sweeping across the city of Florence to the great Apennine Mountains beyond.

Spezi spotted the squad car of the local carabinieri marshal and pulled off next to it. All was quiet: Cimmino and his squad hadn't arrived, nor had the medical examiner or anyone else. The carabinieri officer guarding the site knew Spezi well and did not stop him as he nodded a greeting and walked past. He continued down a small dirt path through an olive grove to the foot of a lonely cypress. There, just beyond, he saw the scene of the crime, which had not been secured or sealed off.

The scene, Spezi told me, would be forever engraved in his mind. The Tuscan countryside lay under a sky of cobalt blue. A medieval castle, framed by cypress trees, crowned a nearby rise. In the vast distance, in the haze of early summer, he could spy the terra-cotta vault of the Duomo rising above the city of Florence, the physical embodiment of the Renaissance. The boy seemed to be sleeping in the driver's seat, his head leaning on the side window, eyes closed, face smooth and untroubled. Only a little black mark on his temple, which lined up with a hole in the spiderwebbed window, indicated that a crime had occurred.

On the ground, in the grass, lay a straw purse, wide open and upside down, as if someone had rummaged through it and flung it aside.

He heard the swish of feet in the grass and the carabinieri officer came up behind him.

"The woman?" Spezi asked him.

The cop gestured with his chin behind the car. The girl's body lay some distance away, at the foot of a little embankment, amid wildflowers. She had also been shot and lay on her back, naked except for a gold chain around her neck, which had fallen between her parted lips. Her blue eyes were open and seemed to be looking up at Spezi with surprise. Everything was unnaturally composed, immobile, with no signs of struggle or confusion—like a museum diorama. But there was a singular horror: the pubic area below the victim's abdomen simply wasn't there anymore.

Spezi turned back and found the cop behind him. The man seemed to understand the question in Spezi's eyes.

"During the night . . . the animals came . . . And the hot sun did the rest."

Spezi fumbled a Gauloise out of his pocket and lit it in the shade of the cypress. He smoked in silence, standing halfway between the two victims, reconstructing the crime in his head. The two people had obviously been ambushed while making love in the car; they had probably come up here after an evening dancing at Disco Anastasia, a hangout for teenagers at the bottom of the hill. (The police would later confirm this was the case.) It was the night of the new moon. The killer would have approached in the dark, silently; perhaps he watched them make love for a while, and then struck when they were at their most vulnerable. It had been a low-risk crime—a cowardly crime—to shoot two people imprisoned in the small space of a car at point-blank range, at a time when they were completely unaware of what was going on around them.

The first shot was for him, through the window of the car, and he may never have known what happened. Her end was crueler; she would have realized. After killing her, the murderer had dragged her away from the car—Spezi could see the marks in the grass—leaving her at the bottom of the embankment. The place was shockingly exposed. It lay right next to a footpath that ran parallel to the road, out in the open and visible from multiple vantage points.

Spezi's musings were interrupted by the arrival of Chief Inspector Sandro Federico and a prosecutor, Adolfo Izzo, along with the forensic squad. Federico had the easygoing manner of a Roman, affecting an air of amused nonchalance. Izzo, on the other hand, was in his first posting and he arrived wound up like a spring. He leapt out of the squad car and charged up to Spezi. "What are you doing here, sir?" he asked angrily.

"Working."

"You must leave the premises immediately. You can't remain here."

"Okay, okay . . ." Spezi had seen all he wanted to see. He shoved his pen and notebook away, got in his car, and drove back to police headquarters. In the hallway outside Cimmino's office he ran into a police sergeant he knew well; they had been able to do each other favors from time to time. The sergeant slipped a photograph out of his pocket and showed it to him. "You want it?"

It was a picture of the two victims, in life, sitting on a stone wall with their arms around each other.

Spezi took it. "I'll bring it back to you later this afternoon, after we've copied it."

Cimmino gave Spezi the names of the two victims: Carmela De Nuccio, twenty-one years old, who worked for the Gucci fashion house in Florence. The man was Giovanni Foggi, thirty, employed by the local electric utility. They were engaged to be married. A policeman on his day off, enjoying a Sunday morning walk in the country, had found the two bodies at ten-thirty. The crime had occurred a little before midnight, and there was a witness of sorts: a farmer who lived across the road. He had heard a tape of John Lennon's "Imagine" coming from a car parked in the fields. The song had been interrupted all of a sudden, in the middle. He hadn't heard any shots from what was evidently a .22 pistol, judging from the shells that were left at the scene of the crime—Winchester series "H" rounds. Cimmino said the two victims were clean, they had no enemies, excluding the man Carmela left when she began dating Giovanni.

"It's frightening," Spezi said to Cimmino. "I've never seen anything like it around here . . . And then, to think what the animals did—"

"What animals?" Cimmino interrupted.

"The animals that came during the night . . . That bloody mess . . . in between the girl's legs."

Cimmino stared at him. "Animals my ass! The killer did that."

Spezi felt his gut freeze. "The killer? What did he do, stab her?"

Inspector Cimmino answered matter-of-factly, perhaps as a way to keep the horror at bay. "No, he didn't stab her. He cut out her vagina . . . and took it away."

Spezi didn't immediately understand. "He took her vagina away? Where?" As soon as the question was out he realized how stupid it sounded.

"It's simply not there anymore. He took it away with him."

CHAPTER
2

The next day, Monday morning, at eleven o'clock, Spezi drove to the Careggi district of Florence, on the outskirts of the city. It was a hundred and five degrees in the shade, with the humidity approaching that of a hot shower. Smog lay like a pall over the city. He drove down a potholed lane toward a large yellow building, a decaying villa now part of a hospital complex, the plaster flaking off in platter-sized pieces.

The reception area of the medical examiner's office was a cavernous room dominated by a massive marble table, on which a computer sat, covered in a white sheet like a corpse. The rest of the table was empty. Behind, in a niche in the wall, a bronze bust of a bearded luminary in the field of human anatomy cast a severe gaze on Spezi.

A marble staircase went up and down. Spezi went down.

The stairway led to an underground passageway, illuminated with humming fluorescent lights and lined with doors. The walls were tiled. The last door was open and from it came the strident whine of a bone saw. A rivulet of a black liquid ran out the door and into the hall, where it disappeared down a drain.

Spezi entered.

"Look who's here!" cried Fosco, the ME's assistant. He closed his eyes, stretched out his arms, and quoted Dante. "*There are not many who seek me here ...*"

"Ciao, Fosco," Spezi said. "Who's this?" He jerked his chin at a cadaver stretched out on a zinc gurney, being worked over by a diener. The circular saw had just opened its cranium. On the gurney, next to the white face of the corpse, stood an empty coffee cup and crumbs from a recently consumed brioche.

"This one? A brilliant scholar, a distinguished professor in the Accademia della Crusca no less.

But, as you can see, tonight yet another disappointment has laid me low; I have just opened the head and what do I find inside? Where is all this wisdom? Boh! Inside it looks just like the Albanian hooker I opened yesterday. Maybe the professor thinks he's better than her! But when I open them up, I find that they're equal! And they both have achieved the same destiny: my zinc gurney. Why, then, did he tire himself out poring over so many books? Boh! Take my advice, journalist: eat, drink, and enjoy yourself—"

A courteous voice sounded from the doorway, silencing Fosco. "Good afternoon, Signor Spezi." It was Mauro Maurri, the medical examiner himself, who looked more like an English country gentleman: light blue eyes, gray hair worn fashionably long, a beige cardigan, and corduroy slacks. "Shall we retire to my office upstairs? We will surely find it more congenial for conversation."

The study of Mauro Maurri consisted of a long, narrow room lined with books and magazines on criminology and forensic pathology. He had left the window shut to keep out the heat and had turned on only a single small lamp on his desk, maintaining the rest of his office in darkness.

Spezi seated himself and slid out a packet of Gauloises, offered one to Maurri, who declined with a light shake of his head, and lit one for himself.

Maurri spoke with great deliberation. "The killer used a knife or some other sharp instrument. The instrument had a notch or tooth in the middle, perhaps a defect, perhaps not. It might have been a certain type of knife that takes that form. It seems to me, although I won't swear to it, that it was a scuba knife. Three cuts were made to remove the organ. The first clockwise, from eleven o'clock to six o'clock; the second counterclockwise, again from eleven o'clock to six. The third cut was made from top to bottom to detach the organ. Three clean, decisive cuts, with an extremely sharp edge."

"Like Jack."

"I beg your pardon?"

"Jack the Ripper."

"I see, of course. Jack the Ripper. No . . . not like him. Our killer is not a surgeon. Nor a butcher. Knowledge of anatomy was not required here. The investigators have been demanding to know, 'Was the operation well done?' What does that mean, 'well done'? Who has ever done an operation of this sort? Certainly it was done by someone with no hesitation, one who perhaps uses certain tools in his professional work. Wasn't the girl a leatherworker for Gucci? Didn't she use a cobbler's knife? Wasn't her father also a leatherworker? Perhaps it was someone in her orbit . . . It had to have been someone with no mean ability with a knife—a hunter or taxidermist . . . Above all, a person with determination and nerves of steel. Although he was working on a dead body, it was, after all, only *just* dead."

"Dr. Maurri," Spezi asked, "do you have any thoughts on what he might have done with this . . . fetish?"

"I pray you, do not ask me this question."

When Monday afternoon sank into an ovenlike grayness and it seemed certain there would be no further developments in the case that day, a large staff meeting was held in the office of the managing editor of *La Nazione.* The publisher was there, the editor, the news director, several journalists, and Spezi. *La Nazione* was the only paper that had information on the mutilation of the corpse; the other dailies knew nothing. It would be a major scoop. The managing editor stated that the particulars of the crime had to be presented in the lead headline. The editor disagreed, maintaining the details were too strong. As Spezi read his notes out loud to help solve the dispute, a young journalist on the crime beat suddenly broke in.

"Excuse me for interrupting," he said, "but I just remembered something. It seems to me there was a similar killing five or six years ago."

The managing editor leapt to his feet. "Now you tell us, right before deadline! Were you waiting for the paper to be in the printing presses before you 'remembered'?"

The reporter was cowed, not realizing the man's fury was all show. "I'm sorry, sir, it just occurred to me now. Do you remember that double homicide near Borgo San Lorenzo?" He paused, waiting for an answer. Borgo San Lorenzo was a town in the mountains about thirty kilometers north of Florence.

"Go on, tell us!" the editor yelled.

"In Borgo, a young couple was murdered. They'd also been having sex in a parked car. Remember the one where the killer stuck a branch up her . . . vagina?"

"I seem to recall it now. What were you doing, sleeping? Bring me the files on it. Write a piece immediately—the similarities, the differences . . . Hurry up! Why are you still here?"

The meeting broke up, and Spezi went to his desk to write up his piece on his visit to the ME's office. Before beginning, he went over the old article that told the story of the Borgo San Lorenzo killing. The resemblances were striking. The two victims, Stefania Pettini, eighteen years old, and Pasquale Gentilcore, nineteen, were killed the night of September 14, 1974, also a Saturday night with no moon. They too were engaged to be married. The killer had taken the girl's purse and turned it upside down, scattering its contents, like the straw purse Spezi had seen in the grass. The two victims had also spent the evening in a discotheque, the Teen Club, in Borgo San Lorenzo.

Shells had been recovered from the earlier killing, and the article stated that they were Winchester series H .22 rounds, the same as used in the Arrigo murders. This detail wasn't quite as significant as it seemed, since those were the most common type of .22 bullets sold in Italy.

The Borgo San Lorenzo killer had not excised

the girl's sex organs. Instead, he had dragged her away from the car and had pricked her body with his knife ninety-seven times in an elaborate design that went around her breasts and pubic area. The killing had taken place next to a vineyard, and he had penetrated her with an old, woody piece of grapevine. In neither case was there any evidence of sexual molestation of the victim.

Spezi wrote the lead while the other reporter wrote a sidebar on the 1974 killings.

Two days later, the reaction came. The police, having read the article, had done a comparison between the shells recovered from the 1974 killings and the current ones. Most handguns, aside from revolvers, eject shells after firing; if the shooter doesn't go to the trouble of retrieving them, they remain at the scene of the crime. The police lab report was definitive: the same pistol had been used in both crimes. It was a .22 caliber Beretta "Long Rifle" handgun, a model designed for target shooting. No silencer. The crucial detail was this: the firing pin had a small defect that left an unmistakable mark on the rim of the cartridge, as unique as a fingerprint.

When *La Nazione* broke the news, it caused

a sensation. It meant that a serial killer was stalking the Florentine hills.

The investigation that followed lifted the lid off a bizarre underworld that few Florentines knew existed in the lovely hills surrounding their city. In Italy, most young people live at home with their parents until they marry, and most marry late. As a result, having sex in parked cars is a national pastime. It has been said that one out of every three Florentines alive today was conceived in a car. On any given weekend night the hills surrounding Florence were filled with young couples parked in shadowy lanes and dirt turnouts, in olive groves and farmers' fields.

The investigators discovered that dozens of voyeurs prowled the countryside spying on these couples. Locally, these voyeurs were known as *Indiani*, or Indians, because they crept around in the dark. Some carried sophisticated electronic equipment, including parabolic and suction-cup microphones, tape recorders, and night vision cameras. The Indiani had divided the hills into zones of operation, each managed by a group or "tribe" who controlled the best posts for vicarious sex-watching. Some posts were highly sought after, either because they allowed for very close observation or because they were where the "good cars" were most commonly found. (A "good car" is exactly what you might imagine.) A good car could also be a source of money, and sometimes good cars were bought and sold on the spot, in a kind of depraved bourse, in which one Indiano would retire with a fistful of cash, ceding his post to another to watch the finish. Wealthy Indiani often paid for a guide to take them to the best spots and minimize the risk.

Then there were the intrepid people who preyed on the Indiani themselves, a subculture within a subculture. These men crept into the hills at night not to watch lovers but to spy on Indiani, taking careful note of their cars, license plate numbers, and other telling details—and then they would blackmail the Indiani, threatening to expose their nocturnal activities to their wives, families, and employers. It sometimes happened that an Indiano would have his voyeuristic bliss interrupted by the flash of a nearby camera; the next day he would receive a call:"Remember that flash in the woods last night? The photo came out beautifully, you look simply marvelous, a likeness that even your second cousin would recognize! By the way, the negative is for sale . . ."

It didn't take long for investigators to flush out an Indiano who had been lurking about Via dell'Arrigo at the time of the double killing. His name was Enzo Spalletti, and he drove an ambulance during the day.

Spalletti lived with his wife and family in Turbone, a village outside of Florence that consisted of a cluster of stone houses arranged in a circle around a windswept piazza, looking not unlike a cowboy town in a spaghetti Western. He was not well liked by his neighbors. They said he put on airs, that he thought he was better than everyone else. His children, they said, took dancing lessons as if they were the children of a lord. The entire town knew he was a voyeur. Six days after the killing, the police came for the ambulance driver. At the time they did not believe they were dealing with the killer, but only with an important witness.

Spalletti was taken to police headquarters and questioned. He was a small man with an enormous mustache, tight little eyes, a big nose, a chin that stuck out like a knob, and a small, sphincterlike mouth. He looked like a man with something to hide. Compounding the impression, he answered the police's questions with a mixture of arrogance, evasion, and defiance. He said he had left the house that evening with the idea of finding a prostitute to his taste, whom he claimed to have picked up in Florence on the Lungarno, next to the American consulate. She was a young girl from Naples, in a short red dress. The girl had gotten into his Taurus and he had driven her to some woods near where the two young people were murdered. When they had finished, Spalletti brought the little prostitute in red back to where he'd found her and dropped her off.

The story was most improbable. For one thing, it was unthinkable that a prostitute would voluntarily get into an unknown person's car and allow herself to be driven twenty kilometers deep into the countryside to a dark wood. The questioners pointed out the many holes in his story, but Spalletti wouldn't budge. It took six hours of solid interrogation before he began to wilt. Finally the ambulance driver admitted, still as cocky and self-assured as ever, what everyone already knew, that he was in fact a Peeping Tom, that he had been out and about the evening of Saturday, June 6, and had, in fact, parked his red Taurus not far from the scene of the crime. "And so what?" he went on. "I wasn't the only one out that evening spying on couples in the area. There were a whole bunch of us." He went on to say that he knew well the copper Fiat belonging to Giovanni and Carmela: it came often and was known as a "good car." He had watched them more than once. And he knew for a fact that there were other people nosing around that field the night of the crime. He was with one of those people for quite a while, who could vouch for him. He gave the police the man's name: Fabbri.

A few hours later Fabbri was hauled downtown to police headquarters to see if he could confirm Spalletti's alibi. Instead, Fabbri stated that there was a period of an hour and a half, right around the time of the crime, when he was not with Spalletti. "Sure," Fabbri told investigators, "Spalletti and I saw each other. As usual we met at the Taverna del Diavolo," a restaurant where the Indiani would gather to do business and swap information before going out for the evening. Fabbri added that he saw Spalletti again at the end of the evening, a little after eleven o'clock, when Spalletti stopped on his way down Via dell'Arrigo. Spalletti must have therefore passed not ten meters from the scene of the crime at around the time investigators estimated it occurred.

There was more. Spalletti insisted that he had immediately returned home after greeting Fabbri. But his wife said that when she went to bed at two o'clock in the morning her husband had still not come back.

The interrogators turned back to Spalletti: where had he been between midnight and at least 2 a.m.? Spalletti had no answer.

The police locked Spalletti up at the famous Florentine prison of Le Murate ("The Immured Ones"), accusing him of *reticenza*, reticence—a form of perjury. The authorities still did not yet believe he was the killer, but they were sure he was withholding important information. A few days in jail might just shake it out.

Forensic crime scene investigators went over Spalletti's car and house with a fine-toothed comb. They found a penknife in his car and in the glove compartment a type of gun called a *scacciacani*, a "dog flattener," a cheap pistol loaded with blanks for scaring off dogs, which Spalletti had bought through an ad on the back of a porn magazine. There were no traces of blood.

They interrogated Spalletti's wife. She was much younger than her husband, a fat, honest, simple country girl, and she admitted that she knew her husband was a Peeping Tom. "Many times," she said, weeping, "he promised me he'd stop, but then he'd get back into it. And it's true that the night of June 6 he went out to 'have a look,' as he used to call it." She had no idea when her husband had returned, except that it was after two. She went on, protesting that her husband had to be innocent, that he could never have committed such a terrible crime, since "he's got a terror of blood, so much so that at work, when there's been a highway accident, he refuses to get out of the ambulance."

In the middle of July, policed finally charged Spalletti with being the killer.

Having first broken the original story, Spezi continued to cover it for *La Nazione*. His articles for the paper were skeptical and they pointed out the many holes in the case against Spalletti, among them the fact that there was no direct evidence connecting him with the crime. Nor did Spalletti have any connection to Borgo San Lorenzo, where the first killing occurred in 1974.

On October 24, 1981, Spalletti opened the paper in his prison cell and read a headline that must have brought him great relief:

THE KILLER RETURNS
Young Couple Found Brutally Murdered in Farmer's Field

By killing again, the Monster himself had proved the innocence of the Peeping Tom ambulance driver.

CHAPTER
3

Many countries have a serial killer who defines his culture by a process of negation, who exemplifies his era not by exalting its values, but by exposing its black underbelly. England had Jack the Ripper, born in the fogs of Dickensian London, who preyed on the city's most neglected underclass, the prostitutes who scrabbled for a living in the slums of Whitechapel. Boston had the Boston Strangler, the suave, handsome killer who prowled the city's more elegant neighborhoods, raping and murdering elderly women and arranging their bodies in tableaux of unspeakable obscenity. Germany had the Monster of Düsseldorf, who seemed to foreshadow the coming of Hitler by his indiscriminate and sadistic killing of men, women, and children; his bloodlust was so great that, on the eve of his execution, he called his imminent beheading "the pleasure to end all pleasures." Each killer was, in his own way, a dark embodiment of his time and place.

Italy had the Monster of Florence.

Florence has always been a city of opposites. On a balmy spring evening, with the setting sun gilding the stately palaces lining the river, it can appear as one of the most beautiful and gracious cities in the world. But in late November, after two months of steady rain, its ancient palaces become gray and streaked with damp; the narrow cobbled streets, smelling of sewer gas and dog feces, are shut up on all sides by grim stone façades and overhanging roofs that block the already dim light. The bridges over the Arno flow with black umbrellas held up against the unceasing rain. The river, so lovely in summer, swells into a brown and oily flood, carrying broken trees and branches and sometimes dead animals, which pile up against the pylons designed by Ammanati.

In Florence the sublime and terrible go hand in hand: Savonarola's Bonfires of the Vanities and Botticelli's *Birth of Venus*, Leonardo da Vinci's notebooks and Niccolò Macchiavelli's *The Prince*, Dante's *Inferno* and Boccaccio's *Decameron*. The Piazza della Signoria, the main square, contains an open-air display of Roman and Renaissance sculpture exhibiting some of the most famous statues in Florence. It is a gallery of horrors, a public exhibition of killing, rape, and mutilation unmatched in any city in the world. Heading the show is the famous bronze sculpture by Cellini of Perseus triumphantly holding up the severed head of Medusa like a jihadist on a website video, blood pouring from her neck, her decapitated body sprawled under his feet. Behind Perseus stand other statues depicting famous legendary scenes of murder, violence, and mayhem—among them the sculpture that graces the cover of this book, *The Rape of the Sabine Women* by Giambologna. Inside Florence's encircling walls and on the gibbets outside were committed the most refined and the most savage of crimes, from delicate poisonings to brutal public dismemberments, tortures, and burnings. For centuries, Florence projected its power over the rest of Tuscany at the cost of ferocious massacres and bloody wars.

The city was founded by Julius Caesar in

AD 59 as a retirement village for soldiers from his campaigns. It was named Florentia, or "Flourishing." Around AD 250 an Armenian prince named Miniato, after a pilgrimage to Rome, settled on a hill outside Florence and lived as a hermit in a cave, from which he sallied forth to preach to the pagans in town. During the Christian persecutions under the emperor Decius, Miniato was arrested and beheaded in the city square, whereupon (the legend goes) he picked up his head, placed it back on his shoulders, and walked up the hill to die with dignity in his cave. Today, one of the loveliest Romanesque churches in all of Italy stands at the spot, San Miniato al Monte, looking out across the city and the hills beyond.

In 1302, Florence expelled Dante, an act it has never lived down. In return, Dante populated hell with prominent Florentines and reserved some of the most exquisite tortures for them.

During the fourteenth century, Florence grew rich in the woolen cloth trade and banking, and by the end of the century it was one of the five largest cities in Europe. As the fifteenth century dawned, Florence hosted one of those inexplicable flowerings of genius that have occurred fewer than half a dozen times in human history. It would later be called the Renaissance, the "rebirth," following the long darkness of the Middle Ages. Between the birth of Masaccio in 1401 and the death of Galileo in 1642, Florentines largely invented the modern world. They revolutionized art, architecture, music, astronomy, mathematics, and navigation. They created the modern banking system with the invention of the letter of credit. The gold florin, with the Florentine lily on one side and John the Baptist wearing a hairshirt on the other, became the coin of Europe. This landlocked city on an unnavigable river produced brilliant navigators who explored and mapped the New World, and one even gave America its name.

More than that, Florence invented the very *idea* of the modern world. With the Renaissance, Florentines threw off the yoke of medievalism, in which God stood at the center of the universe and human existence on earth was but a dark, fleeting passage to the glorious life to come. The Renaissance placed humanity at the center of the universe and declared this life as the main event. The course of Western civilization was changed forever.

The Florentine Renaissance was largely financed by a single family, the Medicis. They first came to prominence in 1434 under the leadership of Giovanni di Bicci de' Medici, a Florentine banker of great wealth. The Medicis ruled the city from behind the scenes, with a clever system of patronage, alliances, and influence. Although a mercantile family, from the very beginning they poured money into the arts. Giovanni's great-grandson, Lorenzo the Magnificent, was the very epitome of the term "Renaissance man." As a boy, Lorenzo had been astonishingly gifted, and he was given the finest education money could buy, becoming an accomplished jouster, hawker, hunter, and racehorse breeder. Early portraits of Lorenzo il Magnifico reveal an intense young man with furrowed brows, a big, Nixonesque nose, and straight hair. He assumed leadership of the city in 1469, on the death of his father, when he was only twenty years old. He gathered around him such men as Leonardo da Vinci, Sandro Botticelli, Filippino Lippi, Michelangelo, and the philosopher Pico della Mirandola.

Lorenzo ushered Florence into a golden age. But even at the height of the Renaissance, beauty mingled with blood, civilization with savagery, in this city of paradox and contradiction. In 1478 a rival banking family, the Pazzis, attempted a coup d'état against Medici rule. The name Pazzi means, literally, "Madmen," and it was given to an ancestor to honor his insane courage in being one of the first soldiers over the walls of Jerusalem during the First Crusade. The Pazzis had the distinction of seeing two of their members cast into hell by Dante, who gave one a "doggish grin."

On a quiet Sunday in April, a gang of Pazzi murderers set upon Lorenzo the Magnificent and his brother Giuliano at their most vulnerable moment, during the Elevation of the Host at Mass in the Duomo. They killed Giuliano, but Lorenzo, stabbed several times, managed to escape and lock himself in the sacristy. Florentines were enraged at this attack on their patron family and, in a howling mob, went after the conspirators. One of the leaders, Jacopo de' Pazzi, was hanged from a window of the Palazzo Vecchio, his body then stripped, dragged through the streets, and tossed in the Arno River. Despite this setback, the Pazzi family survived, not long afterward giving the world the famed ecstatic nun Maria Maddalena de' Pazzi, who amazed witnesses with her gasping, moaning transports when seized by the love of God during prayer. A fictional Pazzi appeared in the twentieth

century, when the writer Thomas Harris made
one of his main characters in the novel *Hannibal* a Pazzi, a Florentine police inspector who
gains fame and notoriety by solving the case of
the Monster of Florence.

The death of Lorenzo the Magnificent, in
1492, at the height of the Renaissance, ushered
in one of those bloody periods that marked
Florentine history. A Dominican monk by the
name of Savonarola, who lived in the monastery
of San Marco, consoled Lorenzo on his death-
bed, only later to turn and preach against the
Medici family. Savonarola was a strange-looking
man, hooded in brown monk's robes, magnetic,
coarse, ungainly, and muscular, with a hook nose
and Rasputin-like eyes. In the San Marco church
he began to preach fire and brimstone, railing against the decadence of the Renaissance,
proclaiming that the Last Days had come, and
recounting his visions and his direct conversations with God.

His message resonated among common Florentines, who had watched with disapproval the
conspicuous consumption and great wealth of
the Renaissance and its patrons, much of which
seemed to have bypassed them. Their discontent
was magnified by an epidemic of syphilis, car-

ried back from the New World, which burned through the city. It was a disease Europe had never seen before, and it came in a far more virulent form than we know today, in which the victim's body became overspread with weeping pustules, the flesh sagging and falling from the face, the stricken sinking into fulminating insanity before death mercifully carried them off. The year 1500 was approaching, which seemed to some a nice round figure marking the arrival of the Last Days. In this climate Savonarola found a receptive audience.

In 1494, Charles VIII of France invaded Tuscany. Piero the Unfortunate, who had inherited the rule of Florence from his father, Lorenzo, was an arrogant and ineffective ruler. He surrendered the city to Charles on poor terms, without even putting up a decent fight, which so enraged Florentines that they drove out the Medici family and looted their palaces. Savonarola, who had accumulated a large following, stepped into the power vacuum and declared Florence a "Christian Republic," setting himself up as its leader. He immediately made sodomy, a popular and more or less socially acceptable activity among sophisticated Florentines, punishable by death. Transgressors and others were regularly burned in the central Piazza della Signoria or hanged outside the city gates.

The mad monk of San Marco had free reign to stir up religious fervor among the common people in the city. He railed against the decadence, excess, and humanistic spirit of the Renaissance. A few years into his reign, he instigated his famous Bonfires of the Vanities. He sent his minions around door to door, collecting items he thought were sinful—mirrors, pagan books, cosmetics, secular music and musical instruments, chessboards, cards, fine clothes, and secular paintings. Everything was heaped up in the Piazza della Signoria and set afire. The artist Botticelli, who fell under the sway of Savonarola, added many of his own paintings to the bonfire, and several of Michelangelo's works may also have been torched, along with other priceless Renaissance masterpieces.

Under Savonarola's rule, Florence sank into economic decline. The Last Days he kept preaching never came. Instead of blessing the city for its newfound religiosity, God seemed to have abandoned it. The common people, especially the young and shiftless, began openly defying his edicts. In 1497, a mob of young men rioted during one of Savonarola's sermons; the riots spread and became a general revolt, taverns re-opened, gambling resumed, and dancing and music could once again be heard echoing down Florence's crooked streets.

Savonarola, his control slipping, preached ever more wild and condemnatory sermons, and he made the fatal mistake of turning his criticisms on the church itself. The pope excommunicated him and ordered him arrested and executed. An obliging mob attacked the San Marco monastery, broke down the doors, killed some of Savonarola's fellow monks, and dragged him out. He was charged with a slew of crimes, among them "religious error." After being tortured on the rack for several weeks, he was hung in chains from a cross in the Piazza della Signoria, at the same place where he had erected his Bonfires of the Vanities, and burned. For hours the fire was fed, and then his remains were chopped up and re-mixed with burning brush several times over so that no piece of him could survive to be made into a relic for veneration. His ashes were then dumped in the all-embracing, all-erasing Arno River.

The Renaissance resumed. The blood and beauty of Florence continued. But nothing lasts forever, and over the centuries Florence gradually lost its place among the leading cities of Europe. It subsided into a relative backwater, famous for its past but invisible in the present, as other cities in Italy rose to prominence, notably Rome, Naples, and Milan.

Florentines today are a famously closed people, considered by other Italians to be stiff, haughty, class-conscious, excessively formal, backward-looking, and fossilized by tradition. They are sober, punctual, and hardworking. Deep inside, Florentines know they are more civilized than other Italians. They gave the world all that is fine and beautiful and they have done enough. Now they can shut their doors and turn inward, answerable to nobody.

When the Monster of Florence arrived, Florentines faced the killings with disbelief, anguish, terror, and a kind of sick fascination. They simply could not accept that their exquisitely beautiful city, the physical expression of the Renaissance, the very cradle of Western civilization, could harbor such a monster.

Most of all, they could not accept the idea that the killer might be one of them.

CHAPTER
4

The evening of Thursday, October 22, 1981, was rainy and unseasonably cool. A general strike had been scheduled for the following day—all shops, businesses, and schools would be closed in protest of the government's economic policies. As a result it was a festive evening. Stefano Baldi had gone to the house of his girlfriend, Susanna Cambi, eaten dinner with her and her parents, and taken her out to the movies. Afterwards, they went parking in the Bartoline Fields west of Florence. It was a familiar place for Stefano, who had grown up in the area and played in the fields as a child.

By day the Bartoline Fields were visited by old

pensioners who planted tiny vegetable gardens, took the air, and passed the time gossiping. By night there was a continual coming and going of cars with young couples in search of solitude and intimacy. And naturally there were Peeping Toms.

In the middle of the fields, a track dead-ended among vineyards. That is where Stefano and Susanna parked. In front of them rose the massive, dark shapes of the Calvana Mountains, and behind came the faint rumble of traffic on the autostrada. That night the stars and crescent moon were covered with clouds, casting a heavy darkness over everything.

At eleven the next morning, an elderly couple who had come to water their vegetable garden discovered the crime. The black VW Golf blocked the track, and the left-hand door was closed, the window a solid web of cracks, the right-hand door wide open—exactly the arrangement found at the previous two double homicides.

Spezi arrived at the scene of the crime shortly after the police. Again, the police and carabinieri made no effort to secure the site or seal it with crime tape. Everyone was milling around, making bad jokes—journalists, police, prosecutors, the medical examiner—jokes devoid of humor in a useless attempt to stave off the horror of the scene.

Shortly after his arrival, Spezi spotted a colonel he knew from the carabinieri, dressed in a natty jacket of gray leather buttoned to his neck to keep out the autumn chill, chain-smoking American cigarettes. The colonel had in his hand a stone that he had found twenty meters from the murder scene. In the form of a truncated pyramid, it was about three inches on a side and made of granite. Spezi recognized it as a doorstop of a type often found in old Tuscan country houses, used during the hot summers to hold open the doors between rooms to aid in the circulation of air.

Turning the stone over in his hands, the colonel approached Spezi. "This doorstop is the only thing I've found at the site of any possible significance. I'm taking it back as evidence, since it's all I've got. Maybe he used it to break the car window."

Twenty years later that banal doorstop, collected by chance in a field, would become the center of a new and bizarre investigation.

"Nothing else, Colonel?" Spezi asked. "Not a trace? The ground is soaking wet and soft."

"We found the footprint of a rubber boot, of the Chantilly type, on the ground next to the row of grapevines that run perpendicularly to the dirt track, right next to the Golf. We've inventoried the print. But you know as well as I do that anyone could have left that bootprint . . . just like this rock."

Spezi, remembering his duty as a journalist to observe with his own eyes and not report secondhand, went with great reluctance to look at the female victim. Her body had been dragged more than ten meters from the car and worked on in a place that was, as in the previous homicides, surprisingly exposed. She was left in the grass, her arms crossed, with the same mutilation as before.

The victims were examined by Medical Examiner Mauro Maurri, who concluded that the cuts to the pubic region had been made with the same notched knife that resembled a scuba knife. He noted that, as in the previous killings, there was no evidence of rape, no molestation of the body or presence of semen. The mobile squad collected nine Winchester series H shells from the ground and two more inside the car. An examination proved that all had been fired by the same gun used in the previous two double homicides, with the unique mark on the rim made by the firing pin.

Spezi asked the chief of the mobile squad about the apparently anomalous fact that a Beretta .22 can only hold nine rounds in its magazine, and yet there were eleven shells at the scene. The chief explained that a knowledgeable shooter can force a tenth round into the magazine and, with another preloaded in the chamber turn a nine-shot Beretta into an eleven.

The day after the killing, Enzo Spalletti was released.

It would not be an exaggeration to use the word "hysteria" to describe the reaction to this fresh double homicide. The police and carabinieri were swamped with letters, anonymous and signed, which had to be followed up. Doctors, surgeons, gynecologists, and even priests were among those accused, along with fathers, sons-in-law, lovers, and rivals. Up to this time Italians had considered serial killers a northern European phenomenon, something that happened in England, Germany, or Scandinavia—and, of course, in America, where everything violent seemed to be magnified tenfold. But never in Italy.

Young people were terrified. The countryside

at night was utterly deserted. Instead, certain dark streets in the city, especially around the Basilica of San Miniato al Monte above Florence, were packed with cars, bumper to bumper, the windows plastered with newspapers or towels, young lovers inside.

After the killings, Spezi worked nonstop for a month, filing fifty-seven articles for *La Nazione*. He almost always had the scoop, the breaking news first, and the newspaper's circulation skyrocketed to the highest point in its history. Many journalists took to following him around, trying to discover his sources.

Over the years, Spezi had developed many devious tricks for prying information out of the police and prosecutors. Every morning he would make the rounds of the Tribunale and the prosecutor's offices, to see if anything new had turned up. He hung around the hallways, chatting to the lawyers and policemen, picking up crumbs of information. He also called Fosco, the medical examiner's technical assistant, asking if any interesting stiffs had arrived, and he put in a call to a contact in the fire department, because sometimes firemen were called to the scene of a crime to recover a body, particularly if the corpse was floating in water.

But Spezi's finest source of information was a little man who labored in the bowels of the Tribunale building, an insignificant fellow with an insignificant job, completely overlooked by the other journalists. He was charged with dusting and keeping in order the tomes into which were written, every day, the names of people who were *indagato*—that is, under investigation—and the reasons why. Spezi had arranged for this simple functionary to receive a complimentary subscription to *La Nazione*, of which he was inordinately proud, and in return he allowed Spezi to thumb through the books. To keep this mother lode of information secret from the journalists who tailed him, Spezi would wait until 1:30 p.m., when the journalists had gathered in front of the Tribunale to go home to lunch. He would duck into a side street that led by crooked and devious ways to a back entrance to the Tribunale and visit his secret friend.

When Spezi had gathered a few tantalizing pieces of a story—enough to know it was a good one—he would drop by the prosecutor's office and pretend he knew all about it. The prosecutor in charge of the case, anxious to find out just how much he did know, would engage him in conversation, and by skillful parrying, bluff, and feint, Spezi would be able to confirm what he'd been told and fill in the gaps of the rest, while the prosecutor's worst fears would be realized, that the journalist knew everything.

The young defense lawyers who came and went from the Tribunale were a final, indispensable source of information. They were desperate to get their names into the papers; it was a critical part of advancing their careers. When Spezi needed to lay his hands on an important file, such as a trial transcript or an inquest, he would ask one of the lawyers to get it for him, hinting at a favorable mention. If the man hesitated, and the file were crucial enough, Spezi would threaten him. "If you don't do me this favor, I'll see to it that your name won't appear in the newspapers for at least a year." It was a complete bluff, as Spezi had no such power, but a terrifying prospect to a naïve young lawyer. Thus intimidated, the lawyers sometimes let Spezi carry home entire sets of files from an investigation, which he would spend the night photocopying and return in the morning.

There was never a shortage of news in the Monster investigation. Even in the absence of new developments, Spezi always found something to write about in the rumors, conspiracy theories, and general hysteria surrounding the case.

The wildest rumors and unlikeliest conspiracy theories abounded, many involving the medical profession, and Spezi wrote about them all. An unfortunate headline in *La Nazione* fed the feeding frenzy: "The Surgeon of Death Is Back." The headline writer meant to throw out a sensational metaphor, but many people took it literally, and the rumors intensified that the killer must be a doctor. Many physicians suddenly found themselves the subject of vicious rumors and searches.

Some of the anonymous letters police received were specific enough that they felt obliged to investigate, raid, and search certain doctors' offices. They tried to inquire discreetly, to avoid generating more rumors, but in a small city like Florence every investigation seemed to become public, fueling the hysteria and the perception that the killer was a doctor. Public opinion began to gel around a portrait of the Monster: he was a man of culture and breeding, upper-class, and above all a surgeon. Hadn't the medical examiner stated that the operation performed on Carmela and Susanna had been done with "great ability"? Hadn't there been talk that the operation might have been done with a scalpel? And then there was the cold-blooded and highly calculated nature of the crimes themselves, which hinted at a killer of intelligence and education. Similar rumors insisted the killer must be a nobleman. Florentines have always harbored a suspicion of their own nobility—so much so that the early Florentine republic barred them from holding public office.

A week after the killing in the Bartoline Fields, a sudden flood of telephone calls came pouring in to the police, to *La Nazione*, and to the prosecutor's office. Colleagues, friends, and superiors of a prominent gynecologist named Garimeta Gentile were all demanding confirmation of something all of Florence was talking about, but that the press and police refused to admit: that he had been arrested as the killer. Gentile was one of the most prominent gynecologists in Tuscany, director of the Villa Le Rose clinic near Fiesole. His wife, rumor went, had found in his refrigerator, tucked away between the mozzarella and the rucola, the terrible trophies he had taken from his victims. The rumor had started when someone told police that Gentile had hidden the pistol in a safe-deposit box; the police searched the box in great secrecy, finding nothing, but bank employees began to gossip and the word went out. Investigators denied the rumor in the most strenuous terms, but it continued to grow. A disorderly crowd assembled in front of the doctor's house and had to be dispersed by the police. The head prosecutor finally had to go on television to scotch the rumor, threatening to lodge criminal charges against those spreading it.

Late that November, Spezi received a journalistic prize for work he had done unrelated to the case. He was invited to Urbino to collect the prize, a kilo of the finest white Umbrian truffles. His editor allowed him to go only after he promised to file a story from Urbino. Away from his sources and not having anything new to write about, he recounted the histories of some of the famous serial killers of the past, from Jack the Ripper to the Monster of Düsseldorf. He concluded that Florence now had its very own monster—and there, amid the perfume of truffles, he gave the killer a name: *il Mostro di Firenze*, the Monster of Florence.

CHAPTER
5

Spezi became *La Nazione*'s full-time Monster of Florence correspondent. The Monster case offered the young journalist a dazzling wealth of stories, and he made the most of it. As investigators pursued every lead, no matter how unlikely, they churned up dozens of odd happenings, curious characters, and bizarre incidents that Spezi, a connoisseur of human foible, seized on and wrote up—stories that other journalists passed over. The articles that fell from his pen were highly entertaining, and even though many involved wacky and improbable events, all were true. Spezi's articles became famous for their dry turns of phrase and that one wicked detail that remained with readers long after their morning espresso.

One day he learned from a beat cop that investigators had questioned and released an odd character who had been passing himself off as a medical examiner. Spezi found the story charming and pursued it for the paper. The man was "Dr." Carlo Santangelo, a thirty-six-year-old Florentine, of pleasing appearance, a lover of solitude, separated from his wife, who went about dressed in black wearing eyeglasses with smoked lenses, gripping a doctor's bag in his left hand. His card read:

PROF. DR. CARLO SANTANGELO

MEDICAL EXAMINER

INSTITUTE OF PATHOLOGY, FLORENCE

INSTITUTE OF PATHOLOGY, PISA — FORENSIC SECTION

In the ever-present doctor's bag were the tools of his profession, a number of perfectly honed and glistening scalpels. Instead of maintaining an established residence, Dr. Santangelo preferred to pass his days in various hotels or residences in small towns near Florence. And when he chose a hotel, he made sure it was near a small cemetery. If there was a room with a view of the tombstones, so much the better. Dr. Santangelo's face, eyes covered with thick dark lenses, had become familiar to the staff of OFISA, the most prominent funeral establishment in Florence, where he often passed his hours as if on important business. The doctor with the dark lenses doled out prescriptions, saw patients, and even ran a psychoanalysis business on the side.

The only problem was, Dr. Santangelo wasn't a medical examiner or pathologist. He wasn't even a physician, although he seems to have taken it upon himself to operate on live people, at least according to one witness.

Santangelo was unmasked when a serious car accident took place on the autostrada south of Florence, and somebody remembered that in a hotel nearby there lived a doctor. Dr. Santangelo was fetched to provide first aid, and all were amazed to hear that he was none other than the medical examiner who had performed the autopsies on the bodies of Susanna Cambi and Stefano Baldi, the Monster's latest victims. At least that was what several employees of the hotel said they had heard directly from Dr. Santangelo himself, when he had proudly opened his bag and showed them the tools of his profession.

Santangelo's peculiar claim got back to the carabinieri, and it didn't take them long to find out that he was no doctor. They learned of his predilection for small cemeteries and pathology rooms, and, even more alarming, his penchant for scalpels. The carabinieri promptly hauled Santangelo in for questioning.

The phony medical examiner freely admitted to being a liar and spinner of tall tales, although he wasn't able to explain his love for cemeteries at night. He hotly denied as libel, however, the story his girlfriend told of how he had broken off a night of passionate lovemaking by taking a dose of sleeping pills, saying this was the only way he could resist the temptation to leave his bed of love to take a turn around the tombstones.

The suspicion that Dr. Santangelo was the Monster lasted only a moment. For every night of a double homicide, he had an alibi from the employees of the hotels where he was staying. The doctor, witnesses confirmed, went to bed early, between eight-thirty and nine, in order to rise at three in the morning when the cemeteries called. "I know I do weird things," Santangelo told the magistrate who questioned him. "Sometimes it's occurred to me that I might be a little bit crazy."

The Santangelo story was just one of the many delightful pieces Spezi wrote as the paper's official "Monstrologer." He wrote about the many channelers, tarot card readers, clairvoyants, geomancers, and crystal-ball gazers who offered police their services—and some of whom were actually hired by the police and deposed, the transcripts of their "readings" duly witnessed, notarized, and filed. In middle-class living rooms across the city, an evening would sometimes end with the host and his guests seated around a three-legged table with a small glass upside down on top, questioning one of the Monster's victims and receiving his or her cryptic replies. The results were often sent to Spezi at *La Nazione*, to the police, or circulated feverishly among groups of believers. Next to the official police investigation, there developed a parallel one into the world beyond, which Spezi covered to the great amusement of his readers, as he told of attending readings and séances in graveyards with clairvoyants intent on speaking to the dead.

The case of the Monster so shook the city that

it even seemed to revive the long-dead spirit of the dark monk of San Marco, Savonarola, and his thunderings against the decadence of the age. There were those who seized on the Monster as a way to once again declaim against Florence and its presumed moral and spiritual depravity, its middle-class greed and materialism. "The Monster," wrote one editorial correspondent, "is the living expression of this city of shopkeepers, sinking into an orgy of narcissistic self-indulgence perpetrated by its priests, power brokers, puffed-up professors, politicians, and various self-appointed hacks. . . . The Monster is a cheap middle-class vindicator who hides behind a façade of bourgeois respectability. He is simply a man with bad taste."

Others thought the Monster must be, literally, a monk or priest. One wrote in a letter to *La Nazione* that the shells found at the scenes of the killings were old and discolored "because in a monastery an old pistol and some bullets could have been lying around forgotten in some dark corner almost forever." The letter writer went on to point out something that had already been widely discussed among Florentines: that the murderer might be a Savonarola-like priest visiting the wrath of God upon young people for their fornication and depravity. He pointed out that the woody piece of a grapevine stuck into the first victim might be a biblical message recalling the words of Jesus that the "vines which beareth not fruit He taketh away."

Police detectives also took the Savonarola theory seriously, and quietly began looking into certain priests known to have odd or unusual habits. Several Florentine prostitutes told police that from time to time they entertained a priest with rather eccentric tastes. He paid them generously, not for normal sex, but for the privilege of shaving off their pubic hair. The police were interested, reasoning that here was a man who enjoyed working with a razor in that particular area. The girls were able to give the police his name and address.

One crisp Sunday morning, a small group of police and carabinieri in plainclothes, led by a pair of magistrates, entered an ancient country church perched among cypresses in the lovely hills southwest of Florence. The committee was received in the sacristy, where the priest was in the act of dressing in his robes, taking up the sacred vestments with which he was about to say Mass. They showed him a warrant and told him the reason for their visit, stating their intention to search the church, grounds, confessionals, altars, reliquaries, and tabernacle.

The priest staggered and almost fell to the floor in a faint. He didn't try even for a moment to deny his nocturnal avocation as a barber for ladies, but he swore in the strongest terms that he wasn't the Monster. He said he understood why they had to search the premises, but he begged them to keep the reason for their visit secret and delay the search until after he had said Mass.

The priest was allowed to celebrate Mass before his parishioners, joined by the policemen and investigators, who sat through the service looking and acting just like city folk out enjoying a country Mass. They kept a close eye on the priest so as not to run the risk that, during the service, he might make away with some vital clue.

The search took place as soon as the parishioners had filed out, but all the investigators carried away was the priest's razor, and he was soon cleared.

CHAPTER
6

Despite the huge success of his journalistic career chronicling the Monster case, all was not well for Spezi. The savagery of the crimes preyed heavily on his mind. He began to have nightmares and was fearful for the safety of his beautiful Flemish wife, Myriam, and their baby daughter, Eleonora. The Spezis lived in an old villa that had been converted into apartments high on a hill above the city, in the very heart of the countryside stalked by the Monster. Covering the case raised many unanswerable and excruciating questions in his mind about good and evil, God, and human nature.

Myriam urged her husband to seek help, and

finally he agreed. Instead of going to a psychiatrist, Spezi, a practicing Catholic, turned to a monk who ran a mental health practice out of his cell in a crumbling eleventh-century Franciscan monastery. Brother Galileo Babbini was short, with Coke-bottle glasses that magnified his piercing black eyes. He was always cold, even in summer, and wore a shabby down coat beneath his brown monk's habit. He seemed to have stepped out of the Middle Ages, and yet he was a highly trained psychoanalyst with a doctorate from the University of Florence.

Brother Galileo combined psychoanalysis with mystical Christianity to counsel people recovering from devastating trauma. His methods were not gentle, and he was unyielding in the pursuit of truth. He had an almost supernatural insight into the dark side of the human soul. Spezi would see him for the duration of the case, and he told me that Brother Galileo had saved his sanity, perhaps his life.

The night of the killing in the Bartoline Fields, a couple driving through the area had passed a red Alfa Romeo at a bottleneck in one of the narrow, walled roads so common to the Florentine countryside. The two cars had to inch past each other, and the couple had gotten a clear look at the occupant of the other car. He was a man, they told police, so nervous that his face was contorted with anxiety. They furnished a description to a forensic Identi-Kit team, which used it to create a portrait of a hard-faced man with coarse features. A deeply scored forehead surmounted a strange face with large, baleful eyes, a hooked nose, and a mouth as tight and thin as a cut.

But the prosecutor's office, fearful of the climate of hysteria gripping Florence, decided to keep the portrait secret for fear it would unleash a witch hunt.

A year went by after the murder in the Bartoline Fields, and the investigation made no progress. As summer 1982 approached, anxiety gripped the city. As if on schedule, on the first Saturday of summer with no moon, June 19, 1982, the Monster struck again in the heart of the Chianti countryside south of Florence. His two victims were Antonella Migliorini and Paolo Mainardi. Both were in their early twenties and they were engaged to be married. They spent so much time together that their friends teased them with the nickname Vinavyl, a popular brand of superglue.

The couple came from Montespertoli, a town legendary for its wines and white truffles, as well as for several stupendous castles that crowned the surrounding hills. They spent the early part of the evening with a large gathering of young people in the Piazza del Popolo, drinking Cokes, eating ice cream, and listening to pop music that on warm Saturday nights blared from the ice-cream kiosk.

Afterwards, Paolo managed to persuade Antonella to take a drive in the countryside, despite her oft-stated terror of the Monster. They headed off into the velvety Tuscan night, taking a road that paralleled a rushing torrent that poured from the hills. They passed the gates of the gigantic crenellated castle of Poppiano, owned for nine hundred years by the counts of Gucciardini, and turned into a dead-end lane, the crickets shrilling in the warm night air, the stars twinkling overhead, two dark walls of fragrant vegetation on either side providing privacy.

At that moment, Antonella and Paolo were in the almost exact geographical center of what might be called the map of the Monster's crimes, past and future.

A reconstruction of the crime detailed what happened next. The couple had finished making love and Antonella had moved into the rear seat to put her clothes back on. Paolo apparently became aware of the killer lurking just outside the car, and he stamped on the accelerator and reversed the car at high speed from the dead-end track. The Monster, taken by surprise, fired into the car, striking Paolo's left shoulder. The terrified girl threw her arms around her boyfriend's head, gripping so tightly that later the clasp of her watch was found tangled in his hair. The car backed out of the lane, shot across the main road, and went into the ditch on the opposite side. Paolo threw the car into forward and tried to drive out, but the rear wheels were firmly stuck in the ditch and spun uselessly.

The Monster, standing on the opposite side of the road, was now bathed in the full glare of the car's headlights. He coolly took aim with his Beretta and shot out each headlight, one after the other, with two perfectly placed rounds. Two shells remained by the side of the road to mark the point where he had taken aim. He crossed the road, threw open the door, and fired two more rounds, one into each of the victims' heads. He yanked the boy out of the car, slipped into the driver's seat, and tried to rock the car out of the ditch. It was stuck fast. He gave up and, with-

out committing his usual mutilation, fled up a hill-
side next to the road, tossing the car keys about
three hundred feet from the car. Near the keys,
investigators found an empty medicine bottle
of Norzetam (piracetam), a dietary supplement
sold over the counter, which was popularly believed to improve memory and brain function. It
couldn't be traced.

The Monster took an enormous risk committing the crime next to a main road on a busy Saturday night, and he had saved himself only by
acting with superhuman coolness. Investigators
later determined that at least six cars had passed
in the hour in which the crime had occurred.
A kilometer up the road, two people were jog-
ging, taking advantage of the cool night air, and
next to the turnoff to Poppiano Castle another
couple had parked by the side of the road and
were chatting with the interior light on.

The next passing car stopped, thinking there
had been a road accident. When medics arrived,
the girl was dead. The boy was still breath-
ing. He died in the hospital without regaining
consciousness.

The next morning, a prosecutor on the case,
Silvia Della Monica, called Mario Spezi and a few
other journalists into her office. "You've got to

give me a hand here," she said. "I'd like you all to write that the male victim was taken to the hospital alive and that he may have said something useful. It might be a waste of time, but if it frightens someone and causes him to make a false move, who knows?"

The journalists did as requested. Nothing came of it—or so it seemed at first.

That same day, after a long and contentious meeting, the magistrates in charge of the case decided to release the Identi-Kit portrait of the suspect drawn up after the previous double homicide in the Bartoline Fields. On June 30, the brutal face of the unknown suspect appeared on front pages across Italy along with a description of the red Alfa Romeo.

The reaction boggled investigators. Sacks of mail and countless phone calls flooded the offices of the police, carabinieri, prosecutors, and local newspapers. Many people saw in that crude and vicious face a rival in business or love, a neighbor, a local doctor or butcher. "The Monster is a professor of obstetrics, ex-chief of the Department of Gynecology of the Hospital of ——," went one typical accusation. Another was certain it was a neighbor whose "first wife left him, then a girlfriend, and then another girlfriend, and now he lives with his mother." The police and carabinieri were paralyzed trying to follow up every lead.

Dozens of people found themselves the object of scrutiny and suspicion. The day the portrait was published, a menacing crowd formed in front of a butcher shop near the Porta Romana of Florence, many clutching newspapers with the portrait. When a new person joined the crowd, he would go into the butcher shop to see for himself, then join the crowd milling in front. The butcher shop had to close for a week.

On that same day, a pizza-maker in the Red Pony pizzeria also became the target of suspicion because he bore an uncanny resemblance to the Identi-Kit. A group of boys began making fun of him by coming into the pizzeria with the portrait, putting on a show of comparing it to him, and then rushing out as if in terror. The next day, after lunch, the man cut his own throat.

The police received thirty-two phone calls identifying a certain taxi driver from the old San Frediano quarter of Florence as the Monster. A police inspector decided to check the person out; he called the taxi company and contrived for the driver to pick him up and take him to police headquarters, where his men surrounded the cab and ordered the driver out. When the taxi driver emerged, the men were astonished: the man matched the Identi-Kit portrait so perfectly that it could have been a photograph of him. The inspector had the cabbie brought to his office, and to his surprise the man heaved a great sigh of relief. "If you hadn't brought me down here," he said, "I'd have come myself just as soon as my shift was over. Ever since that picture was published it's been total hell. I've had nothing but clients who suddenly want to get out of the cab in the middle of the ride." An investigation quickly determined that the taxi driver could not have committed the crimes— the resemblance was a coincidence.

A huge crowd attended the funeral of Paolo and Antonella, the two victims. Cardinal Benelli, the archbishop of Florence, gave the homily, turning it into an indictment of the modern world. "Much has been said," he intoned, "in these recent tragic days of monsters, of madness, of crimes of unimaginable viciousness; but we know well that madness does not arise out of nowhere; madness is the irrational and violent explosion of a world, a society, that has lost its values; that every day becomes more inimical to the human spirit. This afternoon," the cardinal concluded, "we stand here, mute witnesses to one of the worst ever defeats of all that is good in mankind."

The engaged couple were buried one next to the other, the only photograph ever taken of them together placed between their tombs.

Among the avalanche of accusations, letters, and telephone calls that arrived at carabinieri headquarters in Florence, one odd letter stood out. Inside an envelope was nothing more than a yellowed, tattered clipping from an old article published in *La Nazione*, which told of a long-forgotten murder of a couple who had been making love in a car parked in the Florentine countryside. They had been shot with a Beretta pistol firing Winchester series H rounds, the shells having been recovered at the scene. Someone had scrawled on the clipping, "Take another look at this crime." The most chilling thing about the clipping was the date it had been published: August 23, 1968.

The crime had been committed fourteen years before.

CHAPTER
7

Due to a serendipitous bureaucratic error, the shells collected from that old crime scene, which should have been tossed out, were still sitting in a nylon pouch in the dusty case files.

Each one bore on the rim the unique signature of the Monster's gun.

Investigators reopened the old case with a vengeance. But they were immediately confounded: the 1968 double murder had been solved. It had been an open-and-shut case. A man had confessed and was convicted of the double homicide, and he could not be the Monster of Florence, as he had been in prison during the first killings and had lived since his release

in a halfway house, under the watchful eye of
nuns, so feeble he could barely walk. There was
no possible way for him to have committed any
of the Monster's crimes. Nor was his confession
false—it contained specific, accurate details of
the double homicide that only a person present
at the scene could have known.

On the surface, the facts of the 1968 killing
seemed simple, squalid, even banal. A married
woman, Barbara Locci, had been having an affair with a Sicilian bricklayer. One night after
going to the movies, they had parked on a quiet
lane afterwards to have sex. The woman's jealous husband had ambushed them in the middle
of the act and shot them to death. The husband,
an immigrant from the island of Sardinia named
Stefano Mele, was picked up a few hours later.
When a paraffin-glove test indicated he had recently fired a handgun, he broke down and confessed to killing his wife and her lover in a fit
of jealousy. He was given a reduced sentence of
fourteen years due to "infirmity of mind."

Case closed.

The pistol used in the killing had never been
recovered. At the time Mele claimed to have
tossed it in a nearby irrigation ditch. But the
ditch and the entire area had been thoroughly

searched the night of the crime and no pistol had been found. At the time, nobody had paid much attention to the missing gun.

Investigators converged on the halfway house near Verona where Mele was living. They questioned him relentlessly. They wanted to know, in particular, what he had done with the gun after the killings. But nothing Mele said made any sense; his mind was half gone. He constantly contradicted himself and gave the impression he was hiding something, his demeanor watchful and tense. They could get nothing of value from him. Whatever secret he was hiding, he was hiding it so tenaciously that it looked like he would take it to the grave.

Stefano Mele was housed in an ugly white building on a flat plain near the Adige River, outside the romantic city of Verona. He lived with other ex-convicts who, having discharged their debt to society, had nowhere to go, no family, and no possibility of gainful employment. The priest running this goodly institution suddenly found himself, among his other pressing concerns, with the additional duty of protecting the diminutive Sardinian from packs of hungry journalists. Every red-blooded journalist in Italy wanted to interview Mele; the priest was equally determined to keep them away.

Spezi, the Monstrologer of *La Nazione*, was not as easily deterred as the rest. He arrived there one day with a documentary filmmaker, on the pretense of shooting a documentary on the halfway house's good work. After a flattering interview with the priest and a series of fake interviews with various inmates, they finally ended up face-to-face with Stefano Mele.

The first glimpse was discouraging: the Sardinian, although not old, paced about the room, taking tiny, nervous steps with rigid legs, almost as if he was about to topple over. To move a chair was almost a superhuman feat for him. An expressionless smile, frozen on his face, revealed a cemetery of rotten teeth. He was hardly the picture of the cold-blooded killer who, fifteen years before, had murdered two people with efficiency and sangfroid.

The interview, at the beginning, was difficult. Mele was on guard and suspicious. But little by little he relaxed, and even began to warm to the two filmmakers, glad to have finally found sympathetic listeners in whom he could confide. He finally invited them back to his room, where he showed them old photographs of his "missus" (as he called his murdered wife, Barbara) as well as pictures of their son, Natalino.

But whenever Spezi approached the old story of the crime of 1968, Mele became vague. His answers were long and rambling, and he seemed to be spouting out whatever came into his head. It seemed hopeless.

At the end, he said something odd. "They need to figure out where that pistol is, otherwise there will be more murders ... *They* will continue to kill ... *They* will continue ..."

When Spezi left, Mele gave him a gift: a postcard showing the house and balcony in Verona said to have been the place where Romeo confessed his love to Juliet. "Take it," Mele said. "I'm the 'couple man' and this is the most famous couple in the world."

They will continue ... Only after he left did the peculiar use of the plural pronoun strike Spezi. Mele had repeatedly used "they" as if referring to more than one Monster. Why would he think there were several? It seemed to imply that he had not been alone when his wife and her lover were killed. He had accomplices. Mele evidently believed that these accomplices had gone on to murder more couples.

That was when Spezi realized something that

the police had also learned: the 1968 killing had not been a crime of passion. It had been a group killing, a clan killing. Mele had not been alone at the scene of the crime: he had accomplices.

Had one or more of those accomplices gone on to become the Monster of Florence?

The police began to investigate who might have been with Mele on that fateful night. This stage of the investigation delved deeply into the strange and violent Sardinian clan to which Mele belonged. It became known as the *Pista Sarda*, the Sardinian Trail.

CHAPTER
8

The Sardinian Trail investigation illuminated a curious and almost forgotten corner of Italian history, the mass emigration in the 1960s from the island of Sardinia to the Italian mainland. Many of these immigrants ended up in Tuscany, changing the character of the province forever.

To go back to Italy in the early sixties is to make a journey much longer and deeper than a mere forty-five years. Italy was another country then, a world that has utterly vanished today.

The unified country had been created in 1871, cobbled together from various grand duchies and fiefdoms, ancient lands awkwardly stitched into a new nation. The inhabitants spoke some six hundred languages and dialects. When the new Italian state chose the Florentine dialect to be official "Italian," only two percent of the population could actually speak it. (Florentine was chosen over Roman and Neapolitan because it was the language of Dante.) Even in 1960, fewer than half of the citizens could speak standard Italian. The country was poor and isolated, still recovering from the massive destruction of World War II, mired in hunger and malaria. Few Italians had running water in their homes, owned cars, or had electricity. The great industrial and economic miracle of modern Italy was just beginning.

In 1960, the poorest, most backward area in all of Italy was the barren, sunbaked interior mountains of the island of Sardinia.

This was a Sardinia long before the Costa Smeralda, the harbors and yacht clubs, the rich Arabs and golf courses and million-dollar seaside villas. It was an isolated culture that had turned its back on the sea. Sardinians had always been afraid of the sea, because in centuries past it brought them only death, pillage, and rape. "He who comes from the sea, robs," went an ancient Sardinian expression. From the sea came ships bearing the Christian cross of the

Pisans, who cut the Sardinian forests to build their navy. From the sea arrived the black feluccas of Arab pirates who carried off women and children. And many centuries ago—so the legends went—also from the sea came a giant tsunami that wiped out the seaside towns, driving the inhabitants forever into the mountains.

The police and carabinieri charged with investigating the *Pista Sarda*, the Sardinian Trail, went back into those mountains, back in time to the town of Villacidro, where many of the Sardinians connected to the Mele clan had originated.

In 1960, almost nobody in Sardinia spoke Italian, using instead a language all their own, Logudorese, considered to be the oldest and least contaminated of all the Romance languages. The Sardinians lived with indifference to whatever law happened to be imposed by *sos italianos*, as they referred to the people of the mainland. They followed their own unwritten laws, the Barbagian code, born out of the ancient region of central Sardinia called La Barbagia, one of the wildest and least populated areas in Europe.

At the heart of the Barbagian code was the man known as the *balente*, the wily outlaw, the man of cunning, skill, and courage, who takes care of his own. Stealing, particularly of livestock, was an exalted activity under the Barbagian code when it was committed against another tribe, because, aside from mere gain, it was a heroic act, an act of *balentìa*. The thief, by stealing, demonstrated his cunning and his superiority to his adversary, who paid a just price for his incapacity to take care of his own property and flocks. Kidnapping and even murder were justified under similar rules. The *balente* had to be feared and respected.

Sardinians, especially shepherds who lived most of their lives in nomadic isolation, despised the Italian state as an occupying power. If a shepherd, by way of the code of *balentìa*, transgressed the laws inflicted by "foreigners" (Italians), instead of bearing the shame of prison he became an outlaw, joining groups of similar fugitives and brigands who lived in the mountains and raided other communities. Even as an outlaw, he could continue to live secretly in his community, where he was given protection, a welcome, and, beyond that, admiration. To the community, in return, the bandits distributed a share of their spoils, always keeping their depredations away from the home territory. The people of Sardinia viewed the brigand as a person who valiantly defended his rights and the honor of the community against the foreign oppressor, investing in him an almost mythic esteem, a figure of romance and courage.

It was into this clannish environment that the investigators delved as they followed the twists and turns of the Sardinian Trail, prying open an antique culture that made the Sicilian concept of *omertà* seem almost modern.

The village of Villacidro was isolated even by Sardinian standards. Lovely despite its great poverty, it sat on a high plain, divided by the river Leni, ringed by craggy peaks. Deer roamed the oak forests beyond the village and royal eagles soared above its red granite cliffs. The great waterfall of Sa Spendula outside the town, one of the natural wonders of Sardinia, was the inspiration for the poet Gabriele D'Annunzio on a visit to the island in 1882. As he gazed in wonder at the series of falls, tumbling down among boulders, he spied one of the local inhabitants:

> *In the lush valley a watchful shepherd,*
> *wrapped in animal skins,*
> *stands poised on the steep limestone cliffs,*
> *like a bronze faun, silent and still.*

The rest of Sardinia, on the other hand, considered Villacidro a cursed land, a "country of shadows and witches," as an old saying went. Everyone said that the witches up at Villacidro, *is cogas*, covered themselves with long dresses that swept the ground, to hide their tails.

Villacidro was home to a family named Vinci.

There were three Vinci brothers. The oldest, Giovanni, had raped one of his sisters and was shunned by the community. The youngest, Francesco, had a reputation for violence and was known for his ability with a knife—able to kill, skin, gut, and butcher a sheep in record time.

The middle one was named Salvatore. He had married a teenage girl, Barbarina, "Little Barbara," who had given him a baby, Antonio. One night, Barbarina was found dead in her bed, and her death was ruled a suicide by propane gas. But the rumors in Villacidro about this supposed "suicide" were ugly. There were whispers that someone had removed Antonio from his mother's bed after the gas bottle had been turned on, thus saving his life—and leaving the mother to die. Most of the townspeople believed Salvatore had murdered her.

The death of Barbarina was the final straw against the Vinci brothers. The town of Villacidro united against them, and they were compelled to leave. One fine day in 1961 they boarded a ferry for the mainland, joining the great emigration from Sardinia. They landed in Tuscany to begin a new life.

On the other side of the sea, another Barbara awaited them.

CHAPTER
9

When the three Vinci brothers arrived at the docks in Livorno, they were not typical Sardinian immigrants to Tuscany, stepping off the ferry, clutching their cardboard suitcases, with dazed looks on their faces, the first time out of their small mountain village with scarcely a lira in their pockets. The Vincis were self-assured, adaptable, and surprisingly sophisticated.

Salvatore and Francesco were the two brothers who would play a major role in the Monster of Florence story. Physically they resembled each other: short and robust, good-looking, with curly, raven-black hair, their restless eyes peering out of the deep fissures in their rough, arrogant faces. Both were blessed with an intelligence far greater than might be expected from their limited background. But despite their resemblance, the two brothers couldn't have been more different. Salvatore was quiet, reflective, introverted, given to reasoned arguments and discussions that he pursued with a mellifluous, Old World courtesy. He wore a pair of spectacles that gave him the air of a professor of Latin. Francesco, the youngest, was extroverted and cocky, the man of action with a macho swagger, the true *balente* of the two.

Naturally, they hated each other.

Once in Tuscany, Salvatore found work as a bricklayer. Francesco spent most of his time in a bar outside of Florence that was an infamous hangout for Sardinian criminals. It was the unofficial headquarters of three famous Sardinian gangsters who had exported to Tuscany a classic Sardinian business: kidnapping for ransom. These men were partly responsible for the rash of kidnappings that plagued Tuscany in the late sixties and seventies. In one instance, when a ransom was slow in coming, they killed the victim, who was a count, and disposed of the body by feeding it to man-eating pigs—a detail Thomas Harris used to great effect in his novel *Hannibal.* Francesco Vinci, as far as we know, never took part in these kidnappings. He dedicated himself to petty holdups, theft, and another venerable Sardinian tradition, rustling livestock.

Salvatore rented a room in a run-down house occupied by a Sardinian family named Mele, where Stefano Mele lived with his father, siblings, and wife, Barbara Locci. (In Italy, the wife traditionally keeps her maiden name after marriage.) Barbara Locci was slinky and sloe-eyed, with a flattened nose and thick, well-shaped lips. She favored skintight red skirts that showed off a full-bodied figure. When she was a teenager back in Sardinia, her deeply impoverished family had arranged for her to marry Stefano, who came from marginally better circumstances. He was much older than she, and on top of it *uno stupido*, a simpleton. When the Mele family had immigrated to Tuscany, she went along.

Once in Tuscany, the very lively young Barbara set about ruining the Mele family's honor. She often stole money from her in-laws and went out on the town seeking men, giving them money, and sneaking them back into the Mele home. Stefano was completely unable to control her.

In an effort to put an end to her nocturnal

adventures, the patriarch of the Mele family, Stefano's father, put iron bars on the first-floor windows and tried to keep her locked in the house. It didn't work. Barbara soon took up with their lodger, Salvatore Vinci.

Barbara's husband was no obstacle to the affair. He even encouraged it. Salvatore Vinci testified later, "He wasn't jealous. He was the one who invited me to live in their house when I was looking for a place to live. 'Come live with us!' he said. 'We've got a free room.' 'What about money?' 'Give whatever you can.' So I moved into Mele's house. And right away he brought me to meet his wife in bed. Then he urged me to take her to the movies. He said that it didn't matter to him. Or he would go play cards at his social club and leave me alone with her in the house."

At one point Stefano's motorbike was hit by a car and he was laid up in the hospital for several months recuperating. The following year Barbara bore him a son, Natalino, but anyone with the ability to count to nine could see that the paternity of Natalino was in grave doubt.

Fed up with this blight on their honor, the patriarch of the family threw Stefano and his wife out of the house, along with Salvatore. Stefano and Barbara rented a hovel in a working-class suburb west of Florence, where she continued to see Salvatore, with the complete (and indeed enthusiastic) cooperation of her husband.

"What was her attraction?" Salvatore testified later about Barbara. "Well, when she made love she certainly wasn't a statue. She knew what kind of game it was, and she knew how to play it."

In the summer of 1968, Barbara left Salvatore and took up with his brother Francesco, the *balente* who played the macho man. With him, Barbara acted the part of a gangster's moll, going to the Sardinian bar, joking with the tough guys, wiggling her hips. She dressed like a femme fatale. Once she went too far, at least for Francesco's taste, and he seized her by the hair, dragged her into the street, and ripped off the offending dress, leaving her in the middle of a gaping crowd in only her slip and hosiery.

At the beginning of August 1968, a new lover appeared on the scene: Antonio Lo Bianco, a bricklayer from Sicily, tall, heavily muscled, with black hair. He too was married, but that didn't stop him from challenging Francesco: "Barbara?" he was reported to have said. "I'll fuck her in a week." Which he did.

Now both Salvatore and Francesco had reason

to feel angry and humiliated. On top of that, Barbara had just stolen six hundred thousand lire from Stefano, money he had received for the motorbike accident. The Vinci and Mele clan feared she would give it to Lo Bianco. They decided to get it back.

The story of Barbara Locci was reaching its final chapter.

The end came on August 21, 1968. A careful reconstruction of the crime, done years later, revealed what happened. Barbara went with her new lover, Antonio Lo Bianco, to the movies to see the latest Japanese horror flick. She brought along her son, Natalino, six years old. Afterwards the three of them drove off in Lo Bianco's white Alfa Romeo. The car headed out of town and turned in to a little dirt road past a cemetery. They drove a few hundred feet and stopped next to a stand of cane, a place where they often went to have sex.

The shooter and his accomplices were already hidden in the cane. They waited until Barbara and Lo Bianco began having sex—her on top, straddling him. The left rear window of the car was open—it was a warm night—and the shooter approached the car in silence, reached in the window with the .22 Beretta in hand, and took aim. The gun was poised a few feet above the head of Natalino, who was sleeping in the backseat. From almost point-blank range—there was powder tattooing—he fired seven shots: four into him and three into her. Each round was perfectly placed, penetrating vital organs, and they both died immediately. Natalino woke at the first shot and saw, in front of his eyes, the bright yellow flashes.

In the magazine of the gun remained one more shot. The shooter handed the gun to Stefano Mele, who took it, pointed it at his dead wife's body with an unsteady hand, and pulled the trigger. The shot, even from that close range, was wild and it struck the woman in the arm. No matter—she was dead and the shot had served its purpose: it had contaminated Stefano's hand with powder that the paraffin-glove test, then in use, would certainly pick up. Mele, the simpleton, would take the fall for the rest. Someone searched the glove compartment for the missing six hundred thousand lire, but it wasn't found. (Investigators would find it later, hidden elsewhere in the car.)

The remaining problem was the child, Natalino. He couldn't be left in the car with his dead mother. After the killing, he saw his father holding the gun and cried out, "That's the gun that killed Mommy!" Mele threw the gun down and picked up his son, hoisted him to his shoulders, and set off walking. He sang a song to calm him down, "The Sunset." Two and a half kilometers down the road, Stefano dropped him at the front door of a stranger's house, rang the doorbell, and disappeared. When the homeowner leaned out the window, he saw a terrified little boy standing in the light of the front door. "Mama and Uncle are dead in the car," the little boy cried in a high, quavering voice.

CHAPTER
10

Even at the time of the 1968 double homicide, the investigation uncovered many clues that a group of men had committed the killings, clues that were ignored or dismissed.

The police back then had questioned the six-year-old Natalino closely, the only witness to the crime. His story was confused. His father had been there. At one point during his questioning, he said, "I saw Salvatore in the cane." He quickly reversed that, saying it wasn't Salvatore but Francesco, and then he admitted it was his father who told him to say it was Francesco. He described the "shadow" of another man at the crime scene and spoke vaguely about an "Uncle

Piero" as also being present, a man who "parted his hair on the right and worked at night"—which must have been his uncle, Piero Mucciarini, who worked as a baker. Then he said he couldn't remember anything.

One of the carabinieri officers, frustrated by the child's incessant contradictions, threatened him: "If you don't tell the truth, I'll take you back to your dead mother."

The only solid piece of information the investigators felt they had gotten from the boy was that he had seen his father at the crime scene with a gun in hand. As the wronged husband, he was the perfect suspect. They took Stefano Mele in that very night and quickly demolished a pathetic alibi that he had been home sick. The paraffin-glove test revealed traces of nitrate powder between the thumb and index finger of his right hand, the classic pattern of someone who had recently fired a handgun. Even a simpleton like Mele realized that after the test, there was no point in further denial, and he confessed to being present at the scene of the crime. Perhaps it even dawned on him that he had been framed.

Cautiously, fearfully, Mele told the carabinieri interrogators that Salvatore Vinci was the actual killer. "One day," he said, "he told me that he had a pistol . . . It was him, he was the jealous lover of my wife. It was him, who, after she left him, threatened to kill her, he said it more than once. One day when I asked him to give me back some money, do you know what he said? 'I'll kill your wife for you,' that's what he said, 'and that'll even up the debt.' He really said that!"

But then, abruptly, Mele retracted his accusations against Salvatore Vinci and took full responsibility for the murder. As to what had happened to the gun, he never gave a satisfactory answer. "I threw it in the irrigation ditch," he claimed— but a careful search that night of the ditch and the surrounding area revealed nothing.

The carabinieri did not like his story. It seemed improbable that this man who had difficulty finding his way around a room would, by himself, have been able to find the scene of the crime, without a car, many kilometers from his house, ambush the lovers, and place seven shots into them. When they pressed him, Stefano once again turned the accusation against Salvatore. "He was the only one who had a car," he said.

The carabinieri decided to bring the two together to see what might happen. They picked

up Salvatore and brought him down to the carabinieri barracks. Those present have said they
never will forget that meeting.

Salvatore entered the room, suddenly the
balente himself, full of swaggering self-assurance.
He stopped and subjected Mele to a hard, word-
less stare. Bursting into tears, Mele threw himself on the ground at Salvatore's feet, groveling
and sobbing. "Forgive me! Please forgive me!" he
cried. Vinci turned around and left, never having
spoken a word. He possessed an inexplicable
hold over Stefano Mele, the ability to enforce an
omertà so powerful that Mele would risk life
in prison rather than challenge it. Mele immediately retracted his accusations of Salvatore being
the shooter and once again accused Salvatore's
brother Francesco. But when pressed, Mele finally went back to insisting he had committed
the double murder all by himself.

At this point the police and the examining
magistrate (the judge who oversees the investigation) felt satisfied. Regardless of the particulars, the crime was solved in the main: they had
the confession of the wronged husband, backed
up by forensic evidence and the statements of
his son. Mele was the only one charged with
murder.

During the trial in the Court of Assizes, when Salvatore Vinci was brought in to testify, an odd scene occurred. As he was gesturing and speaking, his hand caught the attention of the judge. On one finger he wore a woman's engagement ring.

"What is that ring?" the judge asked.

"It's Barbara's engagement ring," he said, looking not at the judge but giving Mele another hard stare. "She gave it to me."

Mele was convicted as the sole perpetrator of the double homicide and sentenced to fourteen years.

In 1982, investigators began to compile a list of possible accomplices to the 1968 killing. On the list were the two Vinci brothers, Salvatore and Francesco, as well as Piero Mucciarini and the "shadow" mentioned by Natalino.

Investigators felt sure that the gun had not been thrown in the ditch, as Stefano insisted. A gun used in a homicide is almost never casually sold, given away, or tossed. One of Mele's accomplices, they felt, must have taken it home and carefully hidden it. Six years later, that gun had emerged from its hiding place, along with the same box of bullets, to become the Monster of Florence's gun.

Tracing the gun, they realized, was the key to solving the case of the Monster of Florence.

The Sardinian Trail investigation zeroed in on Francesco Vinci first, because he was the *balente*, the cocky one, the guy with a rap sheet. He was violent, he had beaten up his girlfriends, and he hung around with gangsters. Salvatore, on the other hand, seemed quieter, a man who had always worked hard and stayed out of trouble. He had a spotless record. To the Tuscan police, who had no experience with serial killers, Francesco Vinci seemed the obvious choice.

Investigators dug up bits and pieces of circumstantial evidence against Francesco. They established that he had not been far from the scenes of each crime on the dates they were committed. Between robberies, thefts of livestock, and escapades with women, he moved around a great deal. At the time of the 1974 double homicide in Borgo San Lorenzo, for example, they placed him near the scene, due to an argument between him and a jealous husband, in which his favorite nephew, Antonio, the son of Salvatore Vinci, also took part. At the time of the

Montespertoli killing, Francesco had also been nearby, again visiting Antonio, who happened to live at that time in a little town six kilometers from the scene.

A prime piece of evidence against Francesco, however, took a while to surface. In the middle of July, the carabinieri in a town on the southern Tuscan coast reported to investigators in Florence that on June 21 they had discovered a car hidden in the woods, covered with branches. They had finally gotten around to running the license plate and found it belonged to Francesco Vinci.

This seemed highly significant: June 21 happened to be the day that Spezi and other journalists had published the (false) reports that one of the victims of the Montespertoli killings may have survived long enough to talk. Perhaps the news had spooked the Monster after all, prompting him to hide his car.

The carabinieri took Vinci in and asked him for an explanation. He launched into a story about a woman and a jealous husband, but it didn't make much sense and, furthermore, it didn't seem to explain why he had hidden the car.

Francesco Vinci was arrested in August of

1982, two months after the Montespertoli kill-ings. At the time, the examining magistrate said to the press, "The danger now is that a new kill-ing might happen, even more spectacular than before. The Monster, in fact, might be tempted to reassert his paternity claim to the killings by moving yet again into action." It was a strange thing for a judge to say on the arrest of a sus-pect, but it showed a high level of uncertainty among the investigators that they had the right man.

Fall and winter came, and there were no new killings. Francesco Vinci remained in custody. Florentines, however, did not rest easy: Fran-cesco did not look like the intelligent and aris-tocratic Monster they had imagined; he was too much the image of a cheap hustler, ladies' man, and macho charmer.

All of Florence awaited with trepidation the arrival of the warm weather of summer, the time favored by the Monster.

CHAPTER
II

During that fall and winter of 1982-83, Mario Spezi wrote a book on the Monster of Florence case. Entitled *Il Mostro di Firenze*, it was published in May. It told the story of the case from the 1968 killings to the Montespertoli double homicide. The book was devoured by a public terrified of what the coming season might bring. But as the balmy nights of summer settled on the green hills of Florence, no new killings occurred. Florentines began to hope that perhaps the police had gotten the right man after all.

In addition to writing a book and publishing articles on the Monster case, that summer

Spezi wrote a puff piece about a young film-maker named Cinzia Torrini, who had produced a charming little documentary about the life of Berto, the last ferryman across the Arno River—an ancient, wizened man who regaled his passengers with stories, legends, and old Tuscan sayings. Torrini was pleased by Spezi's article, and she read his Monster book with interest. She called him to propose the idea of making a film on the Monster of Florence, and Spezi invited her to dinner at his apartment. It would be a late dinner, even by Italian standards, because Spezi kept journalistic hours.

And so it was that on the evening of September 10, 1983, Torrini found herself driving up the steep hill that led to Spezi's apartment. As might be expected from a cinematographer, Torrini had a vivid imagination. The trees on either side of the road, she said later, looked like the hands of skeletons twisting and clawing in the wind. She could not stop herself from questioning her wisdom at going out in the heart of the Florentine hills on a moonless Saturday night to talk to someone about hideous crimes committed in the Florentine hills on moonless Saturday nights. Around one curve of the winding road, the headlights of her old Fiat 127 spotlighted a whitish thing in the middle of the narrow road. The "thing" spread itself, becoming enormous. It detached itself from the asphalt and rose, noiselessly, like a dirty sheet carried off by the wind, revealing itself to be a great white owl. Torrini felt a tightening of her stomach, because Italians believe, as the Romans did before them, that it is an ugly omen to encounter an owl in the nighttime. She almost turned around.

She parked her car in the small parking area outside the huge iron gates of the old villa turned into an apartment building and rang the bell. As soon as Spezi opened the green door to his apartment, her sense of disquiet vanished. The place was welcoming, warm, and eccentric, with an old seventeenth-century gambling table, called a scagliola, used as a coffee table, old photographs and drawings on the walls, a fireplace in one corner. The dining table had already been set on the terrace, under a white awning, overlooking the twinkling lights sprinkling the hills. Torrini laughed at herself for the absurd uneasiness she had felt on the drive up and put it out of her mind.

They spent much of the evening talking about the possibility of making a film on the case of the Monster of Florence.

"It seems to me it would be difficult," Spezi said. "The story lacks a central character—the killer. I have my doubts the police have the right man, the man they have in prison awaiting trial, Francesco Vinci. It would be a murder mystery without an ending."

Not a problem, Torrini explained. "The main character isn't the killer: it's the city of Florence itself—the city that discovers it harbors a monster within."

Spezi explained why he thought Francesco Vinci was not the Monster. "All they have against him is that he was a lover of the first woman killed, that he beats up his girlfriends, and that he's a crook. In my view, these are elements in his favor."

"Why do you say that?" Torrini asked.

"He likes women. He's a big success with women, and that's enough to convince me he isn't the Monster. He hits them but he doesn't kill them. The Monster *destroys* women. He hates them because he wants them and can't have them. That's his frustration, the thing that damns him, and so he possesses them physically in the only way he can, which is to steal the part most indicative of their femininity."

"If you believe that," Torrini said, "then it must

mean the Monster is impotent. Is that what you think?"

"More or less."

"What do you make of the ritual aspects of the killings, the careful placement of the body? The stick from a grapevine inserted in the vagina, for example, which recalls the words of Saint John that the 'vines which beareth not fruit He taketh away'? A killer who is punishing couples for having sex outside of marriage?"

Spezi blew a stream of smoke toward the ceiling and laughed. "That's a bunch of twaddle. You know why he used an old piece of grapevine? If you look at the crime scene photos, you see that they were parked right next to a vineyard! He simply grabbed the closest stick he could find. To me, his use of a stick to violate a woman seems to confirm that he is not exactly Superman. He didn't and probably can't rape his victims."

Toward the end of the evening, Spezi opened his book and read the last page out loud. "Many investigators feel the case of the Monster of Florence is solved. But if, at the end of a dinner passed in pleasant company, you were to ask me what I thought, I would tell you the truth: that it is with a strong sense of unease that I answer the first ringing of the telephone on a

Sunday morning. Especially if the previous Saturday evening was the night of the new moon."

After Mario set down his book, a silence fell on the terrace that overlooked the Florentine hills.

And then the telephone rang.

It was a lieutenant of the local carabinieri, one of Spezi's contacts. "Mario, they've just found two people killed in a VW camper in Giogoli, above Galluzzo. The Monster? I don't know. The dead are two men. But if I were you, I'd head over there for a look."

CHAPTER
12

To reach Giogoli, Spezi and Torrini took a road that climbed a steep hill behind the great monastery of La Certosa. The road is called Via Volterrana, and it is one of the most ancient in Europe, built by the Etruscans three thousand years ago. At the top of the hill, Via Volterrana makes a gentle turn and runs straight along the ridgeline. Immediately on the right lies a second road, Via di Giogoli, a narrow lane running between mossy stone walls. The wall on the right encloses the grounds of the Villa Sfacciata, which belonged to the noble family Martelli. Sfacciata means "cheeky" or "impudent" in Italian, and the mysterious appellation went back five hundred years, to at least the time when the villa was home to the man who gave America its name.

The left wall of Via di Giogoli encloses a large olive grove. About fifty meters from the beginning of the road, almost opposite the villa, stood a break in the wall, which allowed farm equipment access to the grove. The opening led to a level area that enjoyed a magical view of the southern Florentine hills, over which were sprinkled ancient castles, towers, churches, and villas. A few hundred meters away, on top of the closest hill, stood a famed Romanesque tower known as Sant'Alessandro a Giogoli. On the next hill rose an exquisite sixteenth-century villa called I Collazzi, half hidden behind a cluster of cypress trees and umbrella pines. It belonged to the Marchi family, one of whose heirs by marriage had become the Marchesa Frescobaldi. Being a personal friend of Prince Charles and Lady Diana, she had entertained the royal pair shortly after their marriage.

Beyond this extraordinary view, the Via di Giogoli descended through torturous switchbacks through villages and small farms, ending in the monolithic working-class suburbs of Florence in the valley below. At night, those gray suburbs became a twinkling carpet of lights.

It would have been hard to find a more beautiful place in all of Tuscany.

Later—too late—the city of Florence would post a sign at this spot that said, in German, English, French, and Italian, "No parking from 7:00 p.m. to 7:00 a.m. No camping for reasons of security." On that evening, the night of September 10, 1983, there had been no sign, and someone had camped there.

When Spezi and Torrini arrived, they found the full cast of characters in the Monster investigation. There was Silvia Della Monica, a prosecutor, with the head prosecutor, Piero Luigi Vigna, his handsome face so sunken and gray it looked almost collapsed. The medical examiner, Mauro Maurri, his blue eyes glittering, was working on the two cadavers. Chief Inspector Sandro Federico was also there, pacing about in a state of high nervous tension.

A spotlight fixed to the top of a police car threw a spectral light across the scene, casting long shadows from the group of people arranged in a semicircle around the sky blue VW bus with German license plates. The stark light emphasized the ugliness of the scene, the scratches on the beaten-up old camper, the lines in the faces of the investigators, the screwlike branches of the olive trees looming against the black sky. To the left of the camper, the field sloped away into darkness toward a cluster of stone houses where, twenty years later, I would take up temporary residence with my family.

When they arrived, the left door of the camper stood open and from inside could be heard, just concluding, the music from the film *Blade Runner*. The music had been playing all day long, without ceasing, as the tape player automatically looped the tape over and over. Inspector Sandro Federico approached and opened his hand, showing two .22 caliber shells. On the base was the same unmistakable mark made by the gun of the Monster.

The Monster had struck again, and the number of his victims had now risen to ten. Francesco Vinci, still in jail, could not have committed the crime.

"Why would he strike two men this time?" Spezi asked.

"Take a look inside the camper," said Federico, with a jerk of his head.

Spezi went toward the van. Passing along its side, he noticed that in the high part of the little windows on the side, in a thin band where the glass was transparent, there were bullet holes. To look inside, he had to stand on his tiptoes. The killer, in order to aim properly, would have to have been taller than Spezi, at least five feet ten inches. He also noted bullet holes in the metal side of the van itself.

Around the van's open door stood a number of people; policemen in plainclothes, carabinieri, and crime scene investigators; their footprints lay everywhere on the dew-laden grass, obliterating any sign left by the killer. It was one more example, Spezi thought, of a botched crime scene.

But before he looked inside the van, Spezi's eye was arrested by something scattered about on the ground outside, pages ripped up from a glossy pornographic magazine entitled *Golden Gay*.

A dim light filtered into the interior. The two seats in front were empty: immediately behind was the body of a young man with a thin mustache, his eyes glazed over, lying stretched out on a double mattress, his feet toward the rear of the van. The second body was in the back of the van, in the corner. It was still crouching as if to make itself as small as possible, petrified with terror, its hands clenched, its face covered by a cascade of long blond hair. The hair was streaked with blood, black and congealed.

"Looks like a girl, don't you think?" came the voice of Sandro Federico, shaking Spezi out of his surprise.

"At first we were fooled, too. But it's a man. It seems our friend made the same mistake. Can you imagine how he felt when he discovered it?"

On Monday, September 12, the papers screamed out the news:

TERROR IN FLORENCE
The Monster Chooses His Victims at Random

The two victims, Horst Meyer and Uwe Rüsch, both twenty-four years old, had been traveling around Italy together and had parked their VW bus in this place on September 8. Their almost nude bodies had been discovered around seven o'clock the evening of September 10.

By this time, Francesco Vinci had spent thirteen months in jail, and the public had come to believe he was the Monster of Florence. It seemed that once again, as with Enzo Spalletti, the Monster himself had demonstrated the innocence of the accused.

The Monster of Florence was now international news. The *Times* of London devoted an entire Sunday section to the case. Television crews arrived from as far away as Australia.

"Even after twelve victims,[1] all we know is that the Monster is free and that his .22 caliber Beretta could kill again," wrote *La Nazione*.

Now that the Monster had killed while Francesco Vinci was in prison, his release seemed imminent. But as the days went by, Vinci remained incarcerated. Investigators suspected that the double homicide had been "made to order." Perhaps, they theorized, someone close to Vinci wished to demonstrate that he couldn't be the killer. The crime of Giogoli was anomalous, improvised, different. It seemed strange that the Monster would have made such a grave mistake, given their assumption that he took his time watching the couple having sex before killing them. And then he had killed on a Friday night, not a Saturday, as was his custom.

A new examining magistrate had arrived in Florence shortly before the crime and was now in charge of the Monster investigation. His

---

[1] At the time, many people considered the 1968 double homicide to have been the Monster's first murders—hence twelve victims, not ten.

name was Mario Rotella. He chilled the public with one of his first public statements, in which he said, "We have never identified the so-called Monster of Florence with Francesco Vinci. For the crimes committed after the 1968 homicide he is only a suspect." And then he added, causing a furor, "He is not the only such suspect."

One of the prosecutors, Silvia Della Monica, aroused even more confusion and speculation when she said, "Vinci is not the Monster. But neither is he innocent."

CHAPTER
13

A few days following the Giogoli killings, there was a tense summit meeting in the prosecutor's offices, on the second floor of a Baroque palace in Piazza San Firenze. (The palace is one of the few seventeenth-century edifices in the city—disparaged by Florentines as "new construction.") They met in the small office of Piero Luigi Vigna, the air as thick as a Maremma fog. Vigna was in the habit of breaking his cigarettes in two and smoking both pieces, under the illusion that he was smoking less. Silvia Della Monica was there—small, blonde, herself surrounded by a self-generated cloud of smoke; also in attendance was a colonel of the carabinieri, who had brought two packs of his favorite Marlboros, and Chief Inspector Sandro Federico, who never ceased torturing a withered "toscano" cigar between his teeth. An assistant prosecutor smoked his way through pack after pack of tarry Gauloises. The only nonsmoker in the room was Adolfo Izzo, who merely had to breathe to acquire the habit.

Federico and the carabinieri colonel presented a reconstruction of the Giogoli murders. Using diagrams and flow charts, they showed the sequence of events, how the killer had shot one of the men through the little window and then had fired through the sides of the van, killing the other man where he was crouching in the corner. The Monster then entered the van, fired some more rounds into them, and discovered his mistake. In a rage, he picked up a gay magazine and ripped it up, scattering the pieces outside, and left.

The prosecutor, Vigna, expressed his view that the crime seemed anomalous, ad hoc and improvised—in short, that it had been committed not by the Monster, but by someone else trying to demonstrate the innocence of Francesco Vinci. The investigators suspected that Vinci's nephew, Antonio, had committed the killings as a way to spring his beloved uncle from prison. (Antonio, you will recall, had been the baby saved from the gas back in Sardinia.) Unlike the rest of his family, he seemed tall enough to have taken aim through the clear stripe of glass at the top of the camper's window.

A plan of brutal subtlety was secretly put in motion. Sign of it appeared ten days after the Giogoli killings, when a small and apparently unrelated news item appeared in the back pages of the newspapers, reporting that Antonio Vinci, nephew of Francesco Vinci, had been arrested for illegal possession of firearms. Antonio and Francesco were extremely close, partners in many shady activities and sketchy adventures. The arrest of Antonio was a sign that the investigators were widening their exploration of the Sardinian Trail. The examining magistrate in the Monster case, Mario Rotella, and a lead prosecutor, Silvia Della Monica, were convinced that both Francesco and Antonio knew the identity of the Monster of Florence. They were convinced, in fact, that this terrible secret was shared by the entire clan of Sardinians. The Monster was one of them, and the others knew his identity.

With both men in Florence's Le Murate prison, they could now be played against each other, and perhaps broken. The suspects were kept apart, and artfully crafted rumors were circulated through the prison, designed to arouse suspicions and pit one against the other. A program of interrogation aimed at the two prisoners was set in motion, giving each one the impression that the other had talked. It was "let slip" to each that the other had made serious accusations against him, and that he could save himself only by telling the truth about the other.

It didn't work. Neither one talked. One afternoon, in the ancient interrogation room at Le Murate, the head prosecutor, Piero Luigi Vigna, was fed up. He decided to press Francesco Vinci as hard as he could. Vigna, handsome, dashing, and cultured, with the profile of a hawk, had in the course of his career faced down Mafia dons, murderers, kidnappers, extortionists, and drug kingpins. But he was no match for the small Sardinian.

For half an hour the prosecutor hammered Vinci. With crisp logic, he wove a web of clues and evidence and deductions proving the man's guilt. Then, all of a sudden, using a technique straight out of a Hollywood movie cliché, he shoved his face to within an inch of the black-bearded face of the Sardinian and screamed, spraying him with saliva:

"Confess, Vinci! You're the Monster!"

Francesco Vinci remained utterly calm. He smiled and his carbon-black eyes twinkled. In a calm, low voice he responded with a question that seemed to have nothing to do with anything: "I beg your pardon, sir, but if you want a response from me, tell me first what that thing is on the table. If you please." With a hand he indicated Vigna's pack of cigarettes.

The prosecutor, wanting to follow the man's train of thought, said, "It's a pack of cigarettes, obviously."

"I'm sorry, but isn't it *empty*?"

Vigna agreed that it was.

"Then," said the Sardinian, "it is not a pack of cigarettes. It *was* a pack of cigarettes. Now it is merely a pack. And now, may I ask another favor? Please take it in hand and crush it."

Curious to see where Vinci was leading, Vigna took up the pack and crushed it into a ball.

"There!" said Francesco, showing a mouth full of white teeth. "And now it is no longer even a pack. Your evidence, sir, is like this: you can crush and mangle it to fit any theory you like, but it will always remain the same: empty speculation—never proof."

The nephew Antonio proved just as smart. Not only did he stand up to the interrogations, but at his trial for possession of unregistered firearms he acted as his own lawyer. He pointed out that the guns had not been found in his house, but some distance from it, and that no evidence had been presented that connected him with the firearms in question. Might they not have been planted, perhaps, as a way to imprison him so that he could be pitted against his uncle in a scheme of interrogation?

He promptly won his case and was released.

CHAPTER
14

As time went on, it became increasingly difficult to justify the imprisonment of Franceso Vinci. With his nephew's acquittal and the failure of interrogators to get any of their questions answered, it was only a matter of time before they had to let him go.

Frustrated at the lack of progress, the examining magistrate himself, Mario Rotella, decided to personally interrogate Stefano Mele and make one last attempt to extract information from him. Before making the journey to Verona, Rotella prepared himself well. In a heavy folder he collected a mass of testimony that he had gleaned from old interrogations regarding the

1968 murders, including statements made by little Natalino and his father, Stefano Mele, Mele's brother and his three sisters, and a brother-in-law. He also collected telling statements from more recent interrogations of various participants. He was convinced that the 1968 crime was a clan killing, and that everyone who had participated knew who had taken home the gun. They all knew the identity of the Monster of Florence. Rotella was determined to break the wall of silence.

The new interrogation took place on January 16, 1984. Rotella asked Mele if Francesco Vinci participated in the killings. Mele responded, "No, Francesco Vinci was not with me the night of August 21, 1968. I accused him only to get back at him for being the lover of my wife."

"Tell me, then: who *was* with you that night?"

"Now I don't remember."

He was clearly and deliberately lying. Somebody—the Monster, perhaps—had a tenacious hold over him. Why? What secret did Mele fear more than prison?

Rotella returned to Florence. The press assumed his mission had failed. In reality he had in his file a scrap of paper, handwritten, much soiled, which had been folded and unfolded a hundred times, which he had found hidden in Stefano Mele's wallet. It was a document he considered of the utmost importance.

On January 25, 1984, Rotella sent out word that he would hold an important press conference at 10:30 a.m. in his office the following day. On the twenty-sixth his office was packed with reporters and photographers, most of whom were convinced they would hear the announcement of the release of Francesco Vinci.

Rotella had a surprise in store for them. "The examining magistrate," he read in his pompous voice, "with the agreement of the public minister of the province of Florence, has taken into custody two people for the crimes attributed to Francesco Vinci."

Two hours after the sensational press conference *La Nazione* was first on the newsstands with an extra edition. The headline spanned the entire front page.

ARRESTED!
THE MONSTERS ARE TWO

Above the fold, under the nine-column headline, were plastered the paired photographs that offered to public opinion the faces of the alleged Double Monster: Giovanni Mele, Stefano's brother, and Piero Mucciarini, his brother-in-law.

Most Florentines looked at the newspaper photographs with skepticism. The dimwitted features of the two suspects did not strike them as consistent with the crafty, highly intelligent Monster they had imagined.

The story of why the men were suspected quickly came out. At the end of his interrogation of Mele, Rotella had searched the man's wallet and discovered a tiny piece of paper hidden in a fold. It was a kind of crude memory aid or list of talking points on how he should respond to questions posed by his interrogators. It had been written by his brother, Giovanni Mele, and given to him about two years earlier, when the news first broke connecting the obscure 1968 killing with the Monster of Florence. The writing was weak and tentative, the letters formed with the laboriousness of a second grader, half in capitals and half in cursive. The words were riddled with misspellings resulting from a confusion between Italian and the Sardinian language.

REPORT OF NATALINO regarDING
UNCLE PIETO.

That you woud HAVE SAID the name affter
SERVING THE SENTENSCE.

HOW IT IS Shown FROM Ballistic TEST
of the Shots fired

When Rotella confronted Mele with the paper, he "confessed" that, yes, in fact, his two accomplices in 1968 had been his brother Giovanni and Piero Mucciarini, and that the latter had fired the killing shots—"or rather, no, it was my brother, I can't remember, that was seventeen years ago."

Judge Rotella pored over these enigmatic phrases for days. After much effort, he finally believed he had deciphered them. In the original interrogation of the six-year-old Natalino after the 1968 killing, the little boy had spoken of an "Uncle Pietro or Piero" being present at the murder scene. The details Natalino gave indicated this was his uncle Piero Mucciarini, the baker. But Barbara Locci had a brother named Pietro, and Rotella interpreted the note as an instruction to mislead investigators into thinking that Natalino had spoken about *that* uncle instead. In other words, the paper warned Stefano to say in response to questioning, "I will speak finally, after having served my sentence. Regarding the report of Natalino that Uncle Pieto was at the scene, I can finally say that with me was my wife's brother Pietro and that this was the 'Pieto' he was referring to. The ballistics tests would show he was the shooter."

In other words, the paper instructed Stefano to divert suspicion away from his sister's husband, Piero Mucciarini, to his dead wife's brother, Pietro. Rotella took this to mean that Piero Mucciarini must be guilty, along with Giovanni Mele, the author of the note. Otherwise, why try to divert suspicion? *Quod erat demonstrandum*: both of them were the Monster.

If this logic seems hard to follow, join the club. Hardly anyone except Mario Rotella pretended to understand this convoluted chain of deduction.

Rotella ordered a search of Giovanni's house and car. It brought to light a scalpel, some strange leatherworking knives, ropes coiled up in the trunk of his car, a stack of pornographic magazines, suspicious notes on the phases of

the moon, and a bottle with a perfumed liquid for washing the hands. The investigators
gathered additional details from Giovanni's ex-
girlfriend, who revealed salacious details of his
perverse sexual habits and the extraordinary
dimensions of his member, so large it made
normal sex difficult.

All very suspicious.

The "old" Monster, Francesco Vinci, was still
being kept under lock and key. He was no longer considered the Monster, but Rotella believed he was withholding information. With
the Double Monster and Vinci in prison, three
members of the Sardinian clan were now incarcerated. Once again prosecutors launched into
the old game of rumor and suspicion, in which
the interrogators played one against the other,
hoping to find a crack in the wall of Sardinian
omertà.

Instead, they opened up a crack in their own
investigation.

CHAPTER
15

By this time, the number of prosecutors working on the Monster case had swelled to nearly half a dozen, of whom the most effective and charismatic was Piero Luigi Vigna. These prosecutors played a role much like assistant U.S. attorneys: they directed the investigation, oversaw evidence gathering and analysis, worked up a theory of the crime, and formulated strategies for prosecuting the guilty. In the Italian system, these prosecutors are independent of one another, each one responsible for a part of the case—specifically, the murders that occur when it is his turn to be "on call," so to speak. (In this way the workload is spread among a group of prosecutors, each one taking the cases that occur on his watch.) In addition, another prosecutor holds the august title of *pubblico ministero*, public minister. This prosecutor (who is also usually a judge) represents the interests of the Italian state and argues the case in court. The public minister role in the Monster case changed a number of times during the course of the murders and investigations—as more murders occurred and more prosecutors came into the case.

Overseeing all the prosecutors and the police and carabinieri investigators is the *giudice istruttore*, the instructing judge, or, more properly, the examining magistrate. In the Monster case the examining magistrate was Mario Rotella. His role was to supervise the actions of the police, prosecutors, and public minister and make sure all their activities were carried out legally, correctly, and backed by sufficient evidence. In order for the system to work, the prosecutors, the public minister, and the examining magistrate all had to agree, more or less, on the main thrust of the investigation.

In the Monster case, Vigna and Rotella, the lead prosecutor and the examining magistrate, were very different personalities. It would be hard to find two men less suited to cooperating.

Under the intense pressure to solve the case, they quite naturally began to disagree.

Vigna held court on the second floor of the Tribunale in Florence, in a long file of rooms in a narrow corridor that in centuries past had been the cells of monks. Now these cells were the offices of the prosecutors. Here, in this ancient hall, journalists were always welcome, and they dropped in and joked with the prosecutors, who treated them as friends. Vigna himself had an almost mythical status. He had ended the plague of kidnapping in Tuscany with a simple method: when a person was kidnapped, the state immediately froze the victim's family's bank accounts, preventing the payment of a ransom. Refusing to travel with bodyguards, Vigna also listed his name in the telephone book and on his doorbell, like any common citizen, a gesture of defiance that Italians found admirable. The press ate up his pithy quotes, bons mots, and dry witticisms. He dressed like the Florentine he was, in smartly cut suits and natty ties, and in a country where a pretty face means a great deal, he was exceptionally good-looking, with finely cut features, crisp blue eyes, and an easy smile. His fellow prosecutors were equally charming. A brilliant new arrival, Paolo Canessa, was open and articulate. Silvia Della Monica, spunky and attractive, often regaled journalists with stories of her early cases. A journalist who entered the second floor of the Tribunale always came away with a notebook full of news and trenchant quotations.

On the third floor, there were the same rows of monastic cells, but the atmosphere was entirely different. This was where Mario Rotella held court. He was from the south of Italy, an immediate cause for suspicion among Florentines. His old-fashioned mustache and thick black eyeglass frames made him look more like a greengrocer than a judge. Refined, cultured, and intelligent, he was also a pedant and a bore. He spoke volumes in response to a journalist's question without seeming to say anything. His complex phrases, rich in quotations taken from books of jurisprudence, were untranslatable for the average reader and often incomprehensible even to journalists. When journalists left Rotella's offices, instead of a notebook full of tidbits and quotes easily assembled into an article, they had a miasmic swamp of words that defied any attempt at organization or simplification.

Spezi recorded a typical exchange after the arrest of Giovanni Mele and Piero Mucciarini as the "Double Monster."

"You have proof?" Spezi asked Rotella.

"Yes" was Rotella's laconic response.

Spezi pushed ahead, searching for a headline. "You have two men in jail: is it really true that *both* are the Monster?"

"The Monster doesn't exist as a concept. Someone exists who has reiterated the first killing," replied Rotella.

"Was the testimony of Stefano Mele the clincher?"

"What Mele said was important. There are confirming points. We have not one but five important proofs, and I will only make them known when the moment arrives to send these two new accused persons in front of the Tribunale that will judge them."

The circumlocutions drove Spezi and the other journalists crazy.

Only once did Rotella make a flat statement. "I can tell you one thing at least: Florentines can now rest easy." In a sign that all was not well, he was immediately contradicted by one of the prosecutors on the floor below, who announced to the press that despite what they may have heard from upstairs, "I would cordially invite young people to find some other way of maintaining their health than taking the air of the countryside at night."

The public and the press didn't buy the new Double Monster theory. As the summer of 1984 approached, tensions rose in Florence. The spiderweb of tiny roads and lanes that wound among the hills around the city were empty at night. A young advisor to the city, reacting to the increase in tension, proposed the creation of "villages of love," pleasing places surrounded by gardens that would guarantee intimacy, with certain special services, fenced and furnished with a guard. The idea provoked a scandal, and some replied that Florence might as well open whorehouses. The man defended his idea. "The village of love is a way to affirm that each one of us has the right to a sexual life that is free and happy."

As the first warm days of 1984 tickled the city, anxiety began to climb. By this time the Monster had attracted worldwide attention: many newspapers and television stations aired special reports on the case, including the Sunday *Times* of London and *Asahi Shimbun* of Tokyo. Television documentaries were aired in France, Germany, and Britain. The interest abroad was not merely for the serial killings per se: it was a fascination with the main character in the Monster story—the city of Florence. To most of the world Florence wasn't a real place where real people lived; it was one vast museum, where poets and artists had celebrated the beauty of the female form with its many Madonnas and the beauty of the male form with its proud Davids; a city of elegant palaces, villas perched in the hills, gardens, bridges, fine shopping, and excellent food. It was not a city of dirt, crime, noisy streets, polluted air, graffiti, and drug dealers—let alone serial killers. The presence of the Monster revealed that Florence was not the magical Renaissance city of the tourist brochures—it was tragically and squalidly modern.

As the summer wore on, tensions became almost unbearable. Few in Florence believed the Monster was in jail. Mario Spezi checked his calendar and noted that there was only one Saturday night with no moon during the entire summer: the night of July 28 and 29. A few days before that weekend, Spezi ran into Chief Inspector Sandro Federico at police headquarters. After chatting a while, he said, "Sandro, I'm afraid this Sunday we might see everyone out in the countryside."

The policeman made devil's horns with his fingers, to ward off evil.

Sunday the twenty-ninth came and went peacefully. Early that Monday morning, the thirtieth, it was still dark when the telephone rang in Spezi's house.

CHAPTER
16

It was a stupendous morning, crisp and clear, one that seemed a gift from the gods. Spezi found himself in an idyllic field of flowers and medicinal herbs outside the town of Vicchio, the birthplace of the artist Giotto, forty kilometers northeast of Florence.

The corpses of the new victims, Pia Rontini and Claudio Stefanacci, had been discovered before dawn at the end of a little grassy track by friends who had been searching for them all night. She was nineteen and he had just turned twenty. The place was less than eight kilometers from the field in Borgo San Lorenzo where the Monster had killed his first two victims in 1974.

Claudio was still inside the car, which had been parked by the side of a forested hill called La Boschetta, the Little Wood. Pia had been dragged a few dozen meters back into the open field, another exposed location less than two hundred meters from a farmhouse. She had suffered the same mutilation as the other female victims. But this time the killer had gone even further. He had ripped off—the word "removed" is not appropriate—her left breast. The time of death was established by a witness: a farmer had heard the shots at 9:40 p.m. and assumed it was the backfiring of a motor scooter.

The new crime had occurred while all three main Monster suspects—Francesco Vinci, Piero Mucciarini, and Giovanni Mele—were in prison.

The new double homicide provoked terror, confusion, and an outpouring of bitter recriminations against the police. The case once again hit the front pages of newspapers across Europe. It seemed to people that while the killer steadily added to his list of victims, the police did nothing but arrest suspects whose innocence was then demonstrated by the Monster striking again. Mario Rotella, however, refused to release the three jailed suspects. He was sure they had participated in the 1968 killing and therefore knew the identity of the Monster.

The police and prosecutors involved in the case went into a panic. Vigna pleaded with the public: "Whoever knows must speak," he said. "Certainly there are those who know and who, for whatever reason, aren't talking. Someone with this kind of pathology must at least have left hints or signs in his family."

A fresh tidal wave of anonymous letters poured in, thousands of them, some written with letters cut from magazines, that filled one shelf after another in police headquarters, identifying the Monster as a neighbor, a relative, a friend with strange sexual habits, the local priest, or the family doctor. Once again, gynecologists found themselves targeted by many accusations. Other accusatory letters were signed, some even by well-known intellectuals, offering convoluted theories sprinkled with learned literary quotations and snippets of Latin.

After the double homicide of Vicchio, the Monster of Florence became more than a criminal; he was transformed into a dark mirror reflecting the id of the city itself—its darkest fantasies, its strangest thoughts, its most appalling attitudes and prejudices. Many accusations claimed that behind the killings were esoteric or satanic cults. Various professors and self-appointed experts, who knew absolutely nothing about criminology or serial killers, offered their theories on television and to newspaper journalists. One "expert" echoed a commonly held belief that the Monster might be English. "This is a crime more typically English or of its near neighbor, Germany." Another waxed eloquent about that theory, writing to the newspapers, "Imagine London. The City. A night thick with fog. A model citizen of London, irreproachable, all of a sudden leaps out of the murk and attacks an innocent young couple. Imagine the violence, the eroticism, the powerlessness, the torture . . ."

The advice was never-ending. "You could easily trace, find, and arrest the killer; all you have to do is look in the right places: in the butcher shops and hospitals, since obviously we're dealing with a butcher or a surgeon or nurse."

Another: "He is certainly a bachelor, of about forty; he lives with his mother who knows his 'secret,' but his priest also knows about it from confession, as he attends church regularly."

The feminist interpretation: "The Monster is a woman, a genuine virago, of British origin, who teaches in a Florentine school where there are children up to thirteen years of age."

Hundreds of self-styled private detectives fell upon Florence from all parts of Italy, many with the solution to the crimes already in their pockets; some went about the Florentine hills at night armed to the teeth, looking for the Monster or posing with their guns for fearsome photographs, which were published in the papers.

A number of people showed up at police headquarters claiming to be the Monster. One even managed to break into the radio frequency of the Florentine ambulance service to announce, "I am the Monster, and I will strike again."

Many Florentines were shocked at the outpouring of perversity, conspiracy thinking, and just plain old madness the Monster's killings seemed to arouse in their fellow Florentines. "I never would have thought that in Florence there were such strange people," said Paolo Canessa, one of the prosecutors involved in the investigation.

"The fear is," said Chief Inspector Sandro Federico bitterly, "that somewhere in this swamp of anonymous madness is the very clue we need—and we'll miss it."

Many of the anonymous letters were written

directly to Mario Spezi, the "Monstrologer" of *La Nazione*. One such missive, written in capital letters, stood out. Spezi wasn't sure why, but it chilled him. It was the only one that, to him, had the ring of truth.

> I AM VERY CLOSE TO YOU. YOU WILL NEVER TAKE ME UNLESS I CHOOSE IT. THE FINAL NUMBER IS STILL FAR AWAY. SIXTEEN ARE NOT MANY. I DON'T HATE ANYONE, BUT I HAVE TO DO IT IF I WANT TO LIVE. BLOOD AND TEARS WILL RUN SOON. YOU WILL MAKE NO PROGRESS THE WAY YOU ARE GOING. YOU HAVE GOTTEN EVERYTHING WRONG. TOO BAD FOR YOU. I WILL MAKE NO MORE MISTAKES, BUT THE POLICE WILL. INSIDE OF ME, THE NIGHT WILL LAST FOREVER. I CRIED FOR THEM. EXPECT ME.

The reference to sixteen victims was puzzling, when by that time the double murder near Vicchio made it only twelve (fourteen if you counted the 1968 killings). It suggested another sick fantasist. But someone remembered that in the preceding year, in Lucca, another pair of lovers were killed in their car. The gun wasn't a .22 Beretta and there wasn't any mutilation. That crime was never officially attributed to the

Monster of Florence, but to this day it remains unsolved.

Rumor continued to run riot in Florence until an incident seemed to crystallize public opinion. On the afternoon of August 19, 1984, almost three weeks after the Vicchio killing, Prince Roberto Corsini disappeared in the vast forest surrounding the family castle of Scarperia, a dozen kilometers from Vicchio. The scion of the last surviving princely line in Tuscany, Prince Roberto came from an ancient and wealthy family. The Corsinis had given the world a pope, Clement XII, and had built a huge and beautiful palace in Florence, on the banks of the Arno River. Inside the Palazzo Corsini, the family preserved the sumptuous throne room of their family pope, along with a priceless collection of Renaissance and Baroque art. While the family had run short of cash in latter years—so much so that most of the Palazzo Corsini has not yet been wired for electricity—over the course of centuries the Corsinis had accumulated enormous estates. Roberto's grandfather, Prince Neri, used to brag that he could ride horseback from Florence to Rome—about three hundred kilometers—without leaving his own land.

Prince Roberto was a brusque and silent man

who had no love of the social life or the obliga-
tions of an aristocrat. He preferred to live in the
family castle in the country, seeing only a few
intimate friends. He never married and didn't
seem to have any particular female friends.
Among those who knew him well, he was affec-
tionately referred to as "the Bear" for his gruff
and solitary ways. For others he was simply
strange.

Around four in the afternoon on the Sunday
of August 19, 1984, Prince Roberto left some
German friends staying at his castle and went
alone into the surrounding forest. He wasn't
armed but he carried a pair of binoculars. When
he didn't return by nine in the evening, his
friends became alarmed and called his relatives
and then the carabinieri in the neighboring
town of Borgo San Lorenzo. The carabinieri and
his friends combed the woods for most of the
night. When the search was suspended, no trace
of the prince had been found.

At dawn, the search of the enormous estate
resumed. One of his friends spied a branch covered with blood. The man pushed his way into a
ravine next to a roaring brook, and there he discovered the prince's broken eyeglasses. A little
farther ahead the grass was stained red. Lodged

in the muck of the streambank he found the prince's binoculars. A few feet ahead he found a pheasant killed by a shotgun. And then he came across the dead prince himself, facedown, his lower body in the water, his head wedged in a clefted rock by the current.

The man turned the body over: the prince's face had been obliterated by a shotgun blast at point-blank range.

The rumors swept Florence like wildfire. That the Monster seemed to be clever, cunning, cool, and meticulous had long suggested to some he was a wealthy nobleman. The mysterious killing of a prince known to be strange, who lived alone in a dark and sinister castle in the very area where several Monster killings had taken place, left no doubt in many people's minds: Prince Roberto Corsini had been the Monster of Florence.

Neither investigators nor the press had given the slightest indication that the prince's murder was connected to the Monster of Florence. Public opinion interpreted this silence as further proof of the man's guilt: naturally a great and powerful family like the Corsinis would protect their reputation at all costs. Wasn't it convenient for the family that the prince, being the Monster, was now dead and could never be brought to trial and sully their name?

Two days later a second mysterious event gave the rumors new life. The Corsini castle was broken into, but apparently nothing was taken. No one could fathom why burglars would break into a place that was already swarming with police conducting a murder investigation. Rumor had it that the break-in wasn't by thieves, but by people hired to make away with some important, and perhaps quite gruesome, items in the castle before the police found them.

The rumors continued to grow, even after the prince's murderer was caught four days later—and confessed. He was a young poacher who had been stalking pheasant on the estate. The prince spied him just after he had bagged a bird, and gave chase. The poacher said he had tried to shoot the prince in the legs to foil the pursuit, but Corsini, seeing the shotgun pointed at him, ducked in a gesture of self-defense and received the blast full in the face.

Absurd, said public opinion. Nobody kills a man for so little. The story could not possibly be true—it was, indeed, more proof that the Corsini family was engaged in a cover-up. What's more, the poacher story didn't explain the mysterious break-in at the castle two days later.

From the grand rooms of the Florentine aristocracy to gossip in working-class trattorie, a complicated tale—the *real* story—made the rounds. Prince Roberto Corsini was the Monster of Florence. His family had found out and had done everything they could to cover it up. But someone else—nobody knew who—had also discovered the terrible secret. Instead of reporting it to the police, this person had kept it to himself and blackmailed the prince, periodically extracting large payments for keeping his secret. That Sunday, August 19, twenty days after the Vicchio murders, the two had made an appointment on the banks of the stream, where they argued. A furious struggle had broken out and the blackmailer shot the prince.

There was, it was said, yet another person who knew that Corsini was the Monster. The blackmailing continued, this time directed against the family. But in order for the blackmail to function properly, the blackmailers needed proof that Prince Roberto was the Monster; grisly proof hidden in the depths of the castle. This explained the break-in: the thieves needed to get their hands on evidence, probably the

Beretta, maybe the unfired Winchester series H rounds, and God knows even the trophies that the Monster had cut from the victims.

This rumor, the fruit of the warped imagination of Florence, was utterly false, patently unbelievable, and completely unsupported by anything published in the papers or reported by investigators. The fantasy lasted over a year, until reality destroyed it in the most decisive way possible: with another killing.

CHAPTER
17

By the end of 1984, the case of the Monster of Florence had become one of the most visible and talked about criminal investigations in Europe. A French intellectual and member of the Academy, Jean-Pierre Angremy, who in those years was consul in Florence, became fascinated with the story and published a novel, *Une Ville Immortelle*. The Italian writer Laura Grimaldi wrote a celebrated novel about the case, *The Suspicion*. Madgalen Nabb, the English mystery writer, wrote a book, *The Monster of Florence*. It was the beginning of a literary outpouring that would see the publication of many nonfiction books and novels based on the case. It even

caught the attention of Thomas Harris, who in-
corporated the Monster story into his novel
Hannibal, sequel to *The Silence of the Lambs*.
(In *Hannibal*, Hannibal Lecter has moved to
Florence, where he lives under the pseudonym
of "Dr. Fell." He works as the curator of the archives and library of the Capponi family palace,
after having created the job opening by murdering his predecessor.) The largest Japanese
publishing house asked Spezi to write a book
on the Monster, which he did. (It is still in print,
in its sixth edition.) More than a dozen books
have been published about the Monster case—
as well as a horrific comic book aimed at teenage boys, called *Il Monello* (The Scamp), which
aroused a furor. The creator had wisely avoided
signing his name to it.

Inevitably, films were made about the case, and
in 1984 two were being shot at the same time.
The first director preferred to give the players
fictitious names to avoid legal difficulties, but
the second film was a straight documentary
that offered up an opinion at the end—that the
Monster came from an incestuous family, and
that his mother knew he was the killer. Most Florentines were incensed when they learned the
filmmakers were shooting at the actual scenes

of the crimes. The parents of the victims hired a lawyer to block the documentary. They weren't able to stop it from being made, but the effort produced an odd ruling: a judge declared that the film could be shown anywhere in Italy but Florence.

The police and carabinieri responded to the public outcry by reorganizing the investigation around a special unit, the Squadra Anti-Mostro, or SAM, led by Chief Inspector Sandro Federico. SAM took over much of the fourth floor of police headquarters in Florence. Enormous resources and funds were put at its disposal, including one of those new machines that seemed almost miraculous in its ability to find the answer to any problem: an IBM PC computer. But for a while it sat unused; nobody knew how to operate it.

Around the time of the Vicchio killing, another serial killer appeared to strike Florence. Six prostitutes were murdered in quick succession in the city center. Even with the Monster killings, homicide was still rare in Florence and the city was shocked. Although the MOs of the crimes were different from one another and from the Monster killings, certain elements led the police to think they might be connected. All the prostitutes were murdered in their apartments where they conducted business. The killings were markedly sadistic and the killer or killers never took jewelry or money. Robbery was not a motive.

The medical examiner, Mauro Maurri, who had been in charge of the autopsies of the Monster's victims, was perplexed when he examined the wounds of one of the murdered women, killed with a knife after having been tortured. To Dr. Maurri, the knifework on the victim resembled the wounds on some of the Monster's victims, and was perhaps done with a scuba knife.

Was it possible that the Monster was killing in other ways, choosing different victims?

"I don't know," said Maurri when Spezi posed the question. "It would be worth the trouble to do comparative examinations between the knife wounds on the cadavers of the prostitutes and those of the Monster's victims."

Investigators, for unknown reasons, never requested the comparative examination.

The last prostitute killed lived in a hovel in Via della Chiesa, then a poverty-stricken street in the Oltrarno district of Florence. The apartment was furnished with a few shabby pieces of furniture, the walls covered with simple drawings done by her daughter, whom the state had taken away a few years earlier. They found the prostitute stretched on the floor, next to the window. The killer had used a sweater to tie her arms as in a straitjacket, and had suffocated her by pushing a cloth down her throat.

The police combed every inch of the apartment for clues. They noted that the water heater had been repaired recently and that the firm, Quick House Repair, had affixed its label to the work. One of the detectives, seeing the name and making an important connection, returned to the room where Chief Inspector Sandro Federico was still examining the body of the murdered prostitute.

"Dottore," he said excitedly, "come into the next room; there's something very interesting."

The Quick House Repair outfit, he knew, was owned by Salvatore Vinci.

CHAPTER
18

This discovery prompted the investigators to finally take a closer look at Salvatore Vinci. He was the man whom Stefano Mele had first named as his accomplice in the murder of 1968. Rotella believed that Salvatore was the fourth accomplice in the 1968 killing, who participated along with Piero Mucciarini, Giovanni Mele, and (perhaps) Francesco Vinci. Since three of them had been in prison during the last Monster killing in 1984, Salvatore was the only remaining possibility.

When investigators began looking into Vinci's background, they quickly heard the rumors that he had murdered his wife, Barbarina, back in the town of Villacidro. Rotella reopened the investigation into her death, this time treating it as a homicide, not a suicide. In 1984 investigators traveled to Sardinia where, amid the wild beauty and grinding poverty of Villacidro, they began to uncover the past of a person who seemed quite capable of being the Monster of Florence.

Barbarina was just seventeen years old when she died in 1961. She had been dating a boy named Antonio whom Salvatore detested, and Salvatore had ambushed her in a field and raped her, possibly as a way to humiliate Antonio. She became pregnant and Salvatore had "done his duty" and married her. Everyone in town said that he mistreated her, that he beat her and didn't give her enough money to eat, just enough to buy milk for the baby. The baby was her only happiness. She named him Antonio, after her great love, and continued to see her first lover on the sly.

That name and the baby were a thorn in Salvatore's pride; it was said he doubted he was even the father. With the passing of the years, a hatred would grow between father and son, between Salvatore and Antonio, that would become pitiless and absolute.

The murder of Barbarina—if it was one—had

its origin in November of 1960, when someone surprised her and her lover Antonio in the
countryside and took pictures of them. The be-
trayal became common knowledge in town. Salvatore, in that ancient land of Sardinia ruled by
the Barbagian code, had two ways to recover
his honor—he could either throw his wife out
or kill her.

At first it seemed he would take the former
way out. He told her she had to leave, and she
began looking for work that would take her
away. At the beginning of January 1961, she
received a letter from a nun at an orphanage
offering to take her and her child in if she, in
exchange for room and board, would wait on
tables at the orphanage. She had to present herself on January 21.

She never arrived.

On the evening of January 14, 1961, Barbarina
was alone with her baby in the tiny house she
occupied with Salvatore. He was out as usual, at
the local bar drinking *vermentino* and playing
billiards.

At dinnertime Barbarina found that the propane
tank was empty and she couldn't scald milk for
the baby. She asked a neighbor if she could use
her stove. It was an insignificant episode, but a

few hours later this would become important in refuting what would become the official version of the death of Barbarina—suicide by propane gas. If the tank was empty three hours before she died, and there had been no way to fill it up, how could there have been enough gas in it to kill her?

That evening, just before midnight, Vinci left his brother-in-law at the bar and returned to the house. He later said that he had found the door locked from the inside and had opened it with a hard shove. He turned on the light to see that Antonio's cradle, with the eleven-month-old baby sleeping inside, which would normally have been in the bedroom, had been moved into the kitchen. The door to the bedroom was closed from the inside, and this, he said, worried him. Especially because, he added, he could see light under the door despite the late hour.

"I knocked once and called out to Barbarina," he said several hours later to the carabinieri, "but no one answered. I immediately thought that she was with her lover and so I ran out of the house, fearing an attack."

If this pusillanimous behavior, running away in terror from a man who was cuckolding him in his own bed, seems unlikely today, it appears even more absurd when applied to a twenty-four-year-old Sardinian male in 1961. Salvatore ran to his father-in-law's house and went with him to get his friend at the bar, who happened to be Barbarina's brother. Together they went back to the house.

Years later, one townsperson reflected the general view:"He was only looking for witnesses to his staged suicide."

In front of his father-in-law and brother-in-law, Salvatore opened the door with a simple light shove, the door not offering the slightest resistance. Salvatore promptly shouted that he could smell the odor of gas, although no one else could. The propane tank had been moved next to the bed, the valve open, the tube snaking into the pillow on which Barbarina's head lay. It seemed that Barbarina had killed herself with the tank of propane that, a few hours earlier, had not even contained enough to scald milk. But nobody at the time took note of this discrepancy, not the carabinieri, the medical examiner, or her friends. Nor did the medical examiner treat as significant the bruising around her neck or the faint scratches on her face, as if she had struggled before succumbing to suffocation.

In reopening the case, investigators uncovered all these clues and more that convinced them Salvatore had murdered his wife.

Rotella tried to determine if Salvatore had brought a .22 Beretta with him from Villacidro to Tuscany when he emigrated. Investigators in Villacidro were able to determine that in 1961 there were eleven .22 Berettas in the town, and one of them had indeed been stolen just before Salvatore Vinci left for Tuscany. It belonged to an aged relative of Vinci's who had brought it back from Holland after a stint working there. An investigation conducted in Amsterdam by Interpol could not find the original source of the gun.

At the same time, investigators on the mainland looked into Salvatore Vinci's life after he had arrived in Tuscany in 1961. They found even more evidence that made them think he might be the Monster. It turned out that Salvatore Vinci was a man who, in his sexual tastes and activities, would have aroused envy in the Marquis de Sade.

"We were newly married," Rosina, his new wife, told the carabinieri, "when one evening Salvatore arrived home with a couple of friends and said they would be guests for the night. Fine. Later, when I got up to go to the bathroom, I heard whispering from the room where the couple was sleeping and I recognized my husband's voice. I went in and what did I see? Salvatore in bed with those two! Of course I got mad. I said to the woman and her husband—if he even *was* her husband—to get out quick. And do you know what Salvatore did? He erupted in a terrifying fury, grabbed me by the hair, and forced me to kneel in front of those two and beg their forgiveness! And," she went on, "it wasn't at all over. Another time he introduced me to another young couple, who had just married, and we began to see them. One evening we stayed and slept in their house. And so, that night, I felt a cold hand touching me and I heard a strange sound, as if something fell down. I went to light the lamp and heard my husband's voice telling me not to do it, that nothing had happened. Another hour passed and I felt the same touch again, on my leg, and this time I jumped up and turned on the light. Well, in my bed, in addition to my husband, was also his friend Saverio! I jumped up and went into the kitchen all dazed, trying to understand what was going on. It was then that Salvatore joined me. He tried to calm me down, he said that there was nothing surprising, nothing at all strange, and he invited me to come back to bed. And then, a day later, he began talking about it some more, telling me that he had already had a threesome with Gina, the wife of his friend, and he said for me to do the same thing, that it would be fun, and that on the continent it was the thing to do. So anyway, in the end I found myself in bed with Saverio and Salvatore, who first had sex with me and then with his friend. This went on for a while. If I protested, he hit me. He forced me to have sex with Saverio while he watched, and then we made a four-some. And when it was this way, Salvatore and Saverio were touching each other, caressing each other, each taking their turn as first the man and then the woman, in front of me and Gina! And from that time on Salvatore began to bring me to the homes of his friends, even casual acquaintances, and I had to be with them. He took me to porn films, he'd have his eye on someone, and then he'd introduce me and then perhaps I'd have to have sex with them in the car, but especially at home. And it was worse for me when, in that period, his son Antonio arrived from Sardinia, who was only four years old. They called him Antonello then. I was afraid that he would witness some of these perverse doings with other couples, and our fights, and when he mistreated me."

Eventually Rosina had had enough and ran away to Trieste with another man.

"I can say to you," another of Salvatore's girl-friends told the police, "that Salvatore was the man, the *only* man, who fully satisfied me in terms of sex. He had strange ideas, but what of it? . . . He liked to make love to me while a man did it to him from behind . . ."

Salvatore Vinci picked up the players for his orgies where he could, with the help of his girl-friends, luring them from truck stops on the autostrada, in the red-light districts, and in the Cascine Park on the outskirts of Florence. His sexuality, according to those who knew him, knew no bounds. He would have sex with al-most anyone, man or woman, and employed a wide range of accessories, including vibrators, zucchinis, and eggplants. If a woman was reluc-tant, he slapped her around a bit to get her in the mood.

When Barbara Locci arrived, everything became easier. Salvatore had finally found a woman who fully shared his appetite and tastes. She was so effective at attracting men and boys to orgies that Salvatore began calling her the "Queen Bee."

In the middle of all this, in the same small house, Salvatore's son, Antonio Vinci, was growing up. The young boy heard the rumors that his mother's death wasn't a suicide but a murder, and that his father had done it. Antonio had become deeply attached to Rosina, the second wife of Salvatore. When she fled to Trieste, for Antonio it was like losing his mother all over again. And once again it was his father's fault. He eventually left home and spent much of his free time with his uncle Francesco who became a substitute father to him. This same Antonio would later be arrested on weapons charges, in an attempt to get his uncle Francesco to talk.

The dual investigations in Villacidro and Tuscany convinced Mario Rotella and his carabinieri investigators that they had finally found their man. Salvatore Vinci had been the fourth accomplice at the killing of Barbara Locci. He probably owned a .22 Beretta. He had the only car among the conspirators. He brought the gun to the murder scene, he was the main shooter, and he took the gun home with him. The investigation confirmed he was a cold-blooded killer and sexual maniac.

Salvatore Vinci was the Monster of Florence.

CHAPTER
19

In the middle of all the sound and fury, certain facts stood above the fray, unshakably true, obtained by solid police work and expert analysis.

The first of these was the analysis of the pistol. No fewer than five ballistics analyses were done, and the answer was always the same: the Monster used one gun, a .22 Beretta that was "old and worn," with a defective firing pin that left an incontrovertible mark on the base of each shell. The bullets were the second fact. They were all Winchester series H rounds. All the bullets fired in the crimes had been taken from the same two boxes. This was demonstrated by an examination with a scanning electron microscope of the "H" stamped on the base of each shell—all had the same micro-imperfections, indicative that they were stamped by the same die.The die, which was regularly replaced when it began to wear out, also proved that both boxes were put on sale before the year 1968.

Each box contained fifty cartridges. Counting from the first crime in 1968, after the gun had shot fifty shells from one box, the killer opened a second box.The first fifty were copper-jacketed rounds, and the second were lead. Nothing was ever found that suggested a second gun had been used at the scenes of the crimes or that there was more than one killer. Indeed, the bodies of the victims had all been moved by dragging, which suggested there was no second person around to help lift.

It was the same for the knife used by the killer. Every expert analysis concluded that a single knife had been employed, extremely well honed, with a particular mark or notch in it, and three sawteeth below that of about two millimeters in depth. Some experts speculated it was a *pattada*, the typical knife used by Sardinian shepherds, but the majority of experts spoke, with some uncertainty, of a scuba knife.The experts agreed that the excisions were so nearly identical that they had been made by the same right-handed person.

Finally, the Monster avoided touching his victims, except when necessary, and stripped them by cutting their clothes off with the knife. There was never any sign of rape or sexual molestation.

The psychological experts all agreed on the Monster's psychopathology. "He always works alone," wrote one expert. "The presence of others would take away all flavor from the author of these crimes, which are fundamentally crimes of sexual sadism: the Monster is a serial killer and he only acts alone. . . . The noted absence of any sexual interest not connected to the excision, makes one think of an absolute impotence, or a marked inhibition of coitus."

In September 1984, Rotella finally freed the "Double Monsters" Piero Mucciarini and Giovanni Mele, who had been in prison during the Vicchio killings. Two months later, he released Francesco Vinci, who had also been in prison during the last Monster killings.

The pool of suspects had been reduced to one: Salvatore Vinci. They put his house under observation twenty-four hours a day, seven days a week. His telephone was tapped. When he left his front door, he was often followed.

As the winter passed and the next summer neared—the summer of 1985—a huge feeling of dread built among the investigators and the Florentine public. Everyone was certain that the Monster would strike again. The new elite unit charged with investigating the Monster, the Squadra Anti-Mostro, worked with feverish activity but continued to make little progress.

When Francesco Vinci was released from prison, Mario Spezi, who had often maintained his innocence in his articles, was invited to the homecoming celebration at Vinci's house in Montelupo. Spezi accepted the unusual invitation, hoping to snag an interview on the side. The tables were heaped with spicy salami, strong Sardinian sheep cheese, *vermentino di Sardegna*, and *fil'e ferru*, the potent grappa of the island. At the end of the party, Vinci agreed to an interview with Spezi. He answered the questions with reserve, intelligence, and excessive caution.

"How old are you?"

"Forty-one. Or so I believe."

The interview was unenlightening, except

for one answer that stayed with Spezi for many years. Spezi asked him what he imagined the real Monster to be like.

"He is very intelligent," Vinci said, "someone who knows how to move at night in the hills even with his eyes closed. One who knows how to use a knife much better than most. One," he added, fixing his glittering black eyes on Spezi, "who once upon a time experienced a very, very great disappointment."

CHAPTER
20

The summer of 1985 was one of the hottest in recent memory. A serious drought gripped Tuscany, and the hills of Florence lay stunned and prostrate under the sun, the ground cracking, the leaves turning brown and falling from the trees. The city's aqueducts began to dry up, and priests led their congregations in fervent prayer to the Lord for rain. Along with the heat, fear of the Monster hung over the city like a stifling blanket.

September 8 was another hot, cloudless day in what seemed like an endless string of them. But for Sabrina Carmignani it was a fine day, the day of her nineteenth birthday—a day she would never forget.

That Sunday, around five o'clock, Sabrina and her boyfriend pulled into a small clearing in the woods just off the main road to San Casciano, which was called the Scopeti clearing after the name of the road passing it. The dirt clearing was hidden from Via Scopeti by a curtain of oaks, cypresses, and umbrella pines, and it was well known to young people as a good place to have sex. It lay in the heart of the Chianti countryside, almost within view of the ancient stone house where Niccolò Machiavelli spent his years of exile writing *The Prince*. Today this area of villas, castles, beautifully tended vineyards, and small towns forms one of the most expensive stretches of real estate in the world.

The two young people parked their car next to another, a white VW Golf with French plates. In the center of the rear seat, attached by the seat belts, they noted a child's car seat. A few meters in front of the Volkswagen stood a small dome tent, of a metallic blue. The light struck it in such a way that it was possible to see a human outline in its interior.

"A single person," said Sabrina later, "who was stretched out and perhaps sleeping. The tent seemed shaken up, almost collapsed; the entrance was dirty and there were a lot of flies, and there was a foul dead smell."

They didn't like the look of things and turned around to leave. As they eased out of the clearing, another car was just turning in from the main road. The driver backed up to allow them to pass. Neither Sabrina nor her boyfriend noted the make of the car or saw the person inside.

They had just missed discovering the Monster's new victims.

A day later, at two o'clock in the afternoon on Monday, September 9, an avid mushroom forager drove into the Scopeti clearing. As soon as he stepped out of his car, he was assaulted by "a strange odor along with a loud buzzing of flies. I thought that around there somewhere was a dead cat. Around the tent I didn't notice anything. Then I went toward the thicket of bushes on the opposite side. And in that moment I saw them: two naked feet sticking out of the greenery . . . I didn't have the courage to go any closer."

The newly created squad, SAM, launched into action. The victims were two French tourists who had camped in the Scopeti clearing. For the first time the scene of a Monster crime was properly secured. SAM sealed off not only the

Scopeti clearing, but an area one kilometer in diameter surrounding it. The discovery of a child's seat in the back of the car caused investigators great anguish for some hours, until inquiries to France established that the little daughter of the murdered woman was back in France in the care of relatives.

A helicopter landed at the sealed crime scene carrying on board a famous criminologist who had earlier prepared a psychological and behavioral profile of the Monster. Journalists and photographers were grudgingly allowed in but had been corralled behind a red-and-white plastic fence strung between trees a hundred yards away, under the watchful eyes of two policemen in a ready stance, armed with machine guns. The journalists were angry at not having their usual access. Finally, the assistant prosecutor allowed one, Mario Spezi, to examine the scene and report back to all the others. Spezi climbed over the plastic barrier under the furious gaze of his colleagues. When he saw the Monster's most recent horror, he felt envy for those he had left behind.

The female victim was Nadine Mauriot, thirty-six years old, who owned a shoe store in Montbéliard, France, not far from the French-Swiss border. She had separated from her husband

and for some months had been living with Jean-Michel Kraveichvili, twenty-five years old, an enthusiast of the hundred-meter dash, which he practiced with the local athletic squad. They had taken a camping trip through Italy, and on Monday would have had to be back in France for Nadine's daughter's first day of school.

On hearing the news of the murders, Sabrina and her friend immediately went to the carabinieri to report what they had seen on Sunday afternoon, September 8. The girl recounted exactly the same story years later, in front of a judge of the Corte d'Assise. Twenty years later, in an interview with Spezi, Sabrina was still certain that she had not mistaken the date, given that that Sunday was her birthday.

Her testimony related in a critical way to the date the crime had been committed. It had direct bearing on whether the French couple had been murdered Saturday night, as the evidence suggested, or Sunday night, as investigators would later insist. Her testimony was inconvenient to them, so it was completely ignored— then and now.

There was another weighty clue that the two were killed on Saturday night: if the French couple expected to be home in time to see Nadine's daughter off to her first day of school, they would already have to be driving back to France on Sunday.

The condition of Mauriot's cadaver on that Monday afternoon was frightful. Her face, grotesquely swollen and black, was unrecognizable. The heat had had devastating effects, amplified by being enclosed in a tent, and the body was covered with maggots.

SAM investigators reconstructed how the final killing took place. It was, in a word, horrifying.

The killer had crept up to the dome tent of the two French tourists, who were nude and making love. He advertised his presence by making a seven-inch cut in the fly of the tent with the tip of his knife—without, however, piercing the inner tent. The noise must have frightened the two lovers. They unzipped the door to see what it was. The Monster had already positioned himself, gun at the ready, and as soon as they peered out they were struck by a hail of bullets. Nadine was killed immediately. Four rounds struck Jean-Michel—one in a wrist, one in a finger, one in an elbow, and one grazing his lip, leaving him relatively unscathed.

The young athlete leapt up and charged out the door, perhaps bowling over the Monster in the process, and tore off running in the dark. If he had turned left, a few steps would have taken him to the main road where he might have been saved. But he ran straight ahead, toward the woods. The Monster ran after him. Jean-Michel vaulted a sort of bushy hedge that divided the clearing in two, pursued by the Monster. The Monster reached him in twelve meters, stabbed him in the back, chest, and stomach, and then cut his throat.

Observing the cadaver still under the bushes, Spezi noted that the lowest leaves of the tree above the dead body, six feet up, were splattered with blood.

Having killed Jean-Michel, the Monster returned to the tent. He pulled Nadine out by the feet and performed the two mutilations, removing her vagina and left breast. Then he dragged the body back into the tent and zipped it up. He hid the man's body under trash he collected around the clearing and put the plastic lid of a paint bucket over his head.

Despite diligent evidence collecting in the Scopeti clearing, SAM came up almost empty-handed. It appeared to have been an almost perfect crime.

On Tuesday, a letter arrived at the prosecutor's offices, addressed with letters cut from a magazine.

Inside the envelope, wrapped in tissue paper, was a piece of breast cut from the French tourist.

The letter had been mailed sometime that weekend in a little town near Vicchio, and it entered the postal system on Monday morning.

Silvia Della Monica was the only woman investigator in the Monster case. The arrival of this missive changed her life. It completely terrified her. She immediately resigned from the case and was assigned two bodyguards, who remained in her locked office even at work, for fear that the killer might be a person who could mingle with the people entering the Palazzo di Giustizia and gain access to her office. It was the end of her involvement in the case.

The letter, reproduced in the papers, caused a storm of speculation, because the killer had misspelled the Italian word "REPUBBLICA," using only one "B" instead of two. Was it merely the spelling error of an ignorant person, or did it indicate that the Monster was a foreigner? Among the Romance languages of Europe, only in Italian is the word "Republic" spelled with two "b's.

For the first time, the Monster had made an effort to hide the two bodies. That, combined with the mailing of the note, would have forced a desperate search by the authorities for the victims, if the bodies hadn't already been found. This suggests a reason why the Monster changed his MO—it was a carefully designed plan to humiliate the police.

It almost worked.

CHAPTER
21

After the Scopeti killing, the mayors of Florence and the surrounding towns launched a campaign of prevention. Although the young people of Florence were so thoroughly traumatized that the idea of parking outside the city walls after sunset was now unthinkable, there were still millions of foreigners who poured into Tuscany every year with campers and tents who were unaware of the risk. Throughout the areas where people often camped, signs in multiple languages were posted warning of the danger of remaining there between dusk and dawn. But the mention of a serial killer was carefully avoided, so as not to scare away tourists completely.

The city of Florence printed thousands of posters, designed by the famous graphic artist Mario Lovergine, who drew a staring eye surrounded by leaves. "*Occhio ragazzi*! Watch out kids! Attention! *Jeunes gens, danger*! *Atención chicos y chicas*! *Pericolo di aggressione*! Danger of violence!" warned the poster. Using the same design, tens of thousands of postcards were printed up and passed out at tollbooths, railroad stations, campsites, youth hostels, and on public buses. Television spots reinforced the point.

Despite their most diligent efforts, SAM investigators emerged from the Scopeti clearing with few fresh leads or new evidence. The pressure on them was enormous. Thomas Harris, in his novel *Hannibal*, recounted some of the techniques SAM used to try to catch the Monster. "Some lover's lanes and cemetery trysting places had more police than lovers sitting in pairs in the cars. There were not enough women officers to go around. During hot weather male couples took turns wearing a wig and many mustaches were sacrificed."

The idea of offering a reward had earlier been

rejected, but now it was resurrected by the prosecutor Vigna, who was convinced that the Monster enjoyed the protection of *omertà*, which could only be broken with a very large sum. It was a controversial idea. Rewards and bounties were never part of Italian culture, being something they knew only from American Westerns. Many feared it might incite a witch hunt or bring out a bunch of crazy bounty hunters. The decision was so controversial it had to be made by the prime minister of Italy himself, who set the reward at half a billion lire—a large sum at the time.

The reward was posted, but no one stepped forward with information to claim it.

As before, SAM was plagued with anonymous accusations and unfounded rumors that had to be followed up, no matter how unlikely. Among them was a letter the police received, dated September 11, 1985. It suggested that the police "question our fellow citizen, Pietro Pacciani, born in Vicchio." The note went on, "This individual is said by many to have been in prison for having killed his own fiancée. He has a thousand skills: a shrewd man, cunning, a farmer with big clumsy feet but a quick mind. He keeps his entire family hostage, the wife is a fool, the daughters are never allowed out, they have no friends."

Investigators looked into it. It wasn't true that Pacciani had killed his fiancée, but in 1951 he had killed a man he caught seducing his fiancée in a parked car and had served a long prison sentence for it. Pacciani lived in Mercatale, a half dozen kilometers from the Scopeti clearing. The police conducted a routine search of his house and found nothing of interest.

Still, the old farmer's name remained on the list.

A few weeks later, a rumor made the rounds, this one from Perugia, a hundred and fifty kilometers away. A young doctor, Francesco Narducci, the scion of one of the city's richest families, apparently committed suicide by drowning himself in Lake Trasimeno. Immediately rumormongers began speculating that Narducci had been the Monster, who, overcome with remorse, had done away with himself. A quick investigation showed there could be no truth to it, and investigators shelved it along with the other false leads that plagued the case.

Meanwhile, in 1985, the investigation, under relentless pressure to show results, began to crumble. A rift between the lead prosecutor,

Piero Luigi Vigna, and the examining magistrate, Mario Rotella, was widening.

The disagreement centered on the Sardinian Trail investigation. Rotella was convinced that the gun used in the 1968 clan killing had never left the circle of Sardinians, and that one of them had gone on to become the Monster. His suspicions had settled on Salvatore Vinci, and he was painstakingly building the case against him with the help of the carabinieri. Vigna, on the other hand, felt the Sardinian Trail had reached a dead end. He wanted to throw everything out and start the investigation anew. The *polizia*, the police, agreed with Vigna.

The special unit known as SAM was composed of both polizia and carabinieri allegedly working together. The problem was, the carabinieri and the police rarely got along and were often antagonistic to each other. The Polizia di Stato are a civilian agency and the carabinieri are a branch of the military; both are charged with domestic law enforcement. When a major crime occurs, such as a murder, often the two agencies will rush to the scene and each try to claim the crime as their own. One story, perhaps apocryphal, tells of a bank robbery in which both carabinieri and police chased down and caught the escaping criminals. An argument broke out in front of the robbers about who should get the collar, finally settled when they divided up the spoils, the police getting the robbers and the carabinieri hauling away the getaway car, cash, and guns.

The disagreement between Vigna and Rotella, which became increasingly bitter, was kept a deep secret among the investigators for many years. Outwardly, the Sardinian Trail continued to be the major line of inquiry, but criticism of it, and of Judge Mario Rotella, began to grow.

In 1985 Rotella briefly jailed Stefano Mele on trumped-up charges in a final effort to get him to talk. The move caused a chorus of complaints that Rotella was needlessly torturing a broken-down old man whose ravings had already caused untold damage to the investigation and to the individuals he accused. Rotella found himself out on a limb, isolated and under constant attack by the press. The largest newspaper of Sardinia, the *Unione Sarda*, savaged him on a regular basis. "It's always the case," the newspaper wrote, "that whenever the investigation of the Monster of Florence becomes stuck in the mud, they always resurrect the so-called Sardinian Trail." Associations of Sardinian residents of

Tuscany also took up the issue of racism, and a chorus of outrage from all sides assailed the investigation. Rotella's pontifications and circumlocutions only made matters worse.

But Rotella, who as examining magistrate in the Monster case held considerable power, plodded on. His brief arrest and interrogation of Stefano Mele, so roundly criticized, finally revealed one of the central mysteries in the case: why Stefano had protected Salvatore Vinci for so long, even at the cost of going to prison for fourteen years. Why had Mele acquiesced so meekly in being framed for the murders of Barbara Locci and Antonio Lo Bianco, when the crime had been plotted, organized, and executed by Salvatore? Why had he remained silent during the trial, when Salvatore had the impudence to wear his wife's engagement ring when taking the witness stand? Why, even after serving fourteen years in prison, did Mele refuse to tell investigators that Salvatore was one of his accomplices?

The reason, Mele finally broke down and admitted, was shame. He had participated in Salvatore Vinci's sex circus and was fond of sex with men, most especially with Salvatore himself. This was the terrible secret that Salvatore Vinci had held over Mele's head for almost twenty years, enforcing his silence. This was how Vinci, back in 1968, had been able to reduce Mele to groveling and weeping with a single hard stare. He threatened to expose him as a homosexual.

The double homicide of the French tourists in the Scopeti clearing would be the last known crime committed by the Monster of Florence. Although it would be a while before Florentines realized it, the string of murders that had terrorized them for so long had finally come to an end.

The investigation, however, was just getting started. As time went on, it would become a monster in its own right, consuming all in its path, engorged and distended with the many innocent lives it had ruined.

Nineteen eighty-five was only the beginning.

CHAPTER
22

By the end of 1985, Judge Mario Rotella was firmly convinced that Salvatore Vinci was the Monster of Florence. As he examined the files on Vinci, he became more and more frustrated with the many missed opportunities to nail him. For example, Vinci's house had been searched right after the 1984 killing in Vicchio, and the police had found a rag in his bedroom, stuffed in a woman's straw purse, covered with powder residues and spots of blood. Thirty-eight spots of blood. Rotella looked back through the records and saw that the rag had never been analyzed. Furious, he held it up as an egregious example of the incompetence of the investigation. The prosecutor in charge of that evidence tried to explain: it was impossible to believe a man who already knew he was on the list of suspects would keep in his room such an obvious clue.

Rotella demanded an examination of the rag. The lab it was sent to could not establish if the blood came from one or two blood groups, and the experts were unable to compare the blood on the rag to the blood of the victims of the 1984 crime because, incredibly enough, investigators had not conserved any blood from those victims. The rag was sent to the United Kingdom for further analysis, but the lab reported back that it had deteriorated beyond salvation. (Today, DNA testing might still recover important information from the rag, but so far we know of no plans to test it.)

Rotella had another reason to feel frustration. For more than a year the carabinieri had been keeping Salvatore Vinci under tight surveillance, particularly on weekends. Knowing he was being followed, Salvatore had sometimes amused himself by running red lights or pulling other tricks to lose his trackers. And yet the very weekend of the double homicide in the Scopeti clearing, the carabinieri had inexplicably suspended the surveillance. Vinci suddenly found himself free to go where he pleased, unobserved. If the surveillance had continued, Rotella felt, perhaps the double killing might never have occurred in the first place.

At the end of 1985, Rotella served Salvatore Vinci with an *avviso di garanzia*, a notification that he was the official suspect for sixteen homicides—all the killings from 1968 to 1985.

Meanwhile, the main prosecutor, Piero Luigi Vigna, was becoming fed up with the officious, methodical Rotella and his obsessive pursuit of the Sardinian Trail. Vigna and the police were itching to start afresh, and they were waiting, quietly, for Rotella to make a false move.

On June 11, 1986, Mario Rotella ordered the arrest of Salvatore Vinci for murder. To everyone's great surprise, it was not for the Monster's killings, but for the murder of his wife, Barbarina, on January 14, 1961, back in Villacidro. Rotella's strategy was to convict Vinci of murder in a case that seemed simpler and easier to prove, and then to leverage that into a conviction against him for being the Monster of Florence.

For two years, with Salvatore Vinci in prison, Rotella methodically prepared the case against him for the murder of his seventeen-year-old wife. The Monster did not kill again, which further persuaded Rotella that he had the right man.

Salvatore Vinci's trial for the murder of his wife began on April 12, 1988, in Cagliari, the capital of Sardinia. Spezi covered it for *La Nazione*.

Vinci's behavior in the dock was astonishing. Standing all the while, his tight fists wrapped around the bars of the cage in which he was locked, he responded with scrupulous care to the questions of the judges in a courteous, high, almost falsetto voice. During the breaks he conversed with Spezi and the other journalists on such themes as sexual freedom and the role of habeas corpus in a trial.

His son, Antonio, who was then about twenty-seven years old, was brought into the courtroom to testify against his father. He was serving time for an unrelated offense, and he arrived with his hands shackled, his strong, extremely tense presence noted by all. Seated to the right of the judges, on the side opposite his father, the youth never once took off the huge black sunglasses that hid his eyes. His lips remained compressed, and the nostrils of his aquiline nose were dilated with hatred. Even protected by dark lenses, his face always remained fixated on his father, never once turning elsewhere in the courtroom. Throughout this his father remained immobile as he returned his son's stare with a closed and enigmatic face. The two of them remained that way for hours, the courtroom filled with electricity from their taut and silent interaction.

Antonio Vinci refused to speak a word. He just stared. Later, he told Spezi that if there hadn't been carabinieri officers sitting between him and his father in the van as they were driven away, "I would have strangled him."

The trial came to a disastrous end. Salvatore Vinci was unexpectedly acquitted. The crime had taken place too long ago, witnesses had died and others couldn't remember, physical evidence had disappeared, and very little could actually be proved.

Vinci walked out of the courtroom a free man. He paused on the steps to speak to the press. "It was a very satisfying conclusion," he said calmly, and walked on. He went into the interior mountains to visit his birthplace of Villacidro—and then, like a Sardinian bandit of old, he disappeared forever.

The acquittal of Salvatore Vinci raised a firestorm of complaint against Rotella. It was the false move Vigna and his prosecutors had been waiting for, and they moved in like sharks, silently, with no fuss or publicity. For the next few years, a slow parrying with long knives would take place between Vigna and Rotella, the police and the carabinieri, so quietly conducted that it never came to the attention of the news media.

After the acquittal, Vigna and the police went their own way, ignoring Rotella. They decided to throw out everything and start the Monster of Florence investigation all over again, from the beginning. Meanwhile, Rotella and the carabinieri kept the Sardinian Trail investigation going. The two investigations slowly became incompatible, if not mutually exclusive.

Eventually, something would have to give.

CHAPTER
23

The Squadra Anti-Mostro was taken over by a new chief inspector of police, a man named Ruggero Perugini. A few years later, Thomas Harris would create a fictional portrait of Perugini in his novel *Hannibal*, giving him the thinly disguised fictional name of Rinaldo Pazzi. While researching the book, Harris had been a guest in Chief Inspector Perugini's home in Florence. (It was said that Perugini was not pleased with Harris's return on his hospitality, by having his alter ego gutted and hung from the Palazzo Vecchio.) The real chief inspector was more dignified than his sweaty and troubled counterpart in the film version, played by Giancarlo Giannini.

September 1974, the Monster's first crime at Borgo San Lorenzo. *(NewPressphoto)*

Photograph of a *Monster of Florence* comic book. An example of the many comic books published on the Monster in the 1980s. *(Photograph by Massimo Sestini)*

Identi-Kit portrait of the presumed Monster, prepared after the 1981 double murder, which generated mass hysteria, thousands of accusations, and a suicide. *(NewPressphoto)*

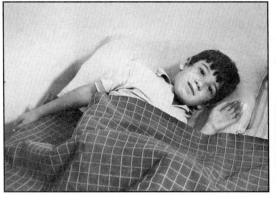

Natalino Mele in the carabinieri barracks, photographed the night he witnessed his mother's murder on August 21, 1968. *(NewPressphoto)*

Stefano Mele, convicted of the 1968 double homicide. *(NewPressphoto)*

Francesco Vinci (right), after his release from prison, with Mario Spezi. *(NewPressphoto)*

Salvatore Vinci in Florence 1968. *(NewPressphoto)*

Piero Luigi Vigna (left), prosecutor in the Monster case, and Mario Spezi, at an exhibition of Spezi's caricatures. (NewPressphoto)

Judge Mario Rotella, the examining magistrate in the Monster case. (Massimo Sestini)

Photograph of the painting allegedly done by Pacciani, used as evidence of his disturbed mind. Spezi later found the real artist, a Chilean painter named Christian Olivares. The painting was originally titled *The Death Knight*. (NewPressphoto)

Pacciani in the dock at his trial.
(Massimo Sestini)

Arturo Minoliti, the
carabinieri officer who
alleged that evidence might
have been planted during the
search of Pacciani's house.
(Massimo Sestini)

Pro-Pacciani T-shirts donned by
many during his trial. The back
says, "A man is innocent until
proven guilty." *(Massimo Sestini)*

Mario Vanni, the ex-postman of
San Casciano, who immortalized the
phrase "picnicking friends." He was
later convicted of participating in the
Monster's killings. *(Massimo Sestini)*

Chief Inspector Michele Giuttari, who directed the Monster investigation for many years. Giuttari ordered the arrest of Spezi and brought in Preston for interrogation. *(Massimo Sestini)*

Mario Spezi with the microphone, transmitter, and GPS devices recovered from his car, planted by the police. *(Massimo Sestini)*

Giancarlo Lotti, the secret witness "Beta," who claimed to have assisted in several of the Monster's killings. He was known as the village idiot of San Casciano. *(Massimo Sestini)*

Dr. Francesco Narducci, the gastroenterologist who drowned in Lake Trasimeno in 1985. His probable suicide was later ruled a murder, and Spezi was accused of involvement in it. *(Massimo Sestini)*

Gabriella Carlizzi, who runs an internet conspiracy website. She accused Spezi of being the Monster. *(NewPressphoto)*

Francesco Calamandrei, on trial for masterminding five of the Monster's double homicides. *(NewPressphoto)*

An old Tuscan doorstop of the kind recovered at one of the murder scenes, which Chief Inspector Michele Giuttari claimed was an "esoteric object used to communicate between this world and the infernal regions." *(Massimo Sestini)*

Preston and Spezi at the site of
the double killing in Vicchio.
(Christine Preston)

Antonio Vinci at
his father's trial for
murdering his mother.
(Massimo Sestini)

Count Niccolò Capponi.
(Christine Preston)

Judge Giuliano Mignini, the
public prosecutor of Perugia,
who interrogated Preston and
indicted him for a string of
crimes; he also sent Spezi to
prison. *(Massimo Sestini)*

Pia Rontini and Claudio
Stefanacci, shortly before
their murder in 1984
near the town of Vicchio.
(NewPressphoto)

Winnie Rontini, the mother of
Pia Rontini. (Massimo Sestini)

Memorial at the
site of the double
murder in the
Bartoline Fields.
(Massimo Sestini)

The real Perugini spoke with a Roman accent, but his movements and dress, and the way he handled his briar pipe, made him seem more English than Italian.

When Chief Inspector Perugini took over SAM, he and Vigna wiped the slate clean. Perugini started with the assumption that the gun and bullets had somehow passed out of the circle of Sardinians before the Monster killings began. The Sardinian Trail was a dead end and he had no more interest in it. He also viewed the evidence collected at the crime scenes with skepticism— and perhaps rightly so. The forensic examination of the crime scenes had been, in general, incompetent. Only the last was actually secured and sealed by the police. In the others, people came and went, picking up the shells, taking pictures, smoking and throwing their butts on the ground, trampling the grass, and shedding their own hair and fibers everywhere. Much of the forensic evidence that was collected—and there was precious little—was never properly analyzed, and some, like the rag, was lost or allowed to spoil. Investigators had not generally kept samples of the victims' hair, clothing, or blood, to see if their presence might be associated with any suspects.

Instead of plodding once again through the

evidence and rereading the thousands of pages of interrogations, Perugini was smitten by the idea of solving the crime in the modern way— with computers. He was in love with the scientific methods used by the FBI to hunt serial killers. He finally dusted off the IBM PC given to SAM by the Ministry of the Interior and booted it up.

He ran through it the names of every man between the ages of thirty and sixty in the province of Florence who had ever been picked up by the police, asking it to spit out all those persons convicted of sexual crimes. Then Perugini matched up their periods of incarceration with the dates of the Monster's homicides, identifying those who were in prison when the Monster didn't kill and out of prison when he did. He winnowed the list down from thousands to a few dozen people. And there, in the middle of this rarefied company, he found the name of Pietro Pacciani—the peasant farmer who had been denounced in an anonymous letter after the Monster's final killings.

Perugini then did another computer screening to see how many of these suspects had lived in or around the areas where the Monster had struck. Once again Pacciani's name surfaced, after Perugini generously expanded the definition of "in or around" to swallow most of Florence and its environs.

The appearance of Pacciani's name in this second screening again reinforced the anonymous message that had arrived on September 11, 1985, inviting the police to "question our fellow citizen Pietro Pacciani born in Vicchio." In this way, the most advanced system of criminal investigation, the computer, was married to the most ancient system, the anonymous letter—both of which fingered the same man: Pietro Pacciani.

Pietro Pacciani became Perugini's preferred suspect. All that remained was to gather the evidence against him.

Inspector Perugini ordered a search of Pacciani's house and came up with what he considered further incriminating evidence. Prime among this was a reproduction of Botticelli's *Primavera*, the famous painting in the Uffizi Gallery, which depicts, in part, a pagan nymph with flowers spilling from her mouth. The picture reminded Perugini of the gold chain lying in the mouth of one of the Monster's first victims. This clue so captivated him that it became the cover of the book he would later publish about the case, which showed Botticelli's nymph vomiting blood instead of flowers. Reinforcing this interpretation, Perugini took note of a pornographic magazine centerfold pinned up in Pacciani's kitchen, surrounded by pictures of the Blessed Virgin and saints, showing a topless woman with a flower clamped provocatively between her teeth.

Right after the Monster's last double homicide, Pietro Pacciani had been sent to prison for raping his daughters. This, for Perugini, was another important clue. It explained why there had been no killings for the past three years.

Most of all, it was the 1951 murder that attracted Perugini's attention. It had taken place near Vicchio, Pacciani's birthplace, where the Monster had struck twice. On the surface it looked like a Monster crime: two young people making love in a car in the Tassinaia woods, ambushed by a killer hidden in the bushes nearby. She was just sixteen, the town beauty and Pacciani's girlfriend. Her lover was a traveling salesman who went from village to village selling sewing machines.

But on a closer look, the crime was quite different—messy, furious, and spontaneous. Pacciani had beaten the man's head in with a stone before knifing him. He then threw his girlfriend into the grass and raped her next to his rival's dead body. Afterwards, he slung the salesman's corpse over his shoulders to carry it to a nearby lake. After struggling for a while he gave up and dumped it in the middle of a field. Criminologists would have called it a "disorganized" homicide, as opposed to the organized ones of the Monster. So disorganized, in fact, that Pacciani was swiftly arrested and convicted.

The murder in the Tassinaia woods had an antique flavor to it, a crime of passion from another age. It may have been the last tale of love and murder to be immortalized in song in the traditional Tuscan manner. At the time, there was one man left in Tuscany who practiced the ancient profession of *cantastorie*, or "story singer," a sort of wandering minstrel who set stories to song. Aldo Fezzi walked about Tuscany dressed in a bright red jacket, even in the heat of August, going from town to town, from country fair to country fair, singing stories in rhyme while showing drawings illustrating the action. Fezzi composed most of his own songs based on stories he collected in his travels; some were hilarious, racy, and off-color, while others were tragic tales of jealousy and murder, desperate love, and savage vendettas.

Fezzi composed a song about the murder in the Tassinaia woods that he sang across northern Tuscany:

> *I sing to you of a great and tragic tale,*
> *In the town of Vicchio in the Mugello,*
> *At the Iaccia farm of the Paterno estate,*
> *There lived a young man, brutal and cruel.*
> *Stay and hear, and your tears will flow,*
> *His name was Pier Pacciani, twenty-six*
> *　years old,*
> *O, listen to the story I am about to tell,*
> *To speak of it will freeze your blood . . .*

Perugini considered it a crucial piece of evidence that Pacciani, spying on the two lovers from the bushes, told investigators he had gone into a frenzy of rage when he saw his girlfriend bare her left breast for her seducer; that was the moment when he had snapped. The story reminded Perugini of the left breast taken from the last two victims. The baring of the left breast, Perugini argued, was the event which first unleashed Pacciani's homicidal fury; it had settled in his unconscious to reappear years later, every time the same circumstances arose—when he saw two young people making love in a car.

Others pointed out that the left breast would be the one most likely seized by a right-handed killer—as the Monster was known to be. But this was far too simple an explanation for Perugini's taste.

Perugini discounted the earlier reconstructions of the Monster's crimes, which seemed to argue very much against Pacciani as the killer. For example, it was difficult to place a fat, short, alcoholic, thickset old peasant, barely five feet three inches tall, at the scene of the crime in Giogoli, in which the killer took aim through a strip of window that was five feet ten inches off the ground. It was even more difficult to put this doddering peasant at the scene of the last crime, in the Scopeti clearing, in which the killer outran a twenty-five-year-old who was an amateur champion of the hundred-meter dash. At the time of the Scopeti crime, Pacciani was sixty years old, had suffered a heart attack, and had undergone a bypass operation. His health records showed he had scoliosis, a bad knee, angina pectoris, pulmonary emphysema, chronic ear infections, multiple slipped discs, spondiloarthrosis, hypertension, diabetes, and polyps in his throat and kidney, among other ailments.

The other incriminating "evidence" Perugini and

his team recovered from Pacciani's house included a round from a hunting rifle, two World War II shell casings (one of which was being used as a flower vase), a photograph of Pacciani as a young man posing with a machine pistol, five knives, a postcard sent from Calenzano, a register book that on its first page had a crude drawing of a road that could not be identified, and a package of pornographic magazines. He also interviewed a series of witnesses who described Pacciani as a violent man, a poacher, a man who at town festivals couldn't keep his hands in his pockets and annoyed all the women.

But the crown jewel of evidence found in Pacciani's house was a disturbing painting. It depicted a large, uncovered cube, inside of which was a centaur. The human half of the centaur showed a general with a skull in place of a head who brandished a saber in his right hand. The animal part was a bull whose horns became a lyre. This strange creature had both male and female sex organs and huge clown feet. There were mummies that looked like policemen, one of which was making a vulgar gesture. A hissing snake was coiled in the corner wearing a hat. And in front of all this, most significantly, were seven little crosses planted in the ground, surrounded by flowers.

Seven crosses. Seven crimes of the Monster.

The painting was signed "PaccianiPietro," and he had given it a misspelled title: "A science-fition dream." Chief Inspector Perugini submitted the painting to an expert for psychological examination. The conclusion: the painting was "compatible with the personality of the so-called Monster."

By 1989, Perugini was closing in on Pacciani. But before he could hang the sign of "Monster" around Pacciani's neck, the chief inspector had to explain how the gun used in the 1968 clan killing ended up in Pacciani's hands. He dealt with the problem in the simplest way possible: he accused Pacciani of committing the 1968 murders too.

Judge Mario Rotella, as the examining magistrate, had watched Perugini's investigation with dismay, viewing it as an effort to construct a monster out of thin air, using as a starting point the conveniently brutal person of Pietro Pacciani. But the attempt to accuse Pacciani of the 1968 double homicide, without a shred of evidence, was going too far. It was a direct challenge to the Sardinian Trail investigation. As examining magistrate, Rotella refused to sanction it.

Inspector Perugini was backed by two powerful

supporters for his investigation of Pacciani: Vigna, the prosecutor, and the police. The carabinieri backed Rotella.

The struggle between Vigna and Rotella, the police and carabinieri, finally came to a head. Vigna led the charge. He argued that the Sardinian Trail investigation was nothing more than the sterile result of paying heed to the ravings of Stefano Mele. It was a red herring that had sidetracked the investigation for more than five years. Rotella and the carabinieri found themselves on the defensive, protecting the Sardinian Trail investigation, but they were on the losing side. They had allowed their primary suspect, Salvatore Vinci, to slip through their fingers after his acquittal in Sardinia. Rotella, with his condescending pontifications and lack of charisma, had become deeply unpopular with the press and the public. Vigna, on the other hand, was seen as a hero. And finally, there was Pacciani himself—brutal murderer, daughter rapist, wife-beater, alcoholic, a man who forced his family to eat dog food—a monstrous human being in every way. To many Florentines, if he wasn't actually the Monster himself, he was close enough.

Vigna won. The carabinieri colonel in charge of the Monster investigation was transferred from

Florence to another posting, and Rotella was ordered to close his files, prepare a final report,
and remove himself from the case. The report,
he was instructed, must clear all the Sardinians
of any involvement in the Monster killings.

The carabinieri were furious at this turn of
events. They officially withdrew from the Monster investigation. "If one day," a colonel of the
carabinieri told Spezi, "the real Monster came to
our barracks with his pistol and perhaps even a
slice of a victim, our response would be: 'Go to
the police station, we've got no interest in you
or your story.'"

Rotella prepared the final report. It was a curious document. In more than a hundred pages
of crisp, logical exposition, it laid out the case
against the Sardinians. It detailed the clan killing of 1968, how it was executed, and who was
involved. It traced the probable arc of the .22
Beretta from Holland to Sardinia to Tuscany,
and placed it in Salvatore Vinci's hands. It built
a persuasive case that the Sardinians who participated in the 1968 killing knew who took the
gun home and, therefore, knew the identity of
the Monster of Florence. And that that person
was Salvatore Vinci.

And then, abruptly, on the last page, he wrote,

"P.Q.M. [*Per questi motivi*, For these reasons] this investigation shall proceed no further." He dismissed all the charges and indictments against the Sardinians and officially absolved them of any involvement in the Monster of Florence killings and the 1968 clan killing. Mario Rotella then resigned from the case and was posted to Rome.

"I had no other way out except for this," Rotella told Spezi in an interview. "This ending is a source of the greatest bitterness to me and many others."

It was clear then—as it is today—that Rotella and the carabinieri, despite all their missteps, were in fact on the right trail. The Monster of Florence was very likely a member of that Sardinian clan.

The official closing of the Sardinian Trail meant that the Monster investigation could now proceed in any direction but the right one.

CHAPTER
24

The carabinieri pulled their men out of SAM, and the special anti-Monster unit was reorganized under Chief Inspector Perugini as an all-police force. Pacciani was now the only suspect, and they pursued him hammer and tongs. The chief inspector was convinced that the end-game was near, and he was determined to force it to a conclusion.

The year was 1989, and the Monster had not killed for four years. Florentines began to think that maybe, finally, the police had gotten their hands on the right man.

Perugini went on a popular television show and became an instant celebrity when, at the end, he fixed his tinted Ray-Bans on the camera and spoke directly to the Monster in firm but not unsympathetic tones: "You're not as crazy as people say. Your fantasies, your impulses, have taken your hand and govern your actions. I know that even in this moment you are trying to fight against them. We want you to know that we will help you overcome them. I know that the past taught you suspicion and silence, but in this moment I am not lying to you and never will, if you decide to free yourself from this Monster who tyrannizes you." He paused. "You know how, when, and where to find me. I will be waiting for you."

The speech, which seemed wonderfully spontaneous to millions of listeners, had actually been written in advance by a team of psychologists. Perugini had memorized it. It was specifically directed at Pacciani himself, who they knew would be at home watching the program. In the days preceding the show, the police had bugged his house in hopes of getting some incriminating reaction from him when Perugini made his carefully crafted speech.

The tape recording from the bug was collected from Pacciani's house after the program and listened to with great interest. There had been, in fact, a reaction. When Perugini concluded his statement on television, Pacciani erupted in a torrent of profanity in a Tuscan dialect so antique, so forgotten, that it would have brought joy to a linguist. He then wailed, still in dialect, "They better not name names, because I'm just a poor, innocent, unfortunate man!"

Three years passed. Between 1989 and 1992, Perugini's investigation against Pacciani made little headway. He could not find a smoking gun. The loot from the searches of his property and house had yielded just enough to satisfy the fantasies of the investigators, but not enough to actually arrest the man for murder.

When Pacciani was interrogated, he responded very differently from the cool and collected Vinci brothers. He loudly denied everything, told lies even about things of no importance, contradicted himself continually, broke down sobbing, and wailed that he was a poor innocent, unjustly persecuted.

The more Pacciani lied and bawled, the more Perugini became convinced of his guilt.

One morning in the early nineties, Mario Spezi, now a freelance writer, dropped by police headquarters and looked up an old friend from his days on the crime beat, hoping to rustle up a story. He had heard rumors that Perugini and SAM, years before, had asked the American FBI for help. The result had been a secret profile of the Monster prepared by the famed Behavioral Science Unit at Quantico. But no one had ever seen the report—if there even was one.

Spezi's contact disappeared and returned a half an hour later with a sheaf of papers. "I'm not giving you anything," he said, handing them to Spezi. "We haven't even seen each other."

Spezi took the file to a café in the loggia of Piazza Cavour. He ordered a beer and began to read. (The report had been helpfully translated into Italian; I have translated it back into English, being unable to get the original report.)

FBI Academy, Quantico, Virginia, 22135. Request for collaboration by the Polizia di Stato Italiana regarding the investigation of THE MONSTER OF FLORENCE, FPC-GCM FBIHQ 00; FBIHQ. The following investigative analysis was prepared by Special Agents John T. Dunn, Jr., John Galindo, Mary Eileen O'Toole, Fernando M. Rivera, Richard Robley and Frans B. Wagner under the direction of Special Agent in Charge

Ronald Walker and other members of the National Center for the Analysis of Violent Crime (NCAVC).

It carried a date of August 2, 1989:"THE MONSTER OF FLORENCE/Our file 163A-3915.

"Please be informed," began the cautionary preface of the American experts, "that the attached analysis is based on an examination of materials furnished by your office and is not to be considered a substitute for a complete and well-conceived investigation and it should not be considered conclusive or comprehensive."

The report stated that the Monster of Florence was not unique. He was a serial killer of a type known to the FBI, on which they had a database: a lone, sexually impotent male with a pathological hatred of women, who satisfied his libidinous cravings through killing. In the dry language favored by law enforcement, the FBI report catalogued the Monster's likely characteristics, explained his probable motive, and speculated as to how and why he killed, how he chose his targets, what he did with the body parts, and even included such details as where he lived and whether or not he owned a car.

Spezi read with growing fascination. It became clear to him why the report had been suppressed: it painted a portrait of a killer very different from Pietro Pacciani.

The report stated that the Monster chose the places, not the victims, and he would kill only in places he knew well.

The aggressor in all likelihood effectuated a surveillance of the victims until they engaged in some form of sexual activity. It is at this point that the aggressor chose to strike, with the advantage of surprise, speed, and the use of a weapon able to incapacitate immediately. This particular method of approach is generally indicative of an aggressor who has doubts about his own ability to control his victims, who feels himself insufficiently prepared to interact with his victims "alive" or who feels himself incapable of confronting them directly.

The aggressor, using a sudden approach, discharged his weapon at close range, concentrating his fire first on the male victim, neutralizing in this way the greater danger to himself. Once the male victim is neutralized, the aggressor feels himself suf-

ficiently secure to perpetrate his attack on the female victim. The use of many rounds indicates that the aggressor wanted to assure himself that both victims were deceased before initiating the mutilation post mortem on the female victim. This is the real objective of the aggressor; the man represents only an obstacle that must be removed.

According to the FBI report, the Monster acted alone. It said the killer may have a record, but only for such things as arson or petty theft. He was not a habitually violent person who would have committed serious crimes of aggression. Nor was he a rapist. "The aggressor is a person who is inadequate and immature in sexual matters, who has had little sexual contact with women in his own peer group." It said that the reason for the mysterious gap in the killings from 1974 to 1981 was probably because the killer was away from Florence during that time. "The aggressor is best described as a person of average intelligence. He would have completed his secondary studies or the equivalent in the Italian educational system. He would be experienced in work that required use of the hands."

Farther on it read, "The aggressor would have lived alone in a working-class area during the years in which the crimes occurred." And he would own his own car.

But the most interesting part, even today, is the manner in which the crimes were committed, which the FBI called his "signature." "The possession and the ritual are very important for this kind of aggressor. This would explain why the female victims were generally moved some meters from the vehicle containing their companion. The necessity of *possession*, as a ritual enacted by the aggressor, betrayed rage toward women in general. The mutilation of the sexual organs of the victims represented either the inadequateness of the aggressor or his resentment of women."

The FBI report noted that this type of serial killer often tried to control the investigation through direct or informal contact with the police, presenting himself as an informant, sending anonymous letters, or contacting the press.

One chapter of the FBI analysis discussed the so-called "souvenirs"—the body parts and perhaps trinkets and jewelry—the Monster took from the victims. "These pieces were taken as souvenirs and helped the aggressor relive the event in his fantasies for a certain period of time. These pieces are kept for a long period of time, and once they are no longer needed by the aggressor they are often left back at the scene of the crime or on the tomb of the victim. Occasionally," the report noted dryly, "the killer may, for libidinous reasons, consume the body parts of the victim to complete the act of possession."

A paragraph was dedicated to the letter that contained the piece of a victim's breast, mailed to the magistrate Silvia Della Monica."The letter may indicate that the aggressor was attempting to mock the police, suggesting that the publicity and attention of this case were important to him, and indicating a growing sense of security on his part."

And about the pistol used by the Monster, the FBI wrote that "for him, perhaps, the pistol was a fetish."The use of the same firearm and boxes of bullets was all part of the ritualized nature of the killing, and probably included specific clothing and other accessories used only for killing, and kept well hidden at other times. "The overall behavior of the aggressor at the scene, including his use of certain accessories and instruments specific to the crime, suggests that the ritual inherent in this series of aggressions is so important to him that he must repeat the offense in the identical manner until he reaches satisfaction."

None of it sounded like Pacciani, so the FBI report was ignored and suppressed.

In the three years from 1989 to 1992, Perugini and his investigators became increasingly frustrated that they could not gather enough evidence to charge Pacciani. They finally decided to organize a massive twelve-day search of the peasant's miserable house and property.

In April of 1992 Perugini and his men launched what would become the longest and most technologically advanced property search in Italian history. From 9:50 a.m. on April 27 to noon on May 8, 1992, a well-armed squad of elite investigators searched Pacciani's hovel and garden: they examined the walls inch by inch, sounded under the paving stones, searched in every possible gap and cavity, looked in every drawer, turned over furniture, beds, chairs, sofas, closets, and bureaus, lifted the roof tiles one by one, excavated with backhoes almost three feet deep in the soil of the garden, and penetrated with ultrasound every square millimeter of the land surrounding the house.

Firemen went over the place with their special knowledge. Representatives of private firms wielded metal detectors and heat-sensing equipment. There were technicians who filmed with precision the places that were being searched. There was a doctor on hand to check on the health of Pacciani, as they feared the excitable peasant might have a heart attack during the search. They brought in an expert in "diagnostic architecture," able to pinpoint the location in a seemingly solid, load-bearing wall where, for example, one might hide a niche or cavity.

At 5:56 p.m. on April 29, when the exhausted police had already decided to abandon the search "under a sky that promised rain," a discovery was made. Ruggero Perugini would later write about this triumphant moment in his book *A Normal Enough Man* (the book that depicted the Botticelli nymph on the cover, vomiting blood). "I caught in the light of the late afternoon an almost imperceptible gleam in the earth," the chief inspector wrote.

It was a Winchester series H cartridge, completely covered with oxidation. It had not been fired, and so the base did not bear the Monster's signature firing-pin mark. It did, however, bear marks that indicated it had been inserted into a firearm. It was analyzed by ballistics experts who concluded that it was "not incompatible" with having been inserted into the Monster's gun."Not incompatible"was as far as they would go despite (as one expert complained later) having been relentlessly pressured.

But it was enough. Pacciani was arrested on January 16, 1993, and charged with being the Monster of Florence.

CHAPTER
25

The trial of Pietro Pacciani began on April 14, 1994. The courtroom bunker was overflowing with a public divided between those who thought him guilty and those who maintained his innocence. Girls paraded around in T-shirts that read in English, "I ♥ Pacciani." There was a veritable caravansary of photographers, filmmakers, and journalists, in the middle of which, protected and led by Chief Inspector Ruggero Perugini, was the writer Thomas Harris.

A trial is perfect theater: a restricted time period, a shut room, recitations by subject, fixed roles—the prosecutor, the lawyers, the judges, the accused. There was no trial that was purer

theater than Pacciani's. It was melodrama worthy of Puccini.

The peasant farmer rocked and sobbed during the proceedings, sometimes crying out in
his antique Tuscan dialect, "I am a sweet little
lamb! ...I am here like Christ on the cross!"
At times he would rise to his full diminutive
height, pull forth from a hidden pocket a little
icon of the Sacred Heart, and wave it in the
judges' faces while the president of the court
banged his gavel and told him to sit down. At
other times he erupted in anger, face on fire,
spittle flying from his lips, cursing a witness or
condemning the Monster himself, invoking God
with his hands joined and eyes rolled to heaven,
hollering, "Burn him in hell forever!"

After only four days of the trial, Spezi broke
the first big story. A central piece of evidence
against Pacciani was his bizarre painting—the
one with the centaur and the seven crosses—
which psychologists said was "compatible" with
the psychopathic personality of the Monster.
The actual image had been kept under wraps,
but Spezi had finally managed to extract a photograph of it from the prosecutor's office. It took
him only a few days to find the actual painter—
a fifty-year-old Chilean artist named Christian

Olivares, exiled to Europe during the Pinochet era. Olivares was outraged when he heard that his painting was being used as evidence against a serial killer. "In this painting," he told Spezi, "I wanted to present the grotesque horror of a dictatorship. To say it is the work of a psychopath is ridiculous. It would be like saying the *Disasters of War* by Goya indicated he was a madman, a monster who needed to be locked up."

Spezi called up Perugini. "Tomorrow," he told the chief inspector, "my paper will publish an article saying that the painting that you attributed to Pacciani was not painted by him, but by a Chilean artist. Would you care to comment?"

The article was a major embarrassment. Vigna, the chief prosecutor, tried to play down the painting. "It was the mass media that exaggerated its importance," he said. Another prosecutor, Paolo Canessa, tried to minimize the damage by explaining that "Pacciani did sign the painting and told some of his friends that it was his own dream."

The trial marched on for six more months. In a corner of the courtroom, cameras with zoom lenses focused in on Pacciani and the witnesses arrayed against him. The images were projected on a screen on the left-hand side of the court, so that even those in poor seats could follow the drama. Every night the highlights of the trial were replayed on television, attracting huge audience numbers. Everyone gathered around the television at dinnertime, watching a drama in installments better than any soap opera.

The high point came when it was time for Pacciani's daughters to speak from the witness stand. All of Tuscany was glued to the television for their testimony.

Florentines have never forgotten the sight of the two daughters (one of whom had joined a convent) weeping as they told, in excruciating detail, how they had been raped by their father. In front of everyone passed a picture of Tuscan country life very different from *Under the Tuscan Sun*. Their testimony portrayed a family in which the women endured insults, drunken abuse, beatings with a stick, and sexual violence.

"He didn't want daughters," said one daughter, weeping. "Once Mamma had a miscarriage and he knew that it was a boy. He said to us, 'You both should have died and he live.' Once he gave us the meat of a groundhog to eat that he had taken for its skin. He beat us when we didn't want to go to bed with him."

None of this had anything to do with the Monster of Florence. When the questioning did turn in that direction, the two daughters weren't able to recall a single damning fact—a glimpse of the gun, a spot of blood, an incautious word dropped during his nightly drinking bouts—that could connect their father with the double homicides of the Monster of Florence.

The prosecutors lined up their meager scraps of evidence. The bullet and a rag were presented. A plastic soapdish found at Pacciani's house was put forward. (The mother of one of the victims said that she thought it looked like one belonging to her son.) A photograph of Botticelli's nymph was propped up in the courtroom, next to a blow-up of the victim with the gold chain in her mouth. A German-made block of sketching paper, also found in Pacciani's house, was advanced as evidence, with relatives saying they thought the German couple might have had one like it. Pacciani claimed he had found it in a Dumpster years before the killing, and notes Pacciani had jotted in it did clearly date to well before the murder. Prosecutors maintained that the wily peasant had added the notes later to divert suspicion. (Spezi pointed out in an article that it would have been far simpler for Pacciani to have thrown the incriminating sketchbook in the fireplace.)

Among the witnesses were Pacciani's old pals from the Casa del Popolo, the communist-built social club and meeting hall for working-class people in San Casciano. His friends were mostly country bumpkins, uneducated, ruined by bad wine and whoring. Among them was a man named Mario Vanni, a dimwitted ex-postman of San Casciano, who had been nicknamed Torsolo, "Apple Core," by his fellow citizens—in other words, the part of the apple that is no good and is thrown away.

In the courtroom Vanni was confused and terrified. In answer to the first question ("What is your current occupation?") instead of answering, he immediately launched into a quavering explanation that, yes, he knew Pacciani, but they were only "picnicking friends" and nothing more. In order to avoid making mistakes the postman had obviously memorized that phrase with which he answered almost every question, whether relevant or not. "*Eravamo compagni di merende*," he kept repeating, "We were picnicking friends."

We were picnicking friends. With those words, the unfortunate postman invented a phrase that would enter the very lexicon of the Italian lan-

guage. *Compagni di merende*,"picnicking friends"
is now a colloquial expression in Italian referring
to friends who pretend to be doing something innocent when in fact they are bent on dark, murderous misdeeds. The phrase became so popular
that it even has its own Italian Wikipedia entry.

"We were picnicking friends," Vanni continued
to repeat after every question, his chin dipping, his
eyes squinting about the vast courtroom.

The prosecutor became more and more irritated with Vanni and that phrase. Vanni went
on to retract everything that he had said in his
earlier interrogations. He denied hunting with
Pacciani, denied various statements he had
made, and ended up denying everything, swearing he knew nothing, protesting loudly that he
and Pacciani were picnicking friends and nothing more. The president of the court finally lost
his temper. "Signor Vanni, you are what we call
reticent, and if you continue this way you risk
being charged with false testimony."

Vanni continued to whine, "But we were just
picnicking friends," while the courtroom audience laughed and the judge banged his gavel.

His behavior on the witness stand aroused the
suspicions of a police officer named Michele
Giuttari, who would later take over the Monster

investigation from Chief Inspector Perugini. Perugini had been rewarded for capturing the Monster (i.e., Pacciani) by being given the plummiest of postings: he had been sent to Washington, D.C., to became the liaison officer between the Italian police and the American FBI.

Giuttari would take the Monster investigation to a new, spectacular, level. But for now he was waiting in the wings, watching and listening, and developing his own theories of the crimes.

The day arrived in the trial that the Italians call the "twist"—that Perry Mason moment when a key witness mounts the stand and seals the fate of the accused. This witness in the Pacciani trial was a man named Lorenzo Nesi, thin and smarmy, with slicked-back hair and Ray-Bans, shirt unbuttoned, gold chains dangling among his chest hair, a smooth talker and small-time ladies' man. Whether it was for the love of attention or the desire to be on the front page, Nesi would become a veritable serial witness, popping up when most needed and suddenly recalling events buried for years. This was his debut appearance; there would be many more.

In his first deposition, spontaneously given, Nesi said that Pacciani had boasted to him of having gone hunting at night with a pistol to shoot pheasants resting in the trees. This was taken as another damning piece of evidence against Pacciani, because it showed the peasant, who denied having a pistol, owned one after all—no doubt "that" pistol.

Twenty days later, Nesi suddenly remembered something else.

On Sunday evening, September 8, 1985, the alleged night of the murder of the two French tourists, Nesi was returning from a trip and was forced to take a detour past the Scopeti clearing because the Florence-Siena superstrada, his usual route, was blocked by construction. (It was later determined, however, that the work interrupting the superstrada occurred on the following weekend.) Between approximately nine-thirty and ten-thirty in the evening, Nesi said, he was about a kilometer from the Scopeti clearing when he stopped at an intersection to let a Ford Fiesta pass. The car was of a rosy or reddish color, and he was ninety percent certain it was driven by Pacciani. There was on board a second individual he didn't know.

Why hadn't he reported this ten years ago?

Nesi replied that at the time he was only seventy to eighty percent certain, and that you should only report things you are certain of.

Now, however, he had become ninety percent certain of his identification, and that, he figured, made it certain enough to be reported. The judge praised him later for his scrupulosity.

One wouldn't normally think that Nesi, being a small dealer in sweaters, would mistake a color. But he had gotten wrong the color of Pacciani's car—it was not "rosy or reddish," it was dead white. (Perhaps Nesi was thinking back to the red Alfa Romeo reported by witnesses that led to the infamous Identi-Kit portrait.)

Nevertheless, Nesi's testimony put Pacciani within a kilometer of the Scopeti clearing on Sunday night, and that was enough to seal the peasant's fate. The judges convicted Pacciani of murder and condemned him to fourteen life sentences. In their opinion, the judges explained Nesi's mistake by the fact that the reflection of the taillights at night made the white car look red. They acquitted Pacciani of the 1968 murders, as prosecutors had presented no evidence linking him with that crime, beyond the fact that it was committed with the same gun. The judges never addressed the question of how, if Pacciani had nothing to do with that killing, he had come into possession of the gun.

At 7:02 p.m. on November 1, 1994, the presi-

dent of the court began to read the verdict. All
the national networks in Italy interrupted their
programming to bring the news. "Guilty of the
murder of Pasquale Gentilcore and Stefania Pettini," the president of the court intoned, "guilty
of the murder of Giovanni Foggi and Carmela
De Nuccio, guilty of the murder of Stefano Baldi
and Susanna Cambi, guilty of the murder of
Paolo Mainardi and Antonella Migliorini, guilty
of the murder of Fredrich Wilhelm Horst Meyer
and Uwe Jens Rüsch, guilty of the murder of Pia
Gilda Rontini and Claudio Stefanacci, guilty of
the murder of Jean-Michel Kraveichvili and Nadine Mauriot."

As the judge's stentorian voice boomed out
the final "guilty," Pacciani placed his hand upon
his heart, closed his eyes, and murmured, "An innocent dies."

CHAPTER
26

One chilly February in 1996, Mario Spezi crossed the little piazza toward the carabinieri barracks in the village of San Casciano. He was out of breath, and not just because of the Gauloises he smoked unceasingly; he was wearing a massive and exceedingly ugly overcoat, in garish colors, dangling with zippers, belts, and buckles that served no purpose except to obscure the real function of the garment. A small button near the collar was a microphone. Behind the silly plastic label on the breast was a video camera. Between the outer material and the lining was a recorder, a battery, and wires. The electronic apparatus hidden among the stuffing did not emit even a faint buzz. A technician from the television station had activated it inside the church of the Collegiata di San Cassiano, behind a stone column between the confessional and the baptismal font. There had been no one in the Collegiata, aside from an old lame woman kneeling on the prayer stand in front of a forest of plastic candles that spread their electric light against the darkness.

In the two years since Pacciani had been convicted, Spezi had written many articles casting doubt on the peasant's guilt. But this one promised to be the scoop to end all scoops.

The video camera would run for an hour. In those sixty minutes Spezi had to convince Arturo Minoliti, the marshal of the carabinieri barracks of San Casciano, to talk. He had to get the man to tell him the truth about Perugini's discovery of the cartridge in Pacciani's vegetable garden. Minoliti, as the local carabinieri official, had been present during the twelve-day search, the only one there not connected with SAM or the police to witness the recovery of the infamous cartridge.

Spezi had always had deep misgivings about this type of journalism, and he had often sworn he would never do it. It was dirty, it was shaking down someone for a scoop. But just before entering the barracks, where Minoliti was waiting, his scruples vanished like holy water on the tip of a finger. Taping Minoliti surreptitiously was, perhaps, the only way to arrive at the truth, or at least a piece of it. The stakes were high: Spezi was convinced that Pacciani was innocent, and that a huge miscarriage of justice had taken place.

Spezi stopped in front of the entrance to the barracks and turned so that his breast would film the sign that read "Carabinieri." He pressed the buzzer and waited. A dog barked somewhere and an icy wind cut his face. He didn't even think for a minute that he ran the risk of being discovered. The desire for a scoop made him feel invincible.

The door was opened by a man in a blue uniform, his eyes wary.

"I'm Mario Spezi. I have an appointment with Marshal Minoliti."

They left him in a small room long enough to smoke another Gauloise. From where he sat Spezi could see the empty office of the minor functionary from whom he hoped to steal the truth. He noted that the seat in front of the writing desk, the one that Minoliti would occupy, was placed on the right-hand side and he calculated that the lens of the camera, on the left side of his chest, would film only a wall. He said to himself that as soon as he sat down, he would have to turn the seat, with a casual gesture, in order to frame the carabinieri officer while he spoke.

Nothing will come if it, Spezi thought, suddenly feeling insecure. *This is like a Hollywood film, and only a bunch of overexcited television people could possibly think that it would succeed.*

Minoliti arrived. Tall, nearly forty, off-the-rack suit, gold-rimmed shades not quite covering the face of an intelligent man. "Sorry that I kept you waiting."

Spezi had worked up a plan for bringing him around to the crucial point. He counted on chipping away at his resistance by arousing his conscience as an upholder and enforcer of the law, and to play a little on his vanity, if he had any.

Minoliti indicated a chair. Spezi took the seat-back and rearranged it with a single, easy move. He seated himself facing the marshal and placed his cigarettes and lighter on the desktop. He was certain he now had Minoliti in the camera's sights.

"I'm sorry for disturbing you," he began hesitatingly, "but tomorrow I have a meeting with my editor in Milan, and I'm looking for something on the Monster of Florence. New stuff, real news. By now, you know better than me, everything and its opposite has been said and nobody gives a damn about it any longer."

Minoliti fidgeted in his seat and twisted his neck in a funny way. He moved his gaze from Spezi to the window and back. In the end he sought help in a cigarette.

"What do you want to know?" he said, blowing the smoke from his nostrils.

"Arturo," Spezi said, leaning forward confidentially. "Florence is small. You and I move in the same circles. We've both heard certain rumors, it's inevitable. Excuse me for being direct, but it seems you have doubts about the investigation against Pacciani. Grave doubts . . . ?"

The marshal took his chin between his hands and, this time, twisted his lips strangely. Then the words came like a gust of relief. "Well, yes . . . In the sense that . . . In short, if there's a strange coincidence, you let it pass. If there are two, you can still let it go. When it gets to three, well, in the end you have to say that it's no longer a coincidence. And here, with the coincidences, or more like strange happenings, there have been a few too many."

Under the lens of the microcamera Spezi's heart began to accelerate.

"What do you mean? Is there something that doesn't seem right about the investigation?"

"Well, yes. Look, I'm convinced that Pacciani is guilty. But it was up to us to prove it . . . You can't cut corners."

"Which is to say?"

"Which is to say . . . the rag, for instance. That rag just doesn't make sense to me, it just doesn't."

The rag he was alluding to was a hard piece of evidence against Pacciani. A month after the maxi-search of his property that had brought to light the cartridge, Minoliti had received an anonymous package. Inside was a spring guide rod from a gun, wrapped in a piece of rag. There was a piece of paper written in capital letters. It said:

THIS IS A PIECE OF THE PISTOL BELONGING TO THE MONSTER OF FLORENCE. IT WAS IN A GLASS JAR REPLACED (SOMEONE HAD FOUND IT BEFORE ME) UNDER A TREE IN LUIANO. PACCIANI USED TO WALK THERE. PACCIANI IS A DEVIL AND I KNOW

HIM WELL AND YOU KNOW HIM TOO. PUNISH HIM
AND GOD WILL BLESS YOU BECAUSE HE IS NOT A MAN
BUT A BEAST. THANK YOU.

The business had seemed decidedly odd right away. And then, a few days after this fact, in the course of yet another search of Pacciani's garage, the agents of SAM had found a similar piece of rag that they had somehow overlooked in the twelve-day search. When the two pieces were brought together, they matched up perfectly.

Perugini theorized that the Monster himself had mailed the letter with the rag, in an unconscious wish to incriminate himself.

"This rag stinks," said Minoliti, turning toward the telecamera hidden on Spezi. "Because I wasn't called when it was found. All the operations were supposed to be conducted jointly by SAM and the carabinieri of San Casciano. But when the rag was found, I wasn't called. Strange. The rag, I say to you, is dirty. We were already in that garage and found many pieces of material, which we took and catalogued. That rag wasn't there."

Spezi lit another Gauloise to control his excitement. This was a major scoop and they had yet to arrive at the bullet found in the garden.

"In your opinion, where did the rag come from?"

The carabiniere opened his arms. "Eh, I don't know. I wasn't there. That's the trouble. And then why send a spring guide rod? Of all the parts of a pistol it's the only one that can't be matched to a specific firearm. And they just happened to mail that one!"

Spezi decided to nudge him toward the Winchester bullet. "And the cartridge. Does that also stink?"

Minoliti took a deep breath and was silent for several seconds. He turned and suddenly began, "It really burned me the way that cartridge was found. I resented how Chief Inspector Perugini put us in such a difficult situation with the truth . . ."

It was all Spezi could do to remain calm, his heart was pounding so hard.

"We were in Pacciani's garden," said the marshal, "I, Perugini, and two other agents of the squad. Those two were scraping the soles of their shoes on a cement grapevine post that lay on the ground and were joking about the fact that they both were wearing the same shoes. At a certain moment, near the shoe of one of them, the base of the cartridge just appeared."

"But," Spezi interrupted in order to make sure that the business was very clear on the tape, "Perugini described it quite differently in his book."

"Right! Right, because he says,'The ray of light made the cartridge glisten.' What ray of light! Look, maybe he just wanted to dress up the discovery a bit."

Spezi asked, "Minoliti, did they put it there?"

The marshal's face darkened. "That's one hypothesis. More than a hypothesis even ... I'm not saying that I'm certain ... I have to consider this against my will. It's a quasi-certainty ..."

"A quasi-certainty?"

"Eh, yes, because in light of the facts I can't find another explanation ...Then, I say, when Perugini wrote about witnessing this glimmer of light, it really frosted me. I say, 'Chief Inspector, you disrespect me. If I go and contradict you, I'm fucked.' What I mean is, who're the judges going to believe? A marshal or a chief inspector? At a certain point I'm forced to back up his story."

Spezi felt like he was filming an Oscar winner, the acting was so superb, and the Neapolitan accent of Minoliti just added that much more color. The journalist saw that he had fifteen minutes of tape by the clock. He had to press him. "Arturo, did they plant it?"

Minoliti was suffering. "I just can't believe that my colleagues, my friends . . ."

Spezi couldn't lose any more time. "Okay, I understand you. But, if for a moment you were to forget they were colleagues you had known for a long time, would the facts cause you to say that this bullet had been planted?"

Minoliti became like stone. "In the light of reason, yes. I must say it was planted. I arrived at that conclusion that certain evidence is dirty: the cartridge, the spring guide rod, and the rag." Minoliti continued to speak in a low tone, almost as if to himself. "I am up against an extremely difficult situation . . . They've got my telephone tapped . . . I'm afraid . . . I am truly afraid . . ."

Spezi tried to find out if he had told anyone of this, by way of confirmation. "You never spoke to anyone?"

"I talked to Canessa." Paolo Canessa was one of the prosecutors.

"And what did he say?"

"Nothing."

A few minutes later, at the door of the barracks, Minoliti said good-bye to Spezi. "Mario," he said, "forget what I told you. It was just venting.

I spoke to you because I trust you. But your colleagues, before they come in here, I order them searched!"

Feeling like a worm, Spezi crossed the piazza and walked along the sidewalk, his left shoulder almost brushing the walls of the houses, his arms rigid. He no longer felt the cold wind.

My God, he thought, *it worked*!

He went into the local Casa del Popolo where the people from the TV channel were waiting for him and drinking beer. Angling over to their table, he seated himself without saying a word. He felt their gaze on him. He continued to say nothing, and they asked him nothing. They all somehow understood it had been a success.

Later that evening, reunited at dinner after having seen the film of Minoliti, they let themselves feel euphoric. It was the scoop of the century. Spezi felt sorry to stick in the meat grinder the unwitting Marshal Minoliti. But, he told himself, even the truth must have its victims.

The next day, the Italian news agency ANSA, which had heard about the taping, ran an item on it. As soon as it was published, all three national television channels called to interview Spezi. At the news hour, Spezi parked himself on the sofa, remote in hand, to see how the news would be reported.

Not one word was aired. The following morning the newspapers did not speak of it, not even a line. Rai Tre, the national television channel that had arranged for the taping of Minoliti, canceled the segment.

Clearly, someone in a position of power had spiked it.

CHAPTER
27

In Italy, a man condemned to a life sentence is automatically granted an appeal before the Corte d'Assise d'Appello, with a new prosecutor and a fresh panel of judges. In 1996, two years after the conviction, Pacciani's case came up for appeal before the Corte d'Assise. The head prosecutor was Piero Tony, an aristocratic Venetian and lover of classical music, bald with a fringe of hair that fell below his collar. The president of the court was the aged and imposing Francesco Ferri, a jurist with a long and distinguished career.

Piero Tony had no stake in the original conviction of Pacciani, no face to save. One of the great strengths of the Italian judicial system is this appeals process, in which none of the players involved in the appeal—prosecutors or judges—have an ax to grind.

Tony, charged with upholding Pacciani's conviction, reviewed all the evidence against the peasant with dispassion and objectivity.

And he was aghast.

"This investigation," he told the court, "if it weren't so tragic, would put one in mind of the Pink Panther."

Instead of prosecuting Pacciani, Tony used his time in court to criticize the investigation and deprecate the evidence against Pacciani, taking it apart with ruthless logic, piece by piece, until not one brick of evidence was left standing on top of another. Pacciani's lawyers, seeing all their arguments usurped by the prosecution, could do little but sit in stunned silence and, when their turn came, express their amazed agreement with the prosecution.

As the trial proceeded, it generated panic and consternation among the investigators. With the prosecutor himself declaring Pacciani's innocence, the peasant would surely be acquitted, which would be an unbearable humiliation and loss of face for the police. Something had to be done—and it fell to Chief Inspector Michele Giuttari to do it.

Six months earlier, at the end of October 1995, Chief Inspector Giuttari had been installed in a sunny office high above the Arno River near the American embassy. He had taken over the Monster of Florence case after Chief Inspector Perugini left for Washington. The Squadra Anti-Mostro had been disbanded, since the case was thought to have been solved, but Giuttari would soon reconstitute a special investigative unit to take over its responsibilities. In the meantime, he had embarked on the herculean task of reading all the files on the case, tens of thousands of them, which included hundreds of interviews with witnesses, masses of expert reports and technical analyses, as well as entire trial transcripts. He also combed through the evidence lockers, examining everything that had been collected at the scenes of the crimes, no matter how irrelevant.

Chief Inspector Giuttari discovered many loose ends, unexplained evidence, and profound mysteries left to resolve. During this process, he came to a fateful conclusion: the case had not been completely solved. Nobody, not even Perugini, had understood the full and terrifying dimensions of the case.

Michele Giuttari was a Sicilian from Messina, dashing and articulate, an aspiring novelist and connoisseur of convoluted conspiracy theories. He went about with half a "toscano" cigar stuck in the corner of his mouth, coat collar flipped up, his long, thick, glistening black hair slicked back. He bore a striking resemblance to Al Pacino in the movie *Scarface*, and there was indeed something cinematic in the way he conducted himself, with style and verve, almost as if a camera were trained on him.

As Giuttari combed the files, he uncovered important but overlooked clues that, in his opinion, pointed to something far more sinister than a lone serial killer. He started with Lorenzo Nesi's claim that he saw Pacciani *with another person* in a red car (that was actually white), on Sunday night a kilometer from the last killing. Giuttari opened an investigation into this shadowy person. Who was he? What was he doing in the car? Had he participated in the murder? By uncovering the truth, the *real* truth, it went without saying that the chief inspector would be doing himself a favor. Perugini had used the Monster as a vehicle for tremendous career advancement and Vigna would soon do the same. There was plenty of mileage left in the Monster of Florence case.

Now, six months later, Pacciani's looming acquittal threatened to undo Chief Inspector Giuttari's nascent theories and carefully laid plans. The chief inspector had to do something to mitigate the damage of Pacciani's acquittal. He developed a plan.

On the morning of February 5, 1996, Chief Prosecutor Piero Tony spent four hours summing up. The case against Pacciani, he said, contained no evidence, no clues, and no proofs. There were no pieces of a pistol connecting him to the killings, there were no bullets planted in the garden capable of convicting, there wasn't a single witness in which he could believe. There was nothing. For Tony, the fundamental fact of the accusation remained unaddressed: nowhere did investigators explain how the infamous .22 Beretta used in the 1968 murder passed from the Sardinian clan into Pacciani's hands.

"Half a clue plus half a clue," Tony thundered, "does not make a whole clue: it makes zero!"

On February 12, Pacciani's lawyers, robbed of their arguments, said little in summation. The following day, Ferri and his associate justices shut themselves up in their chambers to deliberate.

On that same afternoon, Chief Inspector Giut-tari slipped on his black coat, raised his collar, stuck the half"toscano" in his mouth, and gathered together his men. Their unmarked cars blasted out of police headquarters and headed to San Casciano, where they surrounded the house of Mario Vanni—the ex-postman who, at Pacciani's first trial, had mumbled over and over that he and Pacciani were just "picnicking friends." Giut-tari and his men seized Vanni and bundled him into a squad car, not even giving the poor fellow time to put in his false teeth. Vanni, they said, was the "other man" Lorenzo Nesi had seen in the car. They charged him with being Pacciani's accomplice in murder.

The timing was exquisite. On the morning of February 13, the very day the appeals court judges were to announce their verdict, the newspapers were trumpeting the news of Vanni's arrest as Pac-ciani's co-Monster.

As a result, the great bunkerlike courtroom was like a volcano waiting to explode. The arrest of Vanni was a direct challenge to the judges, should they dare acquit Pacciani.

As the proceedings began, a policeman sent

by Chief Inspector Giuttari arrived breathlessly in court, carrying a bundle of papers. He demanded the right to speak. Ferri, the president of the court, was annoyed by this last-minute move. Nevertheless, he coolly invited the emissary from police headquarters to say his piece.

The man announced that four new witnesses in the Monster case had surfaced. He presented them as Greek letters: Alpha, Beta, Gamma, and Delta. For reasons of security, he said, the Tribunale could not render the names. Their testimony was absolutely crucial to the case—because two of these witnesses, the emissary told the stunned court, were *actually present* at the double homicide of 1985 when the French tourists were killed. They had witnessed Pacciani at the very scene of the crime, committing the murders, and one had actually confessed to helping him. The others could corroborate their testimony. These four witnesses, after more than a decade of silence, had suddenly been moved to speak out just twenty-four hours before the final judgment that would decide Pacciani's fate.

A frozen silence fell over the courtroom. Even the Bics of the journalists remained stuck in their notebooks. This was an incredible revela-

tion, the kind of thing you saw in the movies—
never in real life.

If Ferri had been annoyed, now he was incensed. But he maintained an icy calm, his voice
dripping with sarcasm. "We cannot hear Alpha
and Beta. We are not here for a lesson in algebra.
We cannot wait for the Procura [the prosecutor's office] to lift the veil of secrecy from the
names. Either they tell us immediately who this
Alpha, Beta, Gamma, and Delta are and we will
invite them into the courtroom to take their testimony, or else we will ignore this and take no
action whatsoever."

The policeman refused to name the names.
Ferri was livid at what he considered an offense
to the court, and he dismissed the emissary and
his news of witnesses. Then he and the other
judges rose and retired to their chambers to decide their verdict.

Later, it was suggested that Ferri had fallen
into a clever trap. By presenting the witnesses
in a deliberately offensive manner, Giuttari had
provoked Ferri into refusing to hear them—thus
creating grounds to appeal Ferri's verdict to the
Italian Supreme Court.

It was eleven in the morning. By four in the afternoon, the rumors began to circulate that the

appeals court was about to issue its verdict. In all the bars in Italy, the televisions were tuned to the same channel, while pro-Pacciani and anti-Pacciani factions faced off, arguing and laying bets. Many "I ♥ Pacciani" T-shirts were dusted off and donned for the occasion.

Standing, his voice marked with age, President of the Court Ferri announced the absolute and unconditional acquittal of Pacciani for being the Monster of Florence.

The shaky old peasant was freed. He later greeted well-wishers from the shabby window of his house, flanked by his lawyers, weeping and spreading his hands to bless the crowd, as if he were the pope.

The public trial was finished, but the trial of public opinion continued. Giuttari's timely arrest of Vanni and his courtroom gambit had done the trick. Pacciani had been acquitted of a crime that two people had *seen* him commit—his accomplices. There was a public uproar. Pacciani was guilty—he had to be. And yet the court had acquitted him. Ferri came under public criticism. Surely, many said, there must be some way to undo this travesty of justice.

There was: Ferri's refusal to hear the four witnesses. The Italian Court of Cassation (equivalent to the Supreme Court) took up the matter, vacated the acquittal, and opened the door for a new trial.

Giuttari swung into action, marshaling the evidence, preparing for fresh indictments and a trial. Only this time, Pacciani was not a lone serial killer. He had accomplices: his picnicking friends.

CHAPTER
28

Spezi and other journalists immediately rose to the challenge of identifying the four "algebraic" witnesses. The veil of secrecy was easily rent. They turned out to be quite a collection of half-wits and lowlifes. Alpha was a mentally retarded man named Pucci. Gamma was a prostitute named Ghiribelli, in the final stages of alcoholism, known to turn a trick for a twenty-five-cent glass of wine. Delta was a pimp named Galli.

Of them all, Beta would be the most important, as he had confessed to helping Pacciani murder the French tourists. His name was Giancarlo Lotti, and he came from the same town as Vanni, San Casciano. Everyone in San Casciano

knew Lotti. They had given him the racist nickname Katanga, an Italian slang term that might
be loosely translated as "Jungle Bunny," even
though he was white. Lotti was a sort of village
idiot of the classic kind that have largely disappeared from the modern world, a man who
subsisted on the charity of the village, who was
fed, clothed, and housed by his fellow citizens,
and who entertained all with his unwitting an-
tics. Lotti hung about the town square, grinning
and hailing people. He was often subjected to
pranks and taunts by schoolboys. They used
to chase him around: "Katanga! Katanga! Run!
Run! Martians have landed on the soccer field!"
And Lotti would happily start running. He maintained himself in a felicitous state of inebriation,
consuming two liters of wine a day, more on
holidays.

Spezi, in search of information on Lotti, spent
a long evening with the owner of the trattoria where Lotti got a free meal every evening.
The owner regaled him with amusing stories.
He told of the time that one of his waiters—the
same fellow who every evening laid a free bowl
of *ribollita* under the hangdog jowls and blood-
shot eyes of the poor unfortunate—dressed up
as a woman, with a pair of napkins for a hat and

rags stuffed in his shirt for breasts. The waiter, thus decked out, strutted and sashayed in front of Lotti, winking at him lasciviously. Lotti was immediately smitten. "She" pretended to accept an appointment with him in the bushes the following night. The next evening Lotti returned to the trattoria, boasting loudly of his imminent conquest, and he ate and drank with gusto. Then the owner arrived, saying Lotti was wanted on the telephone. Lotti was astonished and pleased to receive a telephone call in a restaurant like a man of affairs. He swaggered to the phone, which in reality was manned by another waiter in the kitchen, who pretended to be the young lady's father.

"If you lay a finger on my daughter," the alleged father roared, "I'll smash your ugly mug!"

"What daughter?" Lotti babbled, terrified, his knees shaking. "I swear I don't know any daughter, you've got to believe me!"

Everyone had a good laugh over that one.

What was not so amusing was the story Lotti and the other algebraic witnesses had told Giuttari, which was soon leaked to the press.

Pucci said that ten years ago, he and Lotti were returning to Florence on Sunday evening, September 8, 1985. This was the night investigators had decided the French tourists were killed, the night that Lorenzo Nesi claimed to have seen Pacciani with another man. They stopped at the Scopeti clearing to relieve themselves.

"I remember well," said Pucci, "that we saw a car of a light color stopped a few meters from a tent, and, to our view, two men who were inside that car got out of it and started to shout at us with menacing gestures, so much so that we went away. The two threatened to kill us if we didn't go away immediately. 'Why did you come here busting our balls, get the hell out or we'll kill both of you!' We were frightened and got out of there."

Pucci claimed that he and Lotti had stumbled across the scene of the Monster's last crime at the very moment when it was being committed. Lotti corroborated the story and added that he clearly recognized both men. They were Pacciani and Vanni—Pacciani waving a pistol and Vanni clutching a knife.

Lotti also implicated Pacciani and Vanni in the 1984 double murder in Vicchio. And then Lotti explained that it was no coincidence they had stopped in the Scopeti clearing that night to take a piss. He knew the crime was scheduled to take place, and he had stopped to assist in the killings. Yes, Lotti said, he had to confess it, he could hold back no longer—he was one of the murderers himself! Along with Vanni, he was one of the accomplices of the Monster of Florence.

Lotti's confession was of enormous importance to the police. As their star witness, they he was well taken care of. They moved him into a secret place that much later was revealed to be police headquarters in Arezzo, a beautiful medieval town south of Florence. After living in the police barracks for many months, Lotti's story, which had begun with many contradictions, began to line up with the facts already ascertained by the police. But Lotti was unable to give the investigators a single objective, verifiable piece of evidence that they didn't already have. The first iteration of Lotti's story, before he had spent months in Arezzo, didn't match the evidence gathered at the crime scene. For example, he swore to having seen Vanni make the cut in the tent. Then he said Pacciani entered the tent through the cut. Kraveichvili jumped out in a flash past Pacciani, and the fat sixty-year-old man pursued him into the woods firing his gun, killing him with the pistol.

None of this agreed with the evidence. The

cut in the tent was only seven inches long, and it was made in the rain fly of the tent, not in the tent itself. Nobody could have entered through the cut. The shells had all been found at the front door of the tent. If it had happened as Lotti claimed, the shells would have been scattered along the path of pursuit. Lotti's initial descriptions of the crime not only contradicted the evidence gathered in the Scopeti clearing, but also contradicted the psychiatric and behavioral analyses, the results of the autopsies, and the reconstructions of the crime.

Even shakier was Lotti's "confession" regarding the killing in Vicchio. Lotti said that the girl was only wounded by the first shots and that Vanni, so as not to dirty himself, had donned a long duster coat. Then, while she screamed, he pulled her out of the car, dragged her into the field of flowers and herbs, and finished her off with a knife. Again, none of this matched the evidence: the girl had been killed by the first shot, a bullet into the brain, and did not have the time even to cry out. The medical examiner had established that all the knife marks had been made post mortem. And there was no evidence at either crime of more than one killer at the scene.

Finally, there was the fundamental question of *when* the killing of the French tourists had taken place. Investigators had settled on Sunday night as the night of the crime. Naturally, Lotti claimed it was Sunday, and Nesi's testimony also involved Sunday night. But there was a great deal of evidence, including the testimony of Sabrina Carmignani, that suggested they had been killed Saturday night.

Why would Lotti make a false confession? The answer isn't hard to see. Lotti had gone from village idiot to star witness and co–Monster of Florence. He was the center of attention of the entire country, his picture on the front page of the newspapers, investigators hanging on his every word. On top of that, he had free room and board in Arezzo and perhaps even a liberal supply of wine.

In addition to the central story, Giuttari and his interrogators took down testimony from the algebraic witnesses of Vanni's sexual depravity. Some of this evidence was inadvertently hilarious. In one such story, the ex-postman had taken the bus to visit a whore in Florence. The bus driver took a curve a little fast, which caused a vibrator to fall out of Vanni's pocket. It rolled and bounced around the bus as Vanni, scrabbling about on his hands and knees, tried to scoop it up.

"The second investigation of the Monster of Florence has passed from an inquiry into serial killings committed by a single individual to a series of killings committed by more than one person," the prosecutor Vigna told the press. Instead of a lone psychopathic killer, a band of Monsters had roamed the Tuscan countryside—the picnicking friends.

Ghiribelli, the alcoholic prostitute, told investigators another story that would eventually loom large in the investigation. She claimed that Pacciani and his picnicking friends frequented the house of a self-styled druid or wizard (whose day job was that of pimp) where they held black masses and worshiped the devil. "In the room just as you entered," said Ghiribelli, "there were old wax candles, a five-pointed star drawn on the floor with carbon, an unspeakable dirtiness and messiness everywhere, condoms, liquor bottles. On the sheets of the big bed there were traces of blood. There were spots as large as a piece of letter paper. These traces I saw every Sunday morning in 1984 and 1985."

The wizard-pimp she named had died ten years before, and it proved impossible to check

Ghiribelli's assertions. Nevertheless, Giuttari took it all down and pushed the case forward, convinced he was finally on the right track.

The president of the appeals court, Francesco Ferri, the man who had acquitted Pacciani, watched the new investigation proceed with growing dismay and anger. He resigned his judgeship to write a book, entitled *The Pacciani Case*, which was rushed into print in late 1996.

In his book, Ferri denounced the new investigation into the picnicking friends. "The worst thing," Ferri wrote about Giuttari's new witnesses, "is not the improbability of their accounts, their lack of believability, but the clear falsity of the accounts. These two individuals [Pucci and Lotti] . . . have described particulars of the homicides, of which they claim to be eyewitnesses, that do not in fact conform to the evidence revealed at the time. . . . It is certain that Pucci and Lotti are coarse and habitual liars. . . . It is very difficult to believe that their stories contain even the minimum basis of truth."

The judge continued, "It smells to high heaven. . . . It is stupefying, however, that no one has up to this time exposed the grave deficiencies of the stories of Pucci and Lotti, neither investigators, defense attorneys, or journalists. . . . The most extraordinary thing, however, and more extraordinary still that nobody has noted it, is that for months Lotti has been kept in custody in an undisclosed location, where he has slept, eaten and perhaps above all drunken, and possibly even received compensation, in a place beyond the reach of the press, like a golden hen from which they ask, from time to time, a golden egg. In this way the revelations dribble out, bit by bit, more or less contradictory."

The judge advanced an explanation. "The mental flexibility of the subjects, their complete absence of morality and the hope of gaining impunity or other advantage is enough to explain their contorted testimony." Ferri concluded, "I could not remain quiet in the face of an investigation so far outside logic and justice, conducted with prejudice and equipped with confessions that are maintained at all cost."

Ferri, unfortunately, was not a compelling wordsmith, and he was innocent in the ways of publishing. He placed his book with a tiny publisher that had little distribution and which printed very few copies. *The Pacciani Case* sank like a stone, virtually unnoticed by the press or the public. The new investigation of the Monster of Florence, under the doughty captainship of Chief Inspector Michele Giuttari, sailed on, untroubled by Ferri's accusations.

In October of 1996, Vigna, the lead prosecutor in the Monster case, was appointed director of the Antimafia Investigation Department in Italy, the most powerful and prestigious law enforcement position in the country. (Perugini, you may recall, had earlier leveraged the Monster case into an appointment in Washington, D.C.) Others responsible for putting Pacciani on trial had also used the case as a springboard to greater things. Regarding the Monster investigation, a highly placed carabinieri officer entertained a unique theory of criminal justice that he shared with Spezi.

"Have you ever considered," he said, "that Pacciani's trial might be nothing more than a case of the acquisition and management of power?"

CHAPTER
29

Pacciani remained free and technically innocent while Giuttari mustered up a new case against him. But the excitement was too much for the Tuscan peasant, and on February 22, 1998, the "sweet little lamb" dropped dead of a heart attack.

It took no time at all for the rumor mill to declare that Pacciani had not died of a heart attack, but had in fact been murdered. Giuttari sprang into action and directed an exhumation of the peasant's body. The remains were tested for poisoning. The results? His death was "compatible" with having been poisoned—by an excess of his own heart medicine. Doctors pointed out that patients, in the throes of a heart attack, often overconsume their heart medicine. But that was far too prosaic an explanation for Chief Inspector Giuttari, who theorized that Pacciani may have been murdered by a person or persons unknown, to keep him from telling what he knew.

The trial of Pacciani's picnicking friends, Vanni and Lotti, began in June of 1997. The evidence against them consisted of Lotti's word, backed up by the feeble-minded Pucci, against Vanni's ineffective and disorganized protestations of innocence. It was a sad spectacle. Vanni and Lotti were convicted of all fourteen Monster killings; Vanni was sentenced to life in prison and Lotti to twenty-six years. Neither the press nor Italian public opinion seemed skeptical of the idea that three quasi-illiterate inebriates of marginal intelligence could have successfully killed fourteen people over a period of eleven years with the goal of stealing the women's sex organs.

The trial, furthermore, never addressed the central motive: why had Pacciani and his picnicking friends stolen those sex organs? Chief Inspector Giuttari, however, had already embarked on an investigation of this very question. And he had an answer: behind the Monster killings lay a satanic cult. This shadowy cabal of wealthy and powerful people, seemingly beyond reproach, who occupied the highest positions in society, business, law, and medicine, had hired Pacciani, Vanni, and Lotti to kill couples in order to obtain the sex organs of girls for use as the obscene, blasphemous "wafer" in their Black Masses.

To investigate this new theory, Chief Inspector Giuttari formed an elite police unit, which he called the Gruppo Investigativo Delitti Seriali, the Serial Killings Investigative Group, or GIDES. They set up shop on the top floor of a monstrous, modern cement structure called Il Magnifico, after Lorenzo il Magnifico, erected near the Florence airport. He assembled a crack team of detectives. Their sole mission: to identify and arrest the *mandanti*, the "masterminds" or instigators behind the killings of the so-called Monster of Florence.

Out of the Everest of evidence in the Monster case, Giuttari had pried out a few pebbles that he felt supported his new theory. First, Lotti had made an offhand statement, ignored at the time, that "a doctor asked Pacciani to do a few little jobs for him." For Giuttari, this revived the old suspicion that a doctor was responsible for the killings—this time not as the killer himself, but as a mastermind. And then there was Pacciani's money. After the old peasant died, it turned out he was rich. He owned two houses and had post office bonds worth more than the equivalent of a hundred thousand dollars. Giuttari was unable to track the source of this wealth. This should not have been all that surprising—a large percentage of the Italian economy at the time was underground and many people had unexplained riches. But Giuttari ascribed a more sinister reason to Pacciani's affluence: the peasant farmer had gotten rich from selling the body parts he and his picnicking friends had collected in their years of labor.

In a later book on the case, Chief Inspector Giuttari explained his satanic sect thesis more particularly. "The best sacrifices for evoking demons are human sacrifices, and *the death most favorable* [emphasis his] for such sacrifices are those that occur during orgasm and are called *mors iusti*. A similar motive led to the killings of the 'monster,' who struck his victims while they were making love. . . . In that precise moment [of orgasm] powerful energies are released, indispensable for the person acting out satanic rituals, which bring power to himself and to the ritual he is celebrating."

Digging deep into medieval lore and legend, the chief inspector found a possible name for this sect: the School of the Red Rose, an ancient, almost forgotten diabolical order that had left its mark across centuries of Florentine history, a perverse Priory of Sion in reverse, all pentacles, black masses, ritual killings, and demonic altars. The school, some said, was a deviant offshoot of an ancient order, Ordo Rosae Rubae et Aurae Crucis, an esoteric Masonic sect connected to the English Golden Dawn, and, therefore, with Aleister Crowley, the most famous satanist of the last century, who called himself "the Great Beast 666" and who in the 1920s founded a church in Cefalù, Sicily, called the Abbey of Thelema. There, it was said, Crowley practiced perverted magical and sexual rituals involving men and women.

There were several other elements that guided Giuttari in the formation of his theory. The most important of them was Gabriella Carlizzi, an energetic little Roman lady with a big smile who ran a conspiracy theory Internet site and had self-published a string of books. Carlizzi claimed to know a great deal of hidden information about many infamous European crimes of the past decades—including the kidnapping and murder

of the former Italian prime minister Aldo Moro
and the Belgian pedophile ring. Behind them all,
she said, was the School of the Red Rose. On the
day of the September 11, 2001, terrorist attacks,
Carlizzi shot a fax out to Italian newspapers: "It
was them, the members of the Red Rose. Now
they want to strike Bush!" The Red Rose was
also behind the Monster killings. Carlizzi had
earlier been convicted of defamation for claiming the well-known Italian writer Alberto Bevilacqua was the Monster of Florence, but since
that time her theories on the Monster had apparently evolved. Her site was also filled with
religious and inspirational stories and a section
in which she detailed her conversations with
the Madonna of Fatima.

Carlizzi became an expert witness for the investigation. Giuttari and his GIDES detectives
called her in and listened to her for hours—perhaps even days—as she recounted her knowledge of the activities of the satanic sect hidden
in the green hills of Tuscany. The police had to
give her a protective escort, she would later
claim, because of the grave danger she faced
from members of the sect intent on silencing
her.

In rummaging through old evidence lockers,

Giuttari found physical evidence to back up his theories that a satanic sect was behind the killings. The first was the doorstop that had been collected a few dozen meters from the place where the Monster had killed a couple in the Bartoline Fields in October 1981. For the chief inspector, that stone was something far more sinister than a doorstop. He described its significance to a reporter for the *Corriere della Sera*, one of Italy's major daily newspapers: it was, he claimed, a "truncated pyramid with an hexagonal base that served as a bridge between this world and Hell." He dug out of an old file some photographs taken by police of some suspicious circles of stones with some berries and a cross where an old gamekeeper claimed the French tourists had camped four days preceding their murder. (Many other witnesses said they had been camping in the Scopeti clearing for at least a week.) Investigators later concluded that the stone circles had no connection with the case. Giuttari did not agree. He turned the photographs over to an "expert" in the occult. The chief inspector reported the expert's conclusions in his book: "When the circle of stones is closed it represents the union of two people, that is to say a pair of lovers, while when it is

open it signifies that the couple has been selected. The photograph of the berries and the
cross show the murder of the two people; the
people are the berries, while their death is represented by the cross. The photograph of the
scattered stones shows the destruction of the
circle after the execution of the two lovers."

Seeing that Pacciani & Co. were all from San
Casciano, Giuttari figured that the satanic sect
must be headquartered in or around that idyllic little Tuscan village, set like a jewel in the
rolling hills of Chianti. Once again he delved
deeply into fusty Monster files and found a
startling clue. In the spring of 1997, a mother
and a daughter had gone to the police with a
strange story. They managed a rest home for old
people in a place called Villa Verde, a beautiful
old country house surrounded by gardens and a
park situated a few kilometers outside San Casciano. The two women complained that a guest
of the villa, a half-Swiss, half-Belgian painter
named Claude Falbriard, had disappeared, leaving behind a huge mess in his room and a pile
of suspicious things—things that might have
something to do with the Monster of Florence,
including an unregistered pistol and hideous
drawings of women with their arms, legs, and

heads cut off. The two women had piled all of Falbriard's belongings in a box and delivered them to the police.

At the time, the police had dismissed it as irrelevant. Giuttari saw the situation in a different light and launched an investigation of the two women and their villa. Right away he struck pay dirt: he discovered that Pacciani had actually worked for a while as a gardener at Villa Verde during the time of the killings!

Giuttari and his investigators now believed that the villa might have served as the headquarters of the Order of the Red Rose, whose members commissioned the gardener, Pacciani, and his friends to collect female body parts for use in satanic rituals at the villa. In Giuttari's scenario, the mother and daughter were actually part of the satanic cult. (Why they would have brought attention to themselves by going to the police was left unexplained.)

Between the time of the murders and Giuttari's investigation, Villa Verde had become a super-luxury hotel with a swimming pool and restaurant, renamed Poggio ai Grilli, Hill of the Crickets. (The sign, almost as soon as it went up, was altered by some Tuscan wag to read "Poggio

ai Grulli," Hill of the Morons.) The new owners
were not at all pleased by the attention.

The press, with *La Nazione* leading the way,
picked up the story with ferocious glee.

OWNERS OF NURSING HOME UNDER SUSPICION
THE VILLA OF HORRORS
ALLEGED TO HAVE HOSTED SECRETS OF
MONSTER OF FLORENCE

*"After ten o'clock, the villa was sealed up
against outsiders. Various people arrived
and performed magical and satanic rites."
So claimed one of the ex-nurses of Poggio
ai Grilli, the villa between San Casciano
and Mercatale where Pietro Pacciani,
once accused of committing the Monster
of Florence killings, had worked as a gardener. During the period of the Tuscan
murders, the "Villa of the Horrors" hosted
a rest home for old people where for several months the painter Claude Falbriard
lived, first investigated for illegal possession of a firearm, who then became a key
witness in the investigation into the pos-*

sible instigators behind the Monster's se-rial killings.

Falbriard at this time was still blithely floating around Europe, completely unaware he was a "key witness" and possibly even a mastermind behind the Monster killings. GIDES enlisted the help of Interpol and they tracked him down in a village on the Côte d'Azur near Cannes. They were disappointed to learn the painter had arrived in Tuscany for the first time in 1996, eleven years after the Monster's final double homicide. Nevertheless, Falbriard was brought to Florence for questioning. He was a disappointing witness—an angry, unhinged, decrepit old man who harangued the police with wild accusations of his own.

"At Villa Verde," he testified, "I was drugged and locked up in a room. They robbed me of billions of lire. Strange things happened, especially at night." The mother and daughter were behind it all, he claimed.

Based on Falbriard's statement, the two women were charged with kidnapping and fraud. *La Nazione* wrote a series of lurid articles on the villa. "From the depositions of the former personnel of the rest home," ran one article, "there came many important clues. In fifty pages of testimony were hidden evidence of disturbing secrets. The old people held at Poggio ai Grilli were left abandoned among their own feces and urine without assistance. At night the aides were absolutely forbidden to set foot in the villa, which was transformed into a place where Black Masses were performed. Giuttari suspects that the genital organs and the parts of the breasts amputated from the victims of the Monster were used to conduct these satanic rituals."

Despite the renovation of the villa, Giuttari hoped that some trace of the Order of the Red Rose might remain, or that the sect might still be active in the villa. Old Tuscan villas have huge basements and underground areas for making and storing wine and aging prosciutto, cheese, and salami, and this is where Giuttari believed the actual room used as the temple of sacrifice might be found—and perhaps still in use.

One fine fall day, GIDES raided Poggio ai Grilli. After searching the enormous villa, the men of GIDES entered the room that their information indicated had been the sanctum sanctorum of the cult, the temple of Satan. In the room they found some cardboard human skeletons, plastic bats hung on strings, and other decorations. The search had come a few days before Halloween and a party had been planned—or so they claimed at the villa.

"Without doubt an attempt to sidetrack the investigation," Giuttari fumed to *La Nazione*.

Giuttari and GIDES made little progress into the satanic sect investigation, and by the year 2000 it seemed to be sputtering out.

Then, in August 2000, I arrived in Italy with my family.

PART II

✤

The Story of Douglas Preston

CHAPTER
30

On November 4, 1966, after forty days of rain, the Arno River burst its banks and laid waste to Florence, one of the most extraordinary cities in the world.

This was no gentle rise of water. The river flash-flooded; it boiled over the Lungarni embankments and tore through the streets of Florence at thirty miles an hour, carrying along tree trunks, smashed cars, and dead cattle. Ghiberti's great bronze doors to the Baptistery were bashed down and knocked to pieces; the Cimabue Crucifix, possibly the greatest example of medieval art in Italy, was reduced to a mound of sodden plaster; Michelangelo's David was fouled to his

buttocks with fuel oil. Tens of thousands of illuminated manuscripts and incunabula in the
Biblioteca Nazionale were buried under muck.
Hundreds of old master paintings stored in the
basement of the Uffizi Gallery flaked apart, leaving layers of paint chips in the mud.

The world watched with horror as the wa-
ters receded, leaving the birthplace of the Renaissance a wasteland of ooze and debris, its
art treasures devastated. Thousands of volunteers—students, professors, artists, and art his-
torians—converged from all over the world to
undertake an emergency salvage effort. They
lived and worked in a city without heat, water,
electricity, food, or services. After a week some
rescuers had to don gas masks to protect themselves from the toxic fumes being released by
rotting books and paintings.

They called the volunteers the Angeli del
Fango, the "Mud Angels."

I had long wanted to write a murder mystery
set at the time of the Florentine flood. The novel,
entitled *The Christmas Madonna*, involved an
art historian who rushes to Florence to volunteer as a Mud Angel. He is an authority on the
mysterious artist Masaccio, the young genius
who single-handedly launched the Italian Re-

naissance with his extraordinary frescoes in the
Brancacci Chapel, and who then died abruptly,
at twenty-six, amid rumors that he had been
poisoned. My character goes to work as a volunteer in the basement of the Biblioteca Nazionale, pulling books and manuscripts out of the
mire. One day he discovers an extraordinary
document, which contains a clue to the whereabouts of a famous lost painting by Masaccio.
Called *The Christmas Madonna*, the painting
was the central panel in a triptych described
vividly by Vasari in the 1600s, which had subsequently disappeared. It is considered to be
one of the most important lost paintings of the
Renaissance.

My art historian abandons his volunteer work
and sets off on a mad search for the painting.
He vanishes. A few days later they find his body
high in the Pratomagno Mountains, dumped by
the side of the road. His eyes have been gouged
out.

The murder is never solved and the painting
is never found. Now, thirty-five years later, we
fast-forward to the present day. His son, a successful artist in New York, hits a midlife crisis.
He realizes there is something he must do: solve
the murder of his father. The way to do it is to

find the lost painting. So he flies to Florence and begins his search—a journey that will take him from crumbling archives to Etruscan tombs and finally to a ruined village high into the Pratomagno Mountains, where a horrifying secret lies buried, and where an even more terrifying destiny awaits him . . .

This was the novel I came to Italy to write. I never did. Instead, I got sidetracked by the Monster of Florence.

Living in Italy was going to be the adventure of a lifetime, for which we were singularly unprepared. None of us spoke Italian. I had spent a few days in Florence the previous year, but my wife, Christine, had never been to Italy in her life. Our children, on the other hand, were at that age of delightful flexibility in which they seemed to meet even the most extraordinary life challenges with a cheerful nonchalance. Nothing in life was out of the ordinary to them, since they hadn't learned what was ordinary to begin with. When the time came, they boarded the plane with complete insouciance. We were a nervous wreck.

We arrived in Florence in August 2000: myself, Christine, and our two children, Aletheia and

Isaac, who were six and five. We enrolled our children in local Italian schools, Aletheia in first grade and Isaac in kindergarten, and we ourselves began taking language classes.

Our transition to Italy was not without its challenges. Aletheia's teacher reported that it was a joy to have such a happy child in class who sang all day long, and she wondered just what it was she was singing. We soon learned:

I don't understand anything she's saying,
She talks and talks all day long,
But I can't understand a word ...

Cultural differences quickly reared up. A few days after Isaac went off to kindergarten, he came back, wide-eyed, and told how the teacher smoked cigarettes during recess and tossed the butts on the playground—and then she spanked (spanked!) a four-year-old who tried to smoke one of them. Isaac called her "the Yelling Lizard." We quickly transferred him and his sister to a private school run by nuns on the other side of town. Nuns, we hoped, wouldn't smoke or spank. We were correct, at least on the former assumption, and came to accept the occasional spanking as a cultural difference we had to live with, along with smokers in restaurants, death-defying drivers, and waiting in line at the post office to pay bills. The school was located in a magnificent eighteenth-century villa hidden behind massive stone walls, which the sisters of the order of San Giovanni Battista had turned into a convent. The schoolchildren took recess in a two-acre formal Italian garden, with cypress trees, clipped hedges, flowerbeds, fountains, and marble statues of naked women. The gardener and the children were constantly at war. Nobody at the school, not even the English teacher, spoke English.

The *direttrice* of the school was a stern, beady-eyed nun who needed only to fix her withering glare on someone, student or parent, to reduce the person to abject terror. She took us aside one day to advise us that our son was *un monello*. We thanked her for the compliment and rushed home to look up the word. It meant "rascal." After that we brought a pocket dictionary to parent-teacher meetings.

As we hoped, our kids began to learn Italian. One day Isaac sat down to dinner, looked at the plate of pasta we'd prepared, made a face, and said, "*Che schifo*!" a vulgar expression meaning "Gross!" We were so proud. By Christmas they were speaking in full sentences, and by the end of the school year their Italian was so good they began making fun of our own. When we had Italian guests for dinner, Aletheia would sometimes march around the room, swinging her arms and bawling an imitation of our atrocious American accent, "How do you do, Mr. and Mrs. Coccolini! What a pleasure it is to meet you! Won't you please come in, accommodate yourselves, and enjoy a glass of wine with us!" Our Italian guests would be helpless with laughter.

And so we adjusted to our new life in Italy. Florence and its surrounding villages turned out to be a delightfully small place, where everyone seemed to know everyone else. Life was more about the process of living than reaching some end result. Instead of a once-a-week, efficient trip to the supermarket, shopping became a shockingly inefficient but charming routine of visiting a dozen or more shops and vendors, each of which sold a single product. This meant exchanging news, discussing the quality of the various choices, and listening to how the shopkeeper's grandmother prepared and served the item under discussion, which was the only way to do it despite what anyone might say to the contrary. Never were you allowed to touch the food being purchased; it was a breach of etiquette to test the ripeness of a plum or place an onion yourself in your shopping bag. For us, shopping was an excellent Italian lesson, but one fraught with danger. Christine made an indelible impression on the handsome *fruttivendolo* (fruit seller) when she asked for ripe *pesce* and *fighe* instead of *pesche* and *fichi* (fish and pussy instead of peaches and figs). It took many months before we felt even a little bit Florentine, although we quickly learned, like all good Florentines, to look with scorn on the tourists who wandered about the city, gaping and slack-jawed, in floppy hats, khaki shorts, and marshmallow athletic shoes, with giant water bottles strapped around their waists as if they were crossing the Sahara Desert.

Life in Italy was a strange mixture of the quotidian and the sublime. Driving the children to school in the morning in the dead of winter, bleary-eyed, I would come over the hill of Giogoli—and there, rising magically from the dawn mists, would be the cloisters and towers of the great medieval monastery of La Certosa. Sometimes, wandering about the cobbled streets of Florence, on a whim I would duck into the Brancacci Chapel and spend five minutes looking at the frescoes that launched the Renaissance, or I would take a turn through the Badia Fiorentina at Vespers to listen to Gregorian chants in the same church where young Dante gazed on his love, Beatrice.

We soon learned about the Italian concept of the *fregatura*, indispensable for anyone living in Italy. A fregatura is doing something in a way that is not exactly legal, not exactly honest, but just this side of egregious. It is a way of life in Italy. We had our first lesson in the fine art of the fregatura when we reserved tickets to see Verdi's *Il Trovatore* at the local opera house. When we got there, the box office informed us they could find no record of our tickets, despite our presentation of the reservation number. There was nothing they could do—the opera was completely and totally sold out. The large crowd seething in front of the box office attested to the truth of that.

As we were leaving, we ran into a shopkeeper from our neighborhood decked out in a mink coat and diamonds, looking more like a countess than the owner of Il Cantuccio, the tiny shop where we bought biscotti.

"What? Sold out?" she cried.

We told her what had happened.

"Bah," she said, "they gave your tickets to someone else, someone important. We'll fix them."

"Do you know somebody?"

"I know nobody. But I *do* know how things work in this town. Wait here, I'll be back in a moment." She marched off while we waited. Five minutes later, she reappeared with a flustered man in tow, the manager of the opera house himself. He rushed over and took my hand. "I am so, *so* sorry, Mr. Harris!" he cried out. "We didn't know you were in the house! No one told us! Please accept my apologies for the mix-up with the tickets!"

Mr. Harris?

"Mr. Harris," said the shopkeeper grandly, "prefers to travel quietly, without a large entourage."

"Naturally!" the manager cried. "Of course!"

I stared dumbfounded. The shopkeeper shot me a warning glance that said, *I got you this far, don't blow it.*

"We had a few tickets in reserve," the manager went on, "and I do hope that you will accept them as compensation, compliments of the Maggio Musicale Fiorentino!" He produced a pair of tickets.

Christine recovered her presence of mind before I did. "How very kind of you." She swiped the tickets from the man's hand, hooked her arm firmly into mine, and said, "Come on, *Tom*."

"Yes, of course," I mumbled, mortified at the deception. "Most kind. And the cost . . . ?"

"*Niente, niente*! The pleasure is ours, Mr. Harris! And may I just say that *The Silence of the Lambs* was one of the finest—one of *the finest*—movies I have ever seen. All of Florence is awaiting the release of *Hannibal*."

Front-center box seats, the finest in the house.

It was a short trip by bicycle or car from our Giogoli farmhouse into Florence through the Porta Romana, the southern entrance to the old city. The Porta Romana opened into a warren of crooked streets and medieval houses that make up the Oltrarno, the most unspoiled part of the old city. As I explored, I often saw a curious figure taking her afternoon *passeggiata* through the narrow medieval streets. She was a tiny ancient woman, sticklike, dressed to the hilt in furs and diamonds, her face rouged, lips coral red, an old-fashioned little hat with netted pearls perched on her diminutive head, walking with assurance in high-heeled shoes over the treacherous cobblestones, looking neither to the right nor left, and acknowledging acquaintances with an almost imperceptible movement of her eyes. I learned she was the Marchesa Frescobaldi, from an ancient Florentine family that owned half the Oltrarno and much of Tuscany besides, a family that had financed the Crusades and given the world a great composer.

Christine often jogged though the city's crooked medieval streets, and one day she stopped to admire one of the grandest palaces in Florence, the Palazzo Capponi, owned by the other great family of the Oltrarno district—and indeed one of the leading noble families of Italy. The palace's rust-red neoclassical façade stretches for hundreds of feet along the banks of the Arno, while its grim, stone-faced, medieval backside runs along the sunken Via de' Bardi, the Street of the Poets. As she was gawking at the grand *portone* of the palazzo, a British woman came out and struck up a conversation with her. The woman worked for the Capponi family, she said, and after hearing about the book I was trying to write about Masaccio, she gave Christine her card and said we should call upon Count Niccolò Capponi, who was an expert in

Florentine history. "He's quite approachable, you know," she said.

Christine brought back the card and gave it to me. I put it away, thinking there was no chance I would make a cold call on Florence's most famous and intimidating noble family, no matter how approachable.

The rambling farmhouse we occupied in Giogoli stood high on the side of a hill, shaded by cypresses and umbrella pines. I turned a back bedroom into a writing studio, where I intended to write my novel. A single window looked past three cypress trees and over the red-tiled roofs of a neighbor's house to the green hills of Tuscany beyond.

The heart of Monster country.

For weeks after hearing the story of the Monster of Florence from Spezi, I found myself wondering about the murder scene so close to our house. One fall day, after a frustrating struggle with the Masaccio novel, I left the house and climbed up through the grove to the grassy meadow to see the spot for myself. It was a lovely little meadow with a sweeping view of the Florentine hills running southward toward some low mountains. The crisp fall air smelled of crushed mint and burning grass. Some claim that evil lingers in such places as a kind of malevolent infection, but I could feel nothing. It was a place outside good and evil. I loitered about, hoping in vain to extract some glimmer of understanding, and almost against my will I found myself reconstructing the crime scene, positioning the VW bus, imagining the tinny sound of the *Blade Runner* score playing endlessly over the scene of horror.

I took a deep breath. Below, in our neighbor's vineyard, the *vendemmia* was in progress, and I could see people moving up and down the rows of vines, heaping clusters of grapes into the back of a three-wheeled motorized cart. I closed my eyes and listened to the sounds of the place—a cock crowing, distant church bells, a barking dog, an unseen woman's voice calling out for her children.

The story of the Monster of Florence was taking hold.

CHAPTER
31

Spezi and I became friends. About three months after we met, unable to shake myself loose from the Monster story, I suggested to him that we collaborate on an article about the Monster of Florence for an American magazine. As a sometime contributor to *The New Yorker*, I called up my editor there and pitched the idea. We got the assignment.

But before putting pen to paper, I needed a crash course from the "Monstrologer." A couple of days a week I shoved my laptop into a backpack, hauled my bike out, and pedaled the ten kilometers to Spezi's apartment. The last kilometer was a murderous ride uphill through groves of knotted olive trees. The apartment he shared with his Belgian wife, Myriam, and their daughter occupied the top floor of the old villa, with a living room, dining room, and a terrace overlooking Florence. Spezi worked in an upstairs garret, crammed with books, papers, drawings, and photographs.

When I arrived, I would find Spezi in the dining room, a Gauloise invariably hanging from his lip, layers of smoke drifting in the air, papers and photographs spread out on the table. While we worked, Myriam would bring us a steady stream of espresso in tiny cups. Spezi would always put away the crime scene photographs before she came in.

Mario Spezi's first job was to educate me about the case. He went through the history chronologically, in minute detail, from time to time plucking a document or a photograph from the heap by way of illustration. All our work was conducted in Italian, as Spezi's English was rudimentary and I was determined to use the opportunity to learn the language better. I took notes furiously on my laptop while he spoke.

"Nice, eh?" he often said when he had finished recounting some particularly egregious example of investigative incompetence.

"*Si, professore,*" I would answer.

His view of the case was not complicated. He had nothing but contempt for the conspiracy theories, alleged satanic rituals, hidden masterminds, and medieval cults. The simplest and most obvious explanation, he felt, was the correct one: that the Monster of Florence was a lone psychopath who murdered couples for his own sick, libidinous reasons.

"The key to identifying him," Spezi said repeatedly, "is the gun used in the 1968 clan killing. Trace the gun and you find the Monster."

In April, when the vineyards were beginning to stripe the hills in fresh green, Spezi took me to see the scene of the 1984 killing of Pia Rontini and Claudio Stefanacci, outside Vicchio. Vicchio lies north of Florence in a region known as the Mugello, where the hills grow steep and wild as they pile up toward the great chain of the Apennines. Sardinian shepherds settled in this area in the early sixties, after the migration to Tuscany, to raise sheep in the mountain meadows. Their pecorino cheese was highly prized, so much so that it became a signature cheese of Tuscany.

We drove along a country road, following a rushing stream. It had been years since Spezi had last been there, and we had to stop several times before we found the place. A turnoff from the road led to a grassy track at a place known locally as La Boschetta, the Little Wood. We parked and walked in. The track dead-ended at the base of a hill covered with oak trees, opening on one side to a field of medicinal herbs. An ancient stone farmhouse with terra-cotta roofs stood a few hundred yards off. A rushing stream, hidden by poplars, ran through the valley below. Beyond the farmhouse the land mounted up, hills upon hills, receding into blue mountains. Emerald-green pastures had been cut into the shoulders and lower slopes of the hills, pastures that the artist Giotto had wandered through as a boy in the late 1200s, tending sheep, daydreaming, and drawing pictures in the dirt.

The track ended at a shrine to the victims. Two white crosses stood in a grassy plot. Plastic flowers, faded by the sun, had been arranged in two glass jars. Coins had been placed on the arms of the crosses; the site had become a place of pilgrimage for young couples from the area, who left the coins as a way to pledge their love for each other. The sun poured in across the valley, bringing with it the scent of flowers and freshly mown fields. Butterflies fumbled about, birds twittered in the woods, and puffy white clouds scudded across a sky of blue.

Gauloise in his hand, Mario sketched out the scene of the crime for me while I took notes. He showed me where the light blue Panda of the two lovers had been parked and where the killer must have been hiding in the dense vegetation. He pointed out where the shells had lain, ejected after each shot, which told the pattern and order of shooting. The boy's body had been found trapped in the rear seat, almost in a fetal position, curled up as if to defend himself. The killer had shot him dead and then, later, stabbed the body several times in the ribs, either to make sure he was dead or as a sign of contempt.

"It happened at about nine-forty," Spezi said. He pointed to a field across the river. "We know that because a farmer, plowing that field at night to escape the heat, heard the shots. He thought it was the backfiring of a *motorino*."

I followed Mario into the open field. "He dragged the body and laid it down here—within full view of the house. An absurdly exposed place." He gestured toward the farmhouse with his cigarette hand, tufts of smoke drifting off. "It was a terrible scene. I'll never forget it. Pia lay on her back, arms thrown wide as if crucified.

Her bright blue eyes were open and staring into sky. It's awful to say this, but I couldn't help noticing how beautiful she was."

We stood in the field, drowsy bees visiting the flowers around us. I had finished taking notes. The whisper of the river came up through the trees. Again, no evil lingered. On the contrary, the place felt peaceful, even holy.

Afterwards we drove into Vicchio. It was a small town set amid lush fields alongside the river Sieve. A ten-foot-tall bronze statue of Giotto, holding his palette and brushes, stood in the center of the cobbled piazza. The shops nearby included a small household appliance store still owned by the Stefanacci family, where Claudio Stefanacci had worked.

We ate lunch in a modest trattoria off the piazza and then walked down a side street to pay a visit to Winnie Rontini, the mother of the murdered girl. We came to a high stone wall with iron gates surrounding a grand in-town villa, one of the most imposing in Vicchio. Through the gates I could see a formal Italian garden gone to seed. Beyond rose the three-story façade of the house, badly run-down, the pale yellow stucco cracked and peeling off. The villa's windows were shuttered. It looked abandoned.

We pressed the buzzer on the iron gate, and a voice quavered out of the tinny speaker. Mario gave his name and the gate clicked open. Winnie Rontini met us at the door and invited us into the darkened house. She moved slowly and heavily, as if under water.

We followed her into a dark sitting room, almost devoid of furniture. One window shutter was partway open, admitting a bar of light like a white wall dividing the darkness, through which drifted dust motes that blazed for a moment and vanished. The air smelled of old fabric and wax polish. The house was almost empty, only a few shabby pieces of furniture left, as all the antiques and silver had been sold long ago to finance the search for her daughter's killer. Signora Rontini was so impoverished she could no longer afford a telephone.

We seated ourselves on the faded furniture, raising a storm of motes, and Signora Rontini seated herself opposite us, settling into a lumpy chair with slow dignity. Her fair skin, fine hair, and sky blue eyes revealed her Danish heritage. Around her neck she wore a gold necklace with the initials of P and C on it, for Pia and Claudio.

She talked slowly, the words spoken as if weights were attached to them. Mario told her about our writing project and our continuing search for the truth. She stated her opinion, almost as if she no longer cared, that it was Pacciani. She told us that her husband, Renzo, a highly paid marine engineer who traveled all over the world, had quit his job to pursue justice for his daughter full-time. Every week he visited police headquarters in Florence, asking for fresh news and consulting with investigators, and on his own he had offered large monetary rewards for information. He had frequently appeared on television or radio, appealing for help. He had been scammed more than once. The effort eventually ruined his health and drained their finances. Renzo died of a heart attack on the street outside the police station after a visit. Signora Rontini remained in the big villa all alone, selling off the furniture piece by piece, and sinking ever deeper into debt.

Mario asked about the necklace.

"For me," she said, touching the necklace, "life ended on that day."

CHAPTER
32

If you believe you are beyond harm, will you go inside? Will you enter this palace so prominent in blood and glory, follow your face through the web-spanned dark ...? Inside the foyer the darkness is almost absolute. A long stone staircase, the stair rail cold beneath our sliding hand, the steps scooped by the hundreds of years of footfalls ...

So it was on a cold January morning that Christine and I found ourselves climbing the stairs so vividly described by Thomas Harris in *Hannibal*. We had an appointment in the Palazzo Capponi to meet Count Niccolò Piero Uberto Ferrante Galgano Gaspare Calcedonio Capponi, and his wife, the Contessa Ross. I had finally made that cold call. *Hannibal* the film, directed by Ridley Scott, had recently been shot in the Palazzo Capponi, where Hannibal Lecter, alias "Dr. Fell," was fictionally employed as the curator of the Capponi library and archives. I thought it would be interesting to interview the real curator of the Capponi archives, Count Niccolò himself, and write a "Talk of the Town" piece about it for *The New Yorker*, to coincide with the release of the film.

The count met us at the top of the stairs and guided us into the library, where the countess was waiting. He was a man of about forty, tall and solid, with curly brown hair, a Vandyke beard, keen blue eyes, and a pair of schoolboy ears. He looked strikingly like a grown-up version of the 1550 portrait of his ancestor Lodovico Capponi by the artist Bronzino, which hangs in the Frick Museum in New York. When the count greeted my wife, he kissed her hand in a most peculiar way, which I later learned was an ancient gesture in which the nobleman takes the lady's hand and with a rapid, elegant twist raises it to within six inches of his lips, while making a crisp half-bow—never, of course, allowing his lips to actually brush the skin. Only titled Florentines greet ladies in this manner. Everyone else shakes hands.

The Capponi library lay at the end of a dim, ice-cold hall decorated with coats of arms. The count settled us in a brace of giant oaken chairs, then perched himself on a metal stepstool behind an old refectory table and fiddled with his pipe. The wall at his back consisted of hundreds of pigeonholes containing family papers, manuscripts, account books, and rent rolls going back eight hundred years.

The count wore a brown jacket, a wine-colored sweater, slacks, and—rather eccentric for a Florentine—beaten-up ugly old shoes. He held a doctorate in military history and taught at the Florentine campus of New York University. He spoke perfect Edwardian English that seemed a relic from an earlier age. I asked him where he had acquired it. English, he explained, had entered his family when his grandfather married an Englishwoman and they raised their children speaking English at home. His father, Neri, in turn, had passed his English on to his children like a family heirloom—and in this way the language of the Edwardian age had been fossilized inside the Capponi family, unchanged for almost a century.

The Countess Ross was American, very pretty, guarded and formal, with a dry sense of humor.

"We had Ridley Scott in here with his cigar," said the count, referring to the director of the movie.

"The group would arrive," the countess said, "led by the cigar, followed by Ridley, followed by an attentive crowd."

"It created quite a bit of smoke."

"There was a lot of fake smoke, actually. Ridley seems to be obsessed with smoke. And busts. He was always needing marble busts."

The count glanced at his watch, then apologized. "I'm not being discourteous. I myself smoke only twice a day, after twelve and after seven."

It was three minutes to twelve.

The count continued: "He wanted more busts in the *Gran Salone* during the shooting. He ordered up papier-mâché busts that were made to look old. But they wouldn't do. So I said that I had a few of my ancestors down in the basement, shall we bring them up? He said marvelous. They were quite dirty, so I asked him, shall we dust them? Oh *no*, he said, please *don't*! One of them was my *quadrisnonna*, my great-great-great-grandmother, born Luisa Velluti Zati of the Dukes of San Clemente, who was a very proper woman. She refused to attend the theater. She thought it was immoral. Now she is appearing as a prop in a movie. And what a movie! Violence, disembowelments, cannibalism."

"You never know, she might be pleased," the countess said.

"The movie crew behaved very well. On the other hand, the Florentines were really bloody-minded while they were filming. Naturally, now that it's over, these same shopkeepers have put up signs in their windows: 'Hannibal was filmed here.'"

He checked his watch, found it had attained *mezzogiorno*, and lit his pipe. A cloud of fragrant smoke rose up toward the distant ceiling.

"Aside from smoke and busts, Ridley was fascinated with Henry the Eighth." The count rose and rummaged through the archives, finally extracting a letter on heavy parchment. It was a letter from Henry VIII to a Capponi ancestor, requesting two thousand soldiers and as many harquebusiers as possible for Henry's army. The letter was signed by Henry himself and from the document dangled something brown and waxy, the size of a squashed fig.

"What is that?" I asked.

"That is Henry the Eighth's broad seal. Ridley quipped that it looked rather more like Henry's left testicle. I made a photocopy for him. Of the document, I mean."

We moved from the library into the Gran Salone, the palace's main reception room, where Hannibal Lecter plays the clavier while Inspector Pazzi, hiding in the Via de' Bardi below, listens. The Salone contained a piano, not a clavier, which Anthony Hopkins played in the film. The room was decorated with dark portraits, fantastical landscapes, marble busts, armor, and weapons. Due to the expense of heating such a vast space, the air temperature hovered just above that of a Siberian torture chamber.

"Most of that armor is fake," said the count, with a dismissive wave. "But this suit over here, this is a good suit of armor. It dates from the 1580s. It probably belonged to Niccola Capponi, who was a knight in the Order of Saint Stephen. It once fit me well. It's quite light. I could do push-ups in it."

There was a lusty wail from a hidden room in the palace and the countess bustled off.

"These are mostly Medici portraits. We have five Medici marriages in our family. A Capponi was exiled from Florence with Dante. But in those days Dante was probably looking down his long nose at us. We were among, as Dante wrote, *la gente nova e i subiti guadagni*—'the new people and the suddenly rich.' Neri Capponi helped bring Cosimo de' Medici back to Florence in 1434 after his exile. It was an enormously profitable alliance for the family. We were successful in Florence because we were never the first family. We were always second or third. There is a Florentine saying: 'The nail that sticks out gets hammered back in.'"

The countess reappeared with a baby, Francesca, named after Francesca Capponi, a great beauty who married Vieri di Cambio de' Medici, and who died in childbirth at the age of eighteen. Her rosy-cheeked portrait, attributed to Pontormo, hung in the next room.

I asked the count who his most famous ancestor was.

"That would be Piero Capponi. All Italian schoolchildren know his story. It's like Washington crossing the Delaware, oft repeated and much embellished."

"He's downplaying the story, as usual," said the countess.

"I am not, my dear. The story *is* largely exaggerated."

"It's largely true."

"Be that as it may. In 1494, Charles the Eighth of France, on his way with his army to claim Naples, passed Florence and, seeing a way to make some fast money, demanded a huge payment from the city. 'We shall blow our trumpets' and attack, he declared, if the ransom were not paid. Piero Capponi's answer was, 'We shall then ring our bells,' meaning they would call up the citizens to fight. Charles backed down. He is reputed to have said, *Capon, Capon, vous êtes un mauvais chapon.* 'Capon, Capon, you are one evil chicken.'"

"Chicken jokes are quite prevalent in the family," the countess said.

The count said, "We eat capons at Christmas. It's a little cannibalistic. On that subject, let me show you where Hannibal Lecter took his meals."

We followed him into the *Sala Rossa*, an elegant drawing room with draped chairs, a scattering of tables, and a mirrored sideboard. The walls were covered in red silk that was woven from cocoons produced on the family's silk-worm estates two hundred and fifty years ago.

"There was a poor woman in the film crew," said the countess. "I had to keep saying to her, 'Don't move anything without permission.' She kept moving everything around. Every day while they were filming, Niccolò's little brother Sebastiano, who runs Villa Calcinaia, the family estate in Chianti, brought up a bottle of their wine, and he would place it in a strategic location in this room. But it never managed to get into the picture. This woman kept moving it out. The producers had an arrangement with Seagram's to use only their brands."

The count smiled. "Nevertheless, by the end of the day the bottle had always managed to get itself uncorked and was empty. It was always the best *riserva*."

Many years ago, when Thomas Harris was researching the Monster of Florence case for his novel *Hannibal*, and attending Pacciani's trial, he met Count Capponi and was invited to the palazzo. Much later Harris called the count and said he would like to make Hannibal Lecter curator of the Capponi archive—would that be all right?

"We had a family meeting," the count said. "I

told him that we agreed, on one condition—that the family would not be the main course."

Niccolò and I became friends. We met for lunch every so often at Il Bordino, a tiny trattoria behind the church of Santa Felicità, where his family's chapel and crypt were located, a short walk from his palazzo. Il Bordino was one of the last old-time trattorias in Florence; small, crowded, with a glass counter displaying the dishes available that day. Its dim interior was more like a dungeon, with blackened stone and plaster walls, scarred wooden tables, and ancient terra-cotta floors. The fare was quintessentially Florentine, simple dishes of meat and pasta accompanied by slabs of coarse bread, served at working-class prices, with tumblers of rough red wine.

One day over lunch, I mentioned to Niccolò that Mario Spezi and I were researching the case of the Monster of Florence.

"Ah," he said, keenly interested. "The Monster of Florence. Are you sure you want to get involved in that business?"

"It's a fascinating story."

"A fascinating story indeed. I should be careful if I were you."

"Why, what could happen? It's an old story. The last killing was twenty years ago."

Niccolò slowly shook his head. "To a Florentine, twenty years is the day before yesterday. And they are still investigating. Satanic sects, black masses, a villa of horrors ... Italians take these things very seriously. Careers have been made—and ruined—over this case. Take care that you and Mario do not poke too vigorously with your sticks into that nest of vipers."

"We'll be careful."

He smiled. "If I were you, I should get back to that delightful novel you described to me about Masaccio—and leave the Monster of Florence well enough alone."

CHAPTER
33

One fine spring day, Monster 101 neared its end.
I knew all the facts that were known, an expert on
the case second only to Spezi and the Monster himself. But there was one point on which Spezi had
been resolutely coy, and that was his opinion as to
who the Monster of Florence might be.

"*Eccoci qua*," said Spezi. "And so here we are:
satanic sects, blasphemous hosts, and hidden
masterminds. What next?" He leaned back in
the chair with a crooked smile and spread his
hands. "Coffee?"

"Please."

Spezi shot back his demitasse of espresso, an

Italian habit I could never quite acquire. I sipped mine.

"Any questions?" His eyes twinkled.

"Yes," I said. "Who do you think is the Monster?"

Spezi flicked the ash off his cigarette. "It's all there." He gestured at the heap of papers. "Who do you think?"

"Salvatore Vinci."

Spezi shook his head. "Let's look at it as Philip Marlowe might. It's all about the Beretta. Who brought the gun to the 1968 crime? Who used it? Who carried it home? And, most important, what happened to it later? It's all there in the story, if you care to look for it."

"The gun belonged to Salvatore Vinci," I said. "He brought it with him from Sardinia, he planned the 1968 killing, he had the car, and he was the shooter."

"Bravo."

"So he must have carried the gun home."

"Exactly. He handed the gun to Stefano Mele to take the last shot, so that Mele would contaminate his hands with powder residue. Afterwards, Mele threw the gun down. Vinci picked it up and took it home. He was no fool. He wasn't about to leave the murder weapon at the scene.

A gun used in a murder is dangerous, because ballistics can connect it to bullets recovered from the victims. A gun like this would never be sold or given away. It would either be destroyed or carefully hidden. Since we know the gun wasn't destroyed, Salvatore Vinci must have hidden it. Along with the boxes of bullets. Six years later it emerged to kill again—in the hands of the Monster of Florence."

I nodded. "So you think Salvatore Vinci is the Monster—just as Rotella did."

Spezi smiled. "Really?" He reached into the pile of papers, withdrew the FBI report. "You've read it. Does it sound like Salvatore Vinci?"

"Not really."

"Not at all! The profile is insistent on one crucial point: the Monster of Florence is impotent, or nearly so. He suffers from sexual dysfunction and would have little or no sexual contact with women his own age. He kills to satisfy his libidinous desires, which can't be satisfied in the normal way. Strong evidence of this is that none of the crime scenes showed any evidence of rape, molestation, or sexual activity. But Salvatore was the opposite of impotent—he was a veritable Priapus. Salvatore doesn't match the rest of the FBI report either, particularly in the psychological details."

"If Salvatore Vinci isn't the Monster," I asked, "then you still have the problem of how the Beretta passed from him to the Monster."

The question hung in the air. Spezi's eyes twinkled.

"Was it stolen from him?" I said.

"Exactly! And who was in the best position to take the gun?"

Although all the clues were there, I could not see them.

Spezi tapped his finger on the table. "I don't have the most important document in the case. I know it exists, because I spoke to someone who'd seen it. I tried *everything* to get it. Can you guess what document that might be?"

"The complaint of the theft?"

"*Appunto*! In the spring of 1974, four months before the Monster's first killing in Borgo San Lorenzo, Salvatore Vinci went to the carabinieri to file a complaint. 'The door of my house was forced and my house was entered.' When the carabinieri asked him what was stolen, he said, 'I don't know.'"

Spezi rose and opened the window. The stream of fresh air eddied the blue layers of smoke in the room. He shook another Gauloise out of a pack lying on the table, stuck it in his mouth and lit it, then turned from the window. "Think about it, Doug. This fine fellow, a Sardinian with a deep and ancient suspicion of authority, probably a murderer, goes to the carabinieri to report a breaking and entering when nothing was stolen. Why? And why would anyone rob his house in the first place? It's a sorry house, poor, there's nothing in there of value. Except ... perhaps ... a .22 Beretta and two boxes of bullets?"

He tapped the ash off the cigarette. I was on the edge of my seat.

"I haven't told you the most extraordinary thing of all. Vinci *named* the person responsible for the breaking and entering. The person he denounced was just a boy. A member of his Sardinian clan, a close relation. The last person he would have thrown to the carabinieri. Why file charges against him if he took nothing? *Because he was afraid of what the thief might do with the gun*. Salvatore Vinci wanted the breaking and entering to be on record, to protect himself. In case the boy did something with the gun that might be ... *terrible*."

Spezi pushed his finger a few inches closer to me, as if sliding the nonexistent document forward. "Right there, on that document, we would find the name that Salvatore Vinci gave the carabinieri. The name of the thief. That person, my dear Douglas, is the Monster of Florence."

"And who is it?"

Spezi smiled teasingly. "*Pazienza*! Back in 1988, after the rift between Rotella and Vigna, the carabinieri officially withdrew from the investigation. But they couldn't leave it well enough alone. They kept it going in secret. And the missing document is one of the things they dug out of God knows what dusty file in the basement of some dingy barracks."

"A secret investigation? Did they find out anything else?"

Mario smiled. "Many things. For example, after the first Monster killing, Salvatore Vinci checked himself into the psychiatric department at Santa Maria Nuova hospital. Why? We don't know— the medical records seem to have disappeared. Perhaps the boy who had stolen his gun had gone and done something terrible with it."

He reached out and shuffled through a pile, extracting the FBI report. "Your FBI, in this report, lists a number of characteristics the Monster is likely to have. Let's apply it to our suspect.

"The report says that the Monster is likely to have a record of petty crimes such as arson and theft, but not crimes such as rape and violence.

Our man has a rap sheet of auto theft, illegal possession of weapons, breaking and entering, and an arson.

"The report says that during the seven years between the crime of 1974 and the next one in 1981, the Monster was not in Florence. Our man left Florence in January of 1975. He returned to Florence at the end of 1980. In several months, the killings started again.

"The report says that the Monster probably lived alone during the period of the crimes. When not living alone, he would probably be found living with an older woman such as an aunt or grandmother. During much of the seven-year period he was away from Florence, our suspect lived with an aunt. Several months after the last killing, in 1985, our man met an older woman and moved in with her. The killings stopped. True, from 1982 to 1985 he was married, but according to a carabinieri officer who was part of the secret investigation into the Monster case, the marriage was annulled for *impotentia coeundi*—nonconsummation. To be fair, *impotentia coeundi* was sometimes invoked as a way to obtain a divorce in Italy at that time, even when it wasn't necessarily true.

"The FBI report says that this type of killer

will often contact the police and try to mislead the investigation, or at least collect news about the crime. Our man offered himself as an informant to the carabinieri.

"Finally, studies of sexual serial killers often turn up a history of maternal abandonment and sexual abuse within the family unit. Our man's mother was murdered when he was one year old. He suffered a second traumatic separation from a mother figure when his father's longtime girlfriend left. And he may have been exposed to his father's bizarre sexual activities. He was living with his father in a small house while his father presided over sex parties involving men, women, and perhaps even children. Did his father force him to participate? There's no evidence that he did . . . or didn't."

I was beginning to see where he was going.

Spezi took a long drag of smoke and exhaled. "The report says the killer probably began in his twenties. However, at the time of the first killing, our man was only fifteen years old."

"Wouldn't that rule him out?"

Spezi shook his head. "The fact is, many serial killers begin at a surprisingly young age." He reeled off the names of famous American serial killers and their ages of debut—sixteen, fifteen, fourteen, seventeen. "He almost botched the first crime in 1974. It was the work of a panicky and impulsive beginner. He managed to pull it off only because the man had been killed by the first shot, but only by accident. The bullet struck his arm and then, deflected by the bone, entered the chest and stopped his heart. The girl had enough time to get out of the car and run. The killer fired after her, but only hit her in the legs. He had to kill her with the knife. Then he lifted her cadaver and moved it behind the car. He tried to possess her, but couldn't do it. 'Sexual inadequacy.' *Impotentia coeundi*. He took a woody vine instead and pushed it into her vagina. He remained with the body and caressed it with the only instrument that gave him a thrill, his knife. He made ninety-seven cuts in her flesh. He may have wanted to sexually molest the corpse but he couldn't. He made the cuts around the breasts and around the pubic area, as if to underline that she was now his."

A long silence in the small dining room. The window at the far end of the table looked out on the very hills the Monster had stalked.

"It says the Monster owned his own car. Our man had a car. The murders were committed in places well known to the killer, near his house or place of work. When you map our man's life and movements, he had either lived near or was familiar with every single place."

Mario's finger touched the table again. "If only I could find that document of the breaking and entering."

"Is he still alive?" I asked.

Spezi nodded. "And I know where he lives."

"Have you ever spoken to him?"

"I tried. Once."

"Well?" I finally asked. "*Who is it*?"

"Are you sure you want to know?" Mario winked.

"Damn it, Mario!"

Spezi took a long drag on his Gauloise and let the smoke trickle out. "The person Salvatore Vinci denounced for breaking and entering in 1974, according to my informant, was his son, *his own son*. Antonio Vinci. The little baby who was rescued from the gas back in Sardinia in 1961."

Of course, I thought. I said, "Mario, you know what we have to do, don't you?"

"What?"

"Interview him."

CHAPTER
34

More than three decades after the murder of Barbara Locci and her lover in 1968, only two people involved in the Sardinian Trail investigation remained alive: Antonio Vinci and Natalino Mele. The rest had died or disappeared. Francesco Vinci's body had been found hogtied and locked in the trunk of a burned car, after he had apparently gotten on the wrong side of the Mafia. Salvatore had disappeared after his acquittal. Stefano Mele, Piero Mucciarini, and Giovanni Mele were long dead.

Before interviewing Antonio Vinci, we decided to speak with Natalino Mele, the six-year-old boy who was in the back of the car in 1968 and witnessed his mother's murder. Natalino agreed to speak to us and chose as a meeting place a duck pond in the Cascine Park in Florence, next to a shabby Ferris wheel and merry-go-round.

The day was overcast and dull, the air smelling of wet leaves and popcorn. Mele arrived, hands shoved in his pockets, a heavy, sad man in his early forties, with black hair and a haunted look in his eyes. He spoke in the excitable, querulous voice of a boy relating an injustice. After his mother was killed and his father imprisoned, his relatives had packed him off to an orphanage, a particularly cruel fate in a country where family means everything. He was alone in the world.

We sat on a bench with the disco beat of the merry-go-round thumping in the background. We asked if he could remember any details of the night of August 21, 1968, the night his mother was murdered. The question set him off.

"I was six years old!" he cried in a high-pitched voice. "What do you want me to say? After all this time, how could I remember anything new? This is what they all keep asking me: What do you remember? *What do you remember?*"

The night of the crime, Natalino said, he was so terrified he couldn't speak at all, until the carabinieri threatened to take him back to his dead mother. Fourteen years later, when the investigators established the connection between the 1968 killing and the Monster's killings, the police took him in for questioning again. They hammered him relentlessly. He had witnessed the 1968 double murder and they seemed to feel he was holding back vital information. The questioning lasted over the course of a year. He told them, over and over, that he couldn't remember anything of that night. The interrogators showed him graphic photographs of the Monster's mutilated victims, yelling at him, "Look at these people. This is your fault! It's your fault, because you can't remember!"

As Natalino spoke of the merciless questioning, his voice filled with anguish, rising in volume. "I *told* them I couldn't remember anything. *Anything.* Except one thing. There is one thing I remembered!" He paused, drawing in breath. "All I remember now is that I opened my eyes in that car and I saw in front of me my mamma, *dead.* That's the only thing I remember of that night. And," he said, his voice quavering, "that's the *only* memory I have of her."

CHAPTER
35

Years earlier, Spezi had called Antonio Vinci on the telephone and tried to arrange an interview. He had been categorically rebuffed. In light of that rejection, we discussed how we should best approach the man. We decided not to call ahead and give him another chance to say no. Instead, we would show up at his door and use false names, to avoid a second refusal and to protect ourselves from possible retaliation after the article was published. I would be an American journalist writing a piece on the Monster of Florence, and Spezi would be a friend giving me a hand as a translator.

We arrived at Antonio's apartment building at

9:40 p.m., late enough to be sure of finding him at home. Antonio lived in a tidy, working-class area west of Florence. His apartment building stood on a side street, a modest structure of stucco with a small flower garden and bicycle rack in front. At the end of the street, beyond a row of umbrella pines, rose the skeletons of abandoned factories.

Spezi buzzed the intercom and a woman answered. "Who is it?"

"Marco Tiezzi," said Spezi.

We were buzzed in with no further questions.

Antonio met us at the door dressed only in a pair of shorts. He stared at Mario. "Ah, Spezi, it's you!" he said, recognizing him instantly. "I didn't hear the name well. I've wanted to meet you for a long time!"

He seated us at the kitchen table with the air of an affable host and offered us a glass of a special Sardinian spirit called *mirto*. His companion, a silent and invisible older woman, finished washing spinach in the sink and left the room.

Antonio was a handsome man with a dimpled smile; his curly black hair was peppered with gray and his body was tanned and heavily muscled. He projected a cocky air of self-confidence and working-class charm. While we chatted about the case, he casually rippled the muscles of his upper arms or slid his hands over them in what seemed an unconscious gesture of self-admiration. He had a tattoo of a four-leaf clover on his left arm and twinned hearts on his right; there was a large scar in the middle of his chest. He spoke in a low, husky, and compelling voice reminiscent of the young De Niro in the movie *Taxi Driver.* His black eyes were animated and at ease, and he seemed amused at our unexpected arrival.

Spezi began the conversation, speaking casually and slipping a tape recorder out of his pocket. "May I use it?" he asked.

Antonio flexed his muscles and smiled. "No," he said, "I am jealous of my voice. It is too velvety, too rich in tone, to be put in that box."

Spezi put the recorder back in his pocket and explained: I was a journalist from the *New Yorker* magazine writing an article on the Monster case. The interview was part of a series, all routine, of those still alive with a connection with the case. Antonio seemed satisfied with the explanation and very much at ease.

Spezi began asking questions of a general nature, and established a friendly, conversational atmosphere, jotting notes in longhand. Antonio had followed the Monster of Florence case closely and had an astonishing command of the facts. After a series of general questions, Spezi began to close in.

"What kind of relationship did you have with your uncle, Francesco Vinci?"

"We were very close. It was a friendship with a bond of iron." He paused for a moment and then said something incredible. "Spezi, I'd like to give you a scoop. Do you know when Francesco was arrested for having hid his car? Well, I was with him that night! Nobody knew that, until now."

Antonio was referring to the night of the double murder in Montespertoli, near Poppiano Castle, in June of 1982. At the time Antonio was living six kilometers away. It was this crime that led to the arrest of Francesco Vinci for being the Monster of Florence, and an important piece of evidence against Vinci was that he had inexplicably hidden his car in the brush around the time of the killing. This was indeed a major scoop: if Antonio had been with Francesco that night, it meant Francesco had had an alibi that he never used—and as a result spent two years in jail needlessly.

"But that means your friend Francesco had a

witness in his favor!" Spezi said. "You could have helped Francesco avoid being accused of being the Monster and of spending years in jail! Why didn't you say anything?"

"Because I didn't want to get mixed up in his affairs."

"And for that you let him serve two years in prison?"

"He wanted to protect me. And I had faith in the system."

Faith in the system. A totally incredible statement coming from him. Spezi moved on.

"And what was your relationship like with your father, Salvatore?"

The faint smile on Antonio's face seemed to freeze a little, but only momentarily. "We never saw eye-to-eye. Incompatibility of character, you might say."

"But were there specific reasons why you didn't get along? Perhaps you held Salvatore Vinci responsible for the death of your mother?"

"Not really. I heard something said about it."

"Your father had strange sexual habits. Perhaps that was a reason you hated him?"

"Back then I knew nothing about that. Only later did I learn about his . . ." He paused. "*Tics.*"

"But you and he had some serious fights. Even

when you were young. In the spring of 1974, for example, your father filed a complaint against you for robbing his house ..." Spezi paused nonchalantly. This was a crucial question: it would confirm if the missing document actually existed—if Salvatore Vinci had indeed filed charges against Antonio just before the Monster killings began.

"That's not quite right,"Antonio said."Since he couldn't say if I'd taken anything, I was charged only for violation of domicile. Another time we had a fight and I pinned him, planting my scuba knife at his throat, but he managed to get away and I locked myself in the bathroom."

We had confirmed a crucial detail: the breaking and entering of 1974. But Antonio had, all of his own accord—almost like a challenge—added a critical fact of his own: that he had threatened Vinci with his "scuba knife." The medical examiner in the Monster case, Mauro Maurri, had written years before that the instrument used by the Monster may have been a scuba knife.

Spezi continued his questions, spiraling in toward our goal.

"Who do you think committed the double murders of 1968?"

"Stefano Mele."

"But the pistol was never found."

"Mele might have sold it or given it to someone else when he left prison."

"That's impossible. The pistol was used again in 1974, when Mele was still in prison."

"Are you sure? I never thought of that."

"They say your father was the shooter in 1968," Spezi went on.

"He was way too much of a coward to do that."

Spezi asked, "When did you leave Florence?"

"In '74. First I went to Sardinia and after to Lake Como."

"Then you returned and got married."

"Right. I married a childhood sweetheart, but it didn't work. We married in 1982 and separated in 1985."

"What didn't work?"

"She couldn't have children."

This was the marriage that had been annulled for nonconsummation: *impotentia coeundi.*

"And then you remarried?"

"I live with a woman."

Spezi assumed an easy tone of voice, as if he were concluding the interview. "Can I ask you a rather provocative question?"

"Sure. I may not answer."

"The question is this: if your father owned the .22 caliber Beretta, you were the person in the best position to take it. Perhaps during the violation of domicile in the spring of 1974."

Antonio didn't answer immediately. He seemed to reflect. "I have proof I didn't take it."

"Which is?"

"If I had taken it"—he smiled—"I would have fired it into my father's forehead."

"Following this line of reasoning," Spezi continued, "you were away from Florence from 1975 to 1980, precisely during the time when there were no killings. When you returned, they began again."

Antonio didn't respond directly to the statement. He leaned back in the chair, and his smile spread. "Those were the best years of my life. I had a house, I ate well, and all those girls . . ." He whistled and made an Italian gesture signifying fucking.

"And so . . ." Spezi said nonchalantly, "you're not . . . the Monster of Florence?"

There was only a brief hesitation. Antonio never stopped smiling for a moment. "No," he said. "I like my pussy alive."

We got up to leave. Antonio followed us to the door. While he opened it, he leaned toward

Spezi. He spoke in a low voice, his tone remaining cordial, and he switched into the informal, "*tu*" form. "Ah, Spezi, I was almost forgetting something." His voice took on a hoarse, threatening tone. "Listen carefully: I don't play games."

CHAPTER
36

Spezi and I submitted the article on the Monster of Florence to *The New Yorker* in the summer of 2001. My family and I went back to the States for the summer, to an old family farm on the Maine coast. I spent much of the summer working with our editor at *The New Yorker*, revising and fact-checking the piece. It was tentatively scheduled for publication the third week of September 2001.

Spezi and I both anticipated a huge reaction in Italy to the publication of the article. Italian public opinion had long ago settled on the guilt of Pacciani and his picnicking friends. Most Italians had also swallowed Giuttari's theory, that Pacciani & Co. had been working for a shadowy, powerful cult. While Americans might scoff at the very idea that a satanic sect was behind the killings, Italians did not find it unusual or unbelievable. From the very beginning, there had been rumors that a powerful and important person must be behind the killings, a doctor or nobleman. The satanic sect investigation seemed a logical extension of this idea, and most Italians believed it was justified.

We hoped to overthrow that complacency.

The New Yorker piece laid out a very strong case that Pacciani was not the Monster. If not, then his self-confessed "picnicking friends" were liars and Giuttari's satanic sect theory, built on their testimony, collapsed. Which would leave only one avenue of investigation left: the Sardinian Trail.

The carabinieri, Mario knew, had continued a secret investigation into the Sardinian Trail. A secret informant in the carabinieri, someone whose identity even I don't know, had told Mario they were awaiting the right moment to unveil the results of their investigation. *"Il tempo è un galantuomo,"* the informant had told Spezi, "Time is a gentleman." Spezi hoped that publication of *The New Yorker* article would spur the carabinieri into action, set the investigation back on the right track—and lead to the unmasking of the Monster.

"Italians," Mario said to me, "are sensitive to American public opinion. If an American magazine of the stature of *The New Yorker* proclaims Pacciani innocent, that will cause a furor, and I mean a *furor.*"

As the summer of 2001 drew to a close, our family made preparations to fly from Boston to Florence on September 14 so the children could make the start of school on the seventeenth.

On September 11, 2001, everything changed.

Around two o'clock on that long and terrible day, I turned off the television in the kitchen of our old farmhouse in Maine. I had to get out of the house. Taking my six-year-old son, Isaac, with me, I went out for a walk. The day glowed with autumnal glory, the last hurrah of life before winter, the air snappish and smelling of wood smoke, the sky a vibrant blue. We crossed the freshly mown fields behind the farmhouse, past the apple orchard, and headed down an abandoned logging road into the woods. A mile in we left the road and plunged into the trees, looking for a beaver pond hidden in the deepest part of the forest, where the moose live. I wanted to get away from any trace of human existence, to escape, to lose myself, to find a place untainted by the horror of the day. We forced our way through stands of spruce and fir and slogged across bogs and carpets of sphagnum moss. Half a mile in, sunlight loomed through the tree trunks and we came to the beaver pond. The surface of the pond was utterly still and black, mirroring the forest leaning over it, here and there splashed with red from the leaves of an autumnal maple crowding the pond's edge. The air smelled of green moss and damp pine needles. It was a primeval place, this nameless pond on an unknown brook, beyond good and evil.

While my son gathered beaver-gnawed sticks, I had a moment to collect my thoughts. I wondered if it was right to leave the country when it was under attack. I considered whether it was safe to fly with my children. And I wondered how this day would affect our lives in Italy if we did return. It occurred to me then, as an afterthought, that the *New Yorker* article

on the Monster of Florence was not likely to
be published.

Like most Americans, we decided to continue our lives as before. We flew back to Italy
on September 18, soon after flights resumed.
Our Italian friends held a dinner for us at an
apartment on Piazza Santo Spirito, overlooking the great Renaissance church built by
Brunelleschi. When we walked into the apartment, it was like arriving at a funeral; our Italian friends came forward and embraced us, one
by one, some with tears in their eyes, offering
their condolences. The evening was somber,
and at the end, a friend who taught Greek at
the University of Florence recited Constantine
Cavafy's poem "Waiting for the Barbarians."
She read it first in the original Greek and then
in Italian. The poem describes the Romans of
the late empire waiting for the barbarians to
come, and I have never forgotten the last lines
she read that evening:

> ... *night is here but the barbarians have*
> *not come.*
> *And some people arrived from the*
> *borders,*

and said that there are no longer any
   barbarians.

And now what shall become of us
   without any barbarians?
Those people were some kind of solution.[1]

As I expected, *The New Yorker* killed the Monster piece, generously paying us in full and releasing the rights back to us so we could publish it elsewhere. I made a few halfhearted attempts to place it with another magazine, but after 9/11 no one was interested in the story of a long-ago serial killer in another country.

In the days following 9/11, many commentators on television and in the newspapers pontificated on the nature of evil. Literary and cultural lions were called upon to express their grave and considered opinions. Politicians, religious leaders, and psychological experts all waxed eloquent on the subject. I was struck by their perfect failure to explain this most mysterious of phenomena, and I began to feel that the very incomprehensibility of evil might be, in fact, one of its fundamental characteristics. You cannot stare evil in the face; it has no face.

[1]Translation from the Greek by George Barbanis.

It has no body, no bones, no blood. Any attempt to describe it ends in glibness and self-delusion.

Maybe, I thought, this is why Christians invented the devil and Monster investigators invented a satanic sect. They both were, as the poem goes, "some kind of solution."

During that time I began to understand my own obsession with the Monster case. In twenty years of writing thrillers involving murder and violence, I had tried and largely failed to understand evil at its core. The Monster of Florence attracted me because it was a road into the wilderness. The case was the purest distillation of evil I had ever encountered, on many levels. It was, first of all, the evil of the depraved killings of a highly disturbed human being. But the case was about other kinds of evil as well. Some of the top investigators, prosecutors, and judges in the case, charged with the sacred responsibility of finding the truth, appeared to be more interested in using the case to leverage their power to greater personal glory. Having committed themselves to a defective theory, they refused to reconsider their beliefs when faced with overwhelming contradictory evidence. They cared more about saving face than saving lives, more about pushing their careers than putting the Monster behind bars. Around the Monster's incomprehensible evil had accreted layer upon layer of additional falsehood, vanity, ambition, arrogance, incompetence, and fecklessness. The Monster's acts were like a metastasized cancer cell, tumbling through the blood to lodge in some soft, dark corner, dividing, multiplying, building its own network of blood vessels and capillaries to feed itself, swelling, expanding, and finally killing.

I knew that Mario Spezi had already struggled with the evil expressed by the Monster case. One day I asked him how he had dealt with the horrors of the case—the evil—which I felt was starting to affect me.

"Nobody understood evil better than Brother Galileo," he told me, referring to the Franciscan monk turned psychoanalyst he had turned to for help when the horrors of the Monster case began to drag him under. Brother Galileo had since died, but Mario credited him with saving his life during the time of the Monster's killings. "He helped me understand what is beyond understanding."

"Do you remember what he said?"

"I can tell you exactly, Doug. I wrote it down."

He dug out his notes of the session where Brother Galileo spoke about evil and read them to me. The old monk began by making a powerful play on words of the fact that the Italian word for "evil" and "sickness" is the same, *male*, and that the word for "speech" and "study" is also the same, *discorso.*

"'Pathology' can be defined as *discorso sul male* [study of sickness (or evil)]," Brother Galileo said. "I prefer to define it as *male che parla* [evil (or sickness) that speaks]. Just so with psychology, which is defined as the 'study of the psyche.' But I prefer 'the study of the psyche struggling to speak through its neurotic disturbances.'

"There is no longer true communication among us, because our very language is sick, and the sickness of our discourse carries us inevitably to sickness in our bodies, to neurosis, if not finally to mental illness.

"When I can no longer communicate with speech, I will speak with sickness. My symptoms are given life. These symptoms express the need for my soul to make itself heard but cannot, because I don't have the words, and because those who should listen cannot get beyond the sound of their own voices. The language of sickness is the most difficult to interpret. It is an extreme form of blackmail which defies all our efforts to pay it off and send it away. It is a final attempt at communication.

"Mental illness lies at the very end of this struggle to be heard. It is the last refuge of a desperate soul who has finally understood that no one is listening or ever will listen. Madness is the renunciation of all efforts to be understood. It is one unending scream of pain and need into the absolute silence and indifference of society. It is a cry without an echo.

"This is the nature of the evil of the Monster of Florence. And this is the nature of the evil in each and every one of us. We all have a Monster within; the difference is in degree, not in kind."

Spezi was crushed by the failure of our article to see print. It was a great blow in his lifelong effort to unmask the Monster. With his disappointment and frustration, his obsession with the case, if anything, deepened. I moved on to other things. That year I began work on a new thriller, *Brimstone*, with my writing partner, Lincoln Child, with whom I had created a series of best-selling novels featuring an investigator named Pendergast. *Brimstone* was set partly in Tuscany and it involved a serial killer, satanic rituals, and a lost Stradivarius violin. The Monster of Florence was dead and I began dissecting the corpse for my fiction.

One day, as I was strolling through Florence, I passed a tiny shop that made hand-bound books. It gave me an idea. I went home and printed out our Monster article in octavo book format and carried it into the shop for binding. The shopkeeper created two handmade volumes, covered in full Florentine leather, with marbled endpapers. Each cover was stamped in gold leaf with the title, our names, and the Florentine lily.

THE MONSTER

SPEZI
&
PRESTON

It was a signed, numbered edition of two. During our next dinner at Spezi's house, sitting at the table on his terrazzo overlooking the hills of Florence, I presented him with copy number one. He was impressed. He turned it over in his hands, admiring the gold tooling and fine leather. After a while, he looked up at me, his brown eyes twinkling. "You know, Doug, with all this work we've already done . . . we *should* write a book about the Monster."

I was immediately smitten with the idea. We talked about it and decided that we would first publish the book in Italy, in Italian. Then we would rework it for an American readership and try to get it published in the United States.

For years my novels had been published in Italian by Sonzogno, a division of RCS Libri, part of a large publishing conglomerate that included Rizzoli and the *Corriere della Sera* newspaper. I called my editor at Sonzogno and she was intrigued, especially after we sent her the ex-*New Yorker* article we had written. She invited Mario and me to Milan to discuss the idea. One day, we took the train to Milan, pitched the idea, and walked away with a handsome contract.

RCS Libri was particularly interested in the idea because they had recently published another book about the Monster case, which had been a major best-seller. The author of the book? Chief Inspector Michele Giuttari.

CHAPTER
37

Meanwhile, Giuttari's investigation, which had stalled badly after the business of the "Villa of Horrors," had began to revive. In 2002, a new line of investigation erupted in the neighboring province of Umbria—in the ancient and beautiful hill town of Perugia, one hundred and fifty kilometers from Florence. The first sign of it was an odd telephone call that Spezi got early that year from Gabriella Carlizzi. Carlizzi, you may recall, was the crank who claimed the cult of the Red Rose had not only ordered the Monster killings but was also behind 9/11.

Carlizzi had quite a story to tell Spezi, the Monstrologer. One day, while providing assistance to the inmates of Rebibbia prison near Rome, she had received an alarming confidence from an inmate who had been a member of the infamous Italian Gang of Magliana. The man had said that a Perugian doctor who drowned in 1985 in Lake Trasimeno had not met his end through accident or suicide, as the inquest had concluded at the time, but had been murdered. He had been killed by the Order of the Red Rose, which the doctor himself belonged to. The other members of the order had eliminated him because he had become unreliable and was about to expose their nefarious activities to the police. To hide the evidence of crime, his body had been substituted for another before dumping it in the lake. Therefore, buried in the doctor's grave wasn't his body, but that of the other person.

Spezi, who had a great deal of experience dealing with conspiracy theorists, had thanked Carlizzi very much and explained that, most regrettably, he was not interested in pursuing the story. He got her off the phone as quickly and politely as possible.

Nevertheless, Spezi vaguely remembered the story of the drowned doctor. One month after the last Monster killing in 1985, a handsome young man from a wealthy Perugian family,

Francesco Narducci, had drowned in Lake Trasimeno. Rumors circulated at the time that he had killed himself because he was the Monster, rumors which were routinely investigated and dismissed.

In early 2002 the indefatigable Carlizzi, turned down by Spezi in her quest for publicity, brought her story to the public minister of Perugia, a man named Giuliano Mignini, whose jurisdiction covered the province of Perugia. (The public minister is the public prosecutor of a region, a position similar to a U.S. attorney or a district attorney. The public minister represents the interests of the state and argues the case in court, as the advocate for the state.) Judge Mignini *was* interested. The story seemed to mesh with another case he was pursuing involving a group of loan sharks who lent money to shopkeepers and professionals at stratospheric interest rates and who, if they didn't get repaid, exacted a brutal revenge. A small shopkeeper who was behind in her payments decided to expose them. She recorded one of their threatening telephone calls and sent the tape to the public minister's office.

One morning, while working in my farmhouse office in Giogoli, I got a call from Spezi. "The

Monster's in the news again," he said. "I'm coming up to your house. Put the coffee on."

He arrived clutching a stack of that morning's newspapers. I began to read.

"Be careful or we'll do to you the same as that dead doctor in Lake Trasimeno," the papers quoted the loan shark as saying in the tape recording of the threatening call. That was it: no names or facts. But Public Minister Giuliano Mignini read a great deal into those words. He concluded, apparently based on information given him by Carlizzi, that Francesco Narducci had been murdered by the loan sharks, some of whom might be in contact with the Red Rose or another diabolical sect. Therefore, the loan sharks and the Narducci killing might be connected in some way with the Monster of Florence murders.

Judge Mignini, the public minister, informed Chief Inspector Giuttari of the connection to the Monster case, and Giuttari and his GIDES squad embarked on a determined effort to prove that Narducci hadn't committed suicide. He had been murdered, to silence him and the terrible secrets he knew. Mignini had ordered the reopening of the Narducci case as a murder investigation.

"I can't follow this at all," I said, trying to read the paper. "It makes no sense."

Spezi nodded, smiling cynically. "In my day they never would have printed this *merda*. Italian journalism is going downhill."

"At least," I said, "it's more fodder for our book."

A while later, more news about the story broke in the papers. This time, still quoting unnamed sources, the papers printed a new version of the so-called tape recording. Now the loan shark was reported to have said, *"Be careful or we'll do to you the same as we did to Narducci and Pacciani!"* This version of the recording directly connected the dead doctor Narducci with the so-called murder of Pacciani—and thus with the Monster case.

Later, Spezi would learn from a source that what was said on the tape was much less specific: *We'll do to you like the dead doctor at the lake.* No mention was made of Narducci or Pacciani. A little digging uncovered the existence of another doctor, a man who had lost more than two billion lire gambling, whose body had been found on the shore of Lake Trasimeno with a bullet in the brain not long before the threatening telephone call. The phrase *"at* the lake" as opposed to the earlier "*in* the lake" seemed to point to this doctor, and not to Narducci, who, after all, had died fifteen years before the call was made.

But by the time this new information came out, the investigation into the dead Dr. Narducci had become a juggernaut, unstoppable. Giuttari and his elite squad, GIDES, looked for—and found!—many links between Narducci's death and the Monster of Florence killings. The new investigative theories offered up succulent gothic scenarios that were leaked to the press. Dr. Narducci, the press reported, had been the guardian of the fetishes cut from the women. He had been killed to keep from spilling the beans. Some of the richest families in Perugia were involved in sinister cults, perhaps under the cover of Freemasonry, a brotherhood to which both Narducci's father and father-in-law belonged.

Giuttari and his investigators from GIDES painstakingly pieced together the final day of Narducci's life, looking for clues.

Dr. Francesco Narducci came from a rich Perugian family, a young man blessed with brains and talent who at age thirty-six was the youngest medical professor in the field of gastroenterology in Italy. In photographs, he is strikingly handsome in a boyish way, tanned and smiling, fit and elegant. Narducci had married Francesca Spagnoli, the beautiful heiress to the fortune of Luisa Spagnoli, the maker of high-fashion clothing for women.

Despite, or perhaps because of, its power and wealth, the Narducci family was not well liked in Perugia. Behind that façade of wealth and privilege there was, as is not unusual, unhappiness. For some time, and in ever-increasing doses, Francesco Narducci had been taking meperidine (Demerol). According to a medical report, by the time of his death he was taking it every day.

The morning of October 8, 1985, was hot and sunny. The doctor made his rounds at the Policlinico di Monteluce in Perugia until about 12:30, when a nurse called him to the telephone. After that, the facts become confused. One witness said that after the call, Narducci cut short his rounds and seemed nervous and preoccupied. Another claimed he finished his rounds in regular order and left the hospital uneventfully, asking a colleague if he wanted to take a spin on Lake Trasimeno in his boat.

At one-thirty he arrived home and ate lunch with his wife. At two o'clock, the owner of the marina where Narducci had a villa received a phone call from the doctor, asking him if his motorboat was ready to go out on the lake. The man answered it was. But as Narducci left his house, he lied to his wife, saying he was going back to the hospital and would be home early.

Narducci took his Honda 400 motocross bike and set off for the lake, but not directly to the marina. First he went into his family's house in San Feliciano. There were rumors, which investigators could not substantiate, that he wrote a letter there and left it on a windowsill, sealed in an envelope. The letter, if it ever existed, never came to light.

At three-thirty the doctor finally arrived at the marina. He jumped in his motorboat, a sleek red Grifo, and fired up the seventy-horsepower engine. The owner of the marina advised him not to go too far, since the gas tank was half empty. Francesco told him not to worry and pointed the boat toward Polvese Island, a kilometer and a half offshore.

He never returned.

At around five-thirty, when it began to grow dark, the marina owner became alarmed and called Francesco's brother. At seven-thirty the carabinieri launched a boat to help with the search.

But Lake Trasimeno is one of the largest in Italy, and it wasn't until the next evening that they found the red Grifo empty and adrift. On board were a pair of sunglasses, a wallet, and a packet of Merit cigarettes, Narducci's brand.

Five days later, they found the body. A single black-and-white photograph was taken of the scene when the body was brought to shore, showing the corpse stretched lengthwise on a dock, surrounded by a group of people.

Carlizzi had told the public minister that the body of Narducci had been substituted for another, which had been tossed in the lake as a decoy. To investigate that statement, Giuttari commissioned an expert analysis of the photograph. Taking as a standard unit of measurement the width of a plank on the dock, the experts concluded that the cadaver in the photograph belonged to a man four inches shorter than Narducci. They also calculated that the dead man's waist was far too large to be that of the trim Narducci.

Other experts disagreed. Some pointed out that a body floating in water for five days does tend to swell. Planks of a dock are not all equal in width, and the dock in question had been replaced. Who knew the width of the planks seventeen years ago? All those in the crowd who were actually standing around the body, including the medical examiner himself, swore the body was Narducci's. At the time, the medical examiner listed the cause of death as drowning, which he estimated had occurred about a hundred and ten hours previously.

Contrary to Italian law, no autopsy had been performed. Narducci's family, led by his father, had managed to bypass the legal requirement. At the time, people in Perugia quietly understood that it was because the family feared that an autopsy would have shown that Narducci was up to his gills in Demerol. But to Giuttari and GIDES, the lack of an autopsy was most significant. They said the family had finagled their way out of an autopsy because it would have shown the body was not that of Narducci at all. The family was somehow complicit, not only in his murder, but in the substitution of his body with another to cover up the crime.

Francesco Narducci—or so Giuttari theorized—had been murdered because he was a member of the satanic sect behind the Monster of Florence killings, to which his father had introduced him. He had been named custodian of the grisly fetishes taken by Pacciani and his picnicking friends. Shaken by the reality into which he had fallen, the young doctor became indecisive, unreliable, prey to depression, and difficult to trust. The leaders of the sect decided he had to be eliminated.

The satanic cult investigation, led by Chief Inspector Giuttari, once moribund, was revived. Giuttari had now identified at least one member of the invidious sect behind the Monster killings—Narducci. All that remained was to find his killer and bring the other members of the sect to justice.

CHAPTER
38

As the Monster investigation heated up, the phone calls from Mario became a regular occurrence. "Did you read the papers this morning?" he would ask me. "Stranger and stranger!" And we would enjoy another coffee up at my place, poring over the news, shaking our heads. At the time, I found it all amusing, even charming.

Spezi was not so charmed. He wanted, more than anything, for the truth in the Monster case to come out. His dedication to unmasking the Monster was a passion. He had seen the dead victims; I had not. He had met most of the families and seen the damage to them. I had wiped away a few tears on leaving Winnie Rontini's dark house, but Spezi had been wiping away tears for more than twenty years. He had seen the lives of innocents ruined by false accusations. What I found deliciously peculiar and even quaint, he found deadly serious. To see the investigators wandering ever deeper into a wilderness of absurdity pained him greatly.

On April 6, 2002, with the press standing by, the coffin of Francesco Narducci was exhumed and opened. His body was inside, instantly recognizable even after seventeen years. A DNA test confirmed it.

This blow to their theories did not stop GIDES, Giuttari, and the public minister of Perugia. Even in the lack of a substituted corpse they found evidence. The body was *too* recognizable for someone who had spent five days in the water and then another seventeen in a coffin. Giuttari and Mignini promptly concluded that the body had been substituted *again*. That's right—Narducci's real body, hidden for seventeen years, had been put back in the coffin and the other body removed, because the conspirators knew ahead of time that the exhumation was coming.

The body of Narducci was shipped off to the medical examiner's office in Pavia to see if it showed signs of murder. That September, the results came in. The medical examiner reported that the left horn of the laryngeal cartilage had been fractured, which made it "more or less probable" that death resulted from a "violent mechanical asphyxiation produced from the constriction of the neck (either from manual strangulation or from strangulation by other homicidal means)."

In other words, Narducci had been murdered.

Once again the newspapers had a field day. *La Nazione* trumpeted:

MURDER IS THEORIZED
BURNING SECRETS

Was Narducci murdered because he knew something or had seen something that he must not see? Almost all the current investigators are by now convinced of the story of secret sects and masterminds behind the double homicides executed by Pacciani and his picnicking friends....A group of persons, around ten, ordered the killings by henchmen composed of Pacciani and his picnicking friends....The search into secret, deviant, and esoteric groups dedi-

cated to horrendous "sacrifices" has even drawn in investigators from Perugia.

Once again, Spezi and I marveled at the banquet of half-baked and ill-formed speculations that constituted press coverage of the case, printed as the wide-eyed truth by journalists who knew absolutely nothing of the history of the Monster of Florence, who had never heard of the Sardinian Trail, and who merely parroted whatever investigators or the prosecutor's office leaked. The conditional tense was hardly ever used, as were qualifiers such as "alleged" and "according to." Question marks were thrown in only for sensationalistic effect. Spezi once again bemoaned the sorry state of Italian journalism.

"Why," he said, "would Narducci's killers concoct such an elaborate scheme of murder? Haven't these journalists asked themselves that obvious question? Why not just drown him and make it look like suicide? Why substitute bodies once, and then yet again? And where on earth did the second body come from? The original ME who examined Narducci's cadaver, along with his family, friends, and all the people in that photograph who saw the dead body insist it was Narducci. They *still* insist it was Narducci!

Were *all* these people in on the conspiracy?" He shook his head sadly.

I read the rest of the article with growing disbelief. The credulous reporter at *La Nazione* never explored any of the obvious discrepancies with the story. He went on to write that the "saponification of the cadaver (internal organs, skin, and hair were in a good state of preservation) was not compatible with immersion in water for five days." More support for the substitution theory.

"What does this mean, 'not compatible'?" I asked Spezi, putting aside the paper. It was a phrase I had seen again and again in the Monster investigation.

Spezi laughed. "Compatible, not compatible, and incompatible are the baroque inventions of Italian experts who don't want to take responsibility. Using 'compatible' is a way to avoid admitting they haven't understood anything. Was the bullet in Pacciani's garden inserted into the Monster's pistol? 'It is compatible.' Was that laryngeal break inflicted by someone who intended to kill? 'It is compatible.' Was the painting done by a monstrous psychopath? 'It is compatible.' Perhaps yes, perhaps no—in short, we don't know! If the experts are chosen by the investigators, they say their results are 'compatible' with the theories of the prosecution; if they are chosen by the defendants they say that their results are 'compatible' with the theories of the defense. That adjective should be outlawed!"

"So where's this going?" I asked. "Where will it end up?"

Spezi shook his head. "The very thought scares me."

CHAPTER
39

Meanwhile, in the picturesque little town of San Casciano, Giuttari opened up yet a new front in the search for the masterminds behind the Monster killings. San Casciano seemed to lie at the very heart of the satanic sect; it was only a few kilometers from Villa Verde, the Villa of Horrors; it had been home to the hapless postman, Vanni, and the village idiot, Lotti, convicted as Pacciani's accomplices.

Spezi called me one morning. "Have you seen the paper? Don't bother buying it, I'm coming over. You won't believe this."

He entered the house, visibly upset, the paper clutched in his hand, Gauloise dangling from his lip. "This is a bit too close to home." He slapped the paper on the table. "Read this."

The article announced that the home of a man named Francesco Calamandrei, the ex-pharmacist of San Casciano, had been searched by GIDES. Calamandrei was suspected of being one of the masterminds behind the Monster killings.

"Calamandrei is an old friend of mine." Spezi said. "He's the man who introduced me to my wife! This is utterly absurd, patently ridiculous. The man wouldn't hurt a fly."

Spezi told me the man's story. He had met Calamandrei back in the mid-sixties, when both were students, Spezi studying law and Calaman-drei studying pharmacology and architecture. A brilliant student, Calamandrei was the son of San Casciano's only pharmacist, which in Italy is a well-paid and high-status profession, all the more so for the Calamandrei family, because San Casciano was a wealthy town with only one phar-macy. Calamandrei cut quite a figure in those days, tooling around Florence in a sleek Lancia Fulvia Coupé, tall, elegant, and handsome, im-peccably dressed in the Florentine style. He had a dry, cutting Tuscan sense of humor and always seemed to have a new girlfriend more beautiful than the last. Calamandrei introduced Mario to his future wife, Myriam ("I've got a nice Belgian girl for you, Mario"), at a famous restaurant; afterwards they all piled into Calamandrei's car and set off on a crazy trip to Venice to play baccarat in the casino. Calamandrei was an expression of that brief period in Italian history known as *La Dolce Vita*, captured so memorably on film by Fellini.

At the close of the sixties Calamandrei married the daughter of a wealthy industrialist. She was a small, high-strung woman with red hair. They had a grand wedding in San Casciano, which Mario and Myriam attended. A few days later the newlyweds stopped by Spezi's house while heading off on their honeymoon. Calamandrei was driving a brand-new cream-colored Mercedes 300L convertible.

That was the last Spezi saw of him for several decades.

He ran into him by chance twenty-five years later and was shocked by the change in his friend. Calamandrei had become morbidly obese and suffered from a deep depression and declining health. He had sold the pharmacy and taken up painting—tragic, anguished pictures, not created with paintbrushes and canvas, but with objects such as rubber hoses, sheet metal, and tar, sometimes putting real syringes and tourniquets in his paintings, and often signing them with his social security number, because, he said, that's all people were in modern Italian society. His son had become a drug addict and then a thief to support his habit. Desperate and not knowing what else to do, Calamandrei had gone to the police and denounced his own son, hoping a stint in prison might shake him up and lead to a turnaround. But the boy continued to take drugs after his release, and then disappeared completely.

What had happened to his wife was equally tragic. She had succumbed to schizophrenia. Once, at a dinner party at a friend's house, she began screaming and breaking objects, stripped off all her clothes, and ran naked into the street. She was hospitalized after that, the first of many such hospitalizations. She was finally declared mentally incompetent and committed to a sanatorium, where she remains to this day.

In 1991, Calamandrei divorced her. She then wrote a letter to the police accusing her husband of being the Monster of Florence. She claimed to have found pieces of the victims hidden in the refrigerator. Her letter—which was completely mad—was duly checked out by investigators at the time and dismissed as absurd.

But Chief Inspector Giuttari, sorting through old police files, came across the wife's handwritten statement, in a strange orthography that sloped ever upward toward the top of the page. To Giuttari, "pharmacist" was close enough to "doctor." The fact that Calamandrei had once been a wealthy and prominent resident of San Casciano, the presumed center of the satanic cult, only whetted Giuttari's interest. The chief inspector opened an investigation of him and several other leading citizens of the town. On January 16, 2004, Giuttari asked for a warrant to search the pharmacist's house; he received it on the seventeenth; on the eighteenth at dawn Giuttari and his men rang the buzzer of the door on Piazza Pierozzi in San Casciano.

On the nineteenth the story of the Monster of Florence was once again all over the news.

Spezi could only shake his head in wonder. "I don't like the way this is moving at all. *Mi fa paura.* It makes me afraid."

Back in Perugia, the inquiry into Narducci's death moved along at a brisk pace. The investigators realized that in order for the bodies to

have been switched twice, a large and powerful conspiracy among influential people must
have taken place. The public minister of Perugia, Judge Mignini, was determined to unmask it.
And in short order he did. Once again, the newspapers, including even the sober *Corriere della
Sera*, dedicated entire pages to it. The news was
sensational: the ex-chief of police of Perugia at
the time of Narducci's death had, it was alleged,
conspired with a colonel in the carabinieri and
with the family's lawyer to prevent the truth of
Narducci's death from coming out, all working
in concert with the father of the dead doctor,
his brother, and the doctor who had signed the
death certificate. Among their crimes were conspiracy, racketeering, and destruction and hiding of a human corpse.

Beyond the conspiracy to cover up the Narducci murder, the investigators also had to
show that Narducci had a connection to Pacciani, his picnicking friends, and the village of
San Casciano, where the satanic cult seemed to
be centered.

They succeeded in this as well. Gabriella Carlizzi made a statement to the police asserting
that Francesco Narducci had been initiated into
the Order of the Red Rose by his father, who

was trying to resolve certain sexual problems in his son—the same diabolical sect, Carlizzi claimed, active for centuries in Florence and its environs. Police and prosecutors seemed to accept Carlizzi's statements as solid, actionable evidence.

As if on cue, Giuttari and his GIDES squad produced witnesses swearing to have seen Francesco Narducci hanging around San Casciano and meeting with Calamandrei. It took a while for the identity of these new witnesses to come out. When Spezi first heard the names, he thought it was a bad joke: they were the same algebraic witnesses, Alpha and Gamma, who had been the surprise witnesses at Pacciani's appeal trial many years before—Pucci, the mentally retarded man who claimed to have witnessed Pacciani killing the French couple, and Ghiribelli, the alcoholic prostitute who would turn a trick for a glass of wine. And then a third witness popped out of the woodwork—none other than Lorenzo Nesi! This was the same fine fellow who had so conveniently remembered Pacciani and a companion in a "reddish" car a kilometer from the Scopeti clearing on Sunday night, the alleged night of the murder of the French tourists.

These three witnesses had earth-shaking new information to impart, which all of them had forgotten to mention eight years earlier when they had first stunned Italy with their extraordinary testimony.

Ghiribelli claimed that the "doctor from Perugia," whose name she did not know, but whose face she recognized as Narducci's from a photograph, came to San Casciano almost every weekend. How could she forget it? She proudly told investigators she had had sex with him four or five times in a hotel and "for each trick he gave me three hundred thousand lire."

In the offices of GIDES, they showed the mentally retarded Pucci photographs of various people and asked him if he had ever seen them before and where. Pucci's recall was phenomenal, crystal clear even when reaching back twenty years, even if he didn't know their names. He recognized Franceso Narducci, "tall and thin, kind of faggoty." He recognized Gianni Spagnoli, brother-in-law of the drowned doctor. He recognized one of the most notable physicians of Florence arrested for child molestation, who had been included in the photo lineup because investigators believed the satanic sect was into pedophilia. He recognized a respected dermatologist and a distinguished gynecologist of San Casciano, both of whom had also fallen under suspicion for being members of the cult. He recognized Carlo Santangelo, the phony ME who liked to wander around cemeteries at night. He recognized a young African-American hairstylist who had died several years before in Florence from AIDS.

But most crucially to the investigation, he recognized the pharmacist of San Casciano, Francesco Calamandrei.

Pucci wasn't stingy with the particulars. "I saw all these people together in San Casciano, in the Bar Centrale under the clock. I can't say if on every occasion I saw them together because it happened that I would see them separately, but anyway these were people who saw each other a lot."

Lorenzo Nesi, the serial witness, also recognized these people and added another. He had seen, palling around with this motley crowd, none other than Prince Roberto Corsini, the nobleman killed by a poacher, who, like Narducci, had been the subject of rumors that he was the Monster.

Gamma, the prostitute Ghiribelli, told another story, one that involved the Villa Sfacciata, near where I lived in Giogoli, across the lane from where the two German tourists had been killed. "In 1981," she said, as recorded in an official statement taken by the police, "there was a doctor who was doing experiments in mummification in the villa ... Lotti also talked about this place on many occasions and always in the eighties, when we went there. He told me that inside, without saying where, there were murals covering entire walls with paintings just like those done by Pacciani. Lotti always told me that this villa had a laboratory underground, where the Swiss doctor did his mummification experiments. I'll explain it better: Lotti said that this Swiss doctor, following his travels in Egypt, got hold of an old papyrus that explained how to mummify bodies. He said the papyrus was missing a piece relating to the mummification of the soft parts and, I mean, among them the sex organs and the breasts. He told me this was why the girls were mutilated in the murders of the Monster of Florence. He explained to me that in 1981 the daughter of this doctor was killed and the death was not reported, so much so that the father had said that he had to go back to Switzerland to explain her absence. The mummification process required that he keep the body of his daughter in that underground laboratory."

Perhaps remembering the embarrassment of the plastic bats and cardboard skeletons, investigators decided not to search the Villa Sfacciata for the Pacciani frescoes, underground laboratory, and mummified daughter.

CHAPTER
40

Dietrologia," said Count Niccolò. "That is the only Italian word you need to know to understand the Monster of Florence investigation."

We were having our usual lunch at Il Bordino. I was eating *baccalà*, salt cod, while the Count enjoyed stuffed *arista*.

"Dietrologia?" I asked.

"*Dietro*—behind. *Logia*—the study of." The count spoke grandly, as if still in the lecture hall, his plummy English accent echoing in the cave-like interior of the restaurant. "Dietrologia is the idea that the obvious thing cannot be the truth. There is always something hidden behind, *dietro*. It isn't quite what you Americans call conspiracy theory. Conspiracy theory implies *theory*, something uncertain, a possibility. The dietrologist deals only in fact. This is how it *really* is. Aside from football, dietrologia is the national sport in Italy. Everyone is an expert at what's really going on, even ... how do you Americans say it? ... even if they don't know jack shit."

"Why?" I asked.

"Because it gives them a feeling of importance! This importance may only be confined to a small circle of idiotic friends, but at least they are *in the know*. *Potere*, power, is that *I* know what *you* do not know. Dietrologia is tied to the Italian mentality of power. You *must* appear to be in the know about all things."

"How does this apply to the Monster investigation?"

"My dear Douglas, it is the very heart of the matter! At all costs, they have to find something behind the apparent reality. There cannot *not* be something. Why? Because it is not possible that the thing you see is the truth. Nothing is simple, nothing is at it seems. Does it look like a suicide? Yes? Well then it must be murder. Somebody went out for coffee? Aha! *He went out for coffee* ... But what was he *really* doing?"

He laughed.

"In Italy," he continued, "there is a permanent climate of witch-hunting. You see, Italians are fundamentally envious. If somebody makes money, there must be a fiddle there somewhere. *Of course* he was in cahoots with someone else. Because of the cult of materialism here, Italians envy the rich and powerful. They're suspicious of them and at the same time want to be them. They have a love-hate relationship with them. Berlusconi is a classic example."

"And that's why the investigators are looking for a satanic sect of the rich and powerful?"

"Precisely. And at all costs they have to find something. Once they've started, to save face they have to go on. For the sake of this idea, they will do anything. They cannot give it up. You *anglosassoni* do not understand the Mediterranean concept of *face*. I was doing historical research in an ancient family archive and I came across some interesting little thing that a distant ancestor had done three hundred years ago. Nothing very bad, just a naughty thing that was already largely known. The head of the family was aghast. He said, 'You can't publish this! *Che figura ci facciamo*! What shame it would cast upon our family!'"

We finished and rose to pay at the counter.

The count as usual insisted on picking up the tab ("They know me," he explained, "and give me *lo sconto*, the discount").

As we stood on the cobbled street outside the restaurant, Niccolò gazed at me gravely. "In Italy, the hatred of your enemy is such that he has to be built up, made into the ultimate adversary, responsible for all evil. The investigators in the Monster case know that behind the simple facts hides a satanic cult, its tentacles reaching into the highest levels of society. This is what they will prove, no matter what. Woe to the person"—he eyed me significantly—"who disputes their theory because that makes him an accomplice. The more vehemently he denies being involved, the stronger is the proof."

He laid a large hand on my shoulder. "Then again, perhaps there is some truth to their theories. Perhaps there *is* a satanic sect. After all, this is Italy ..."

CHAPTER
41

During 2004, our last year in Italy, the Monster investigation picked up a major head of steam. It seemed that almost every month another wildly improbable story would break in the papers. Mario and I continued to work on our book, outlining and gathering information and accumulating a file of newspaper clippings on the latest developments. Mario also continued his own freelance investigative journalism, regularly plying his contacts in the carabinieri for fresh information, poking around, always looking for a new scoop.

Mario called me one day. "Doug, meet me in Bar Ricchi. I've got some splendid news!"

We met once again in our old haunt. My family and I had now been living in Italy for four years, and I was well enough known in Bar Ricchi not only to greet the owner and his family by name, but sometimes to get *lo sconto* myself.

Spezi was late. He had, as usual, parked his car illegally in the piazza, putting in the window his "JOURNALIST" sign, next to the special journalist permit that allowed him to drive into the old city.

He strode in, trailing smoke, and ordered an espresso *"stretto stretto"* and a glass of mineral water. A heavy object weighed down his trench coat.

He tossed his Bogart fedora on the banquette, slid in, and removed an object wrapped in newspaper, which he placed on the table.

"What is it?"

"You shall see." He paused to shoot down his coffee. "Ever seen the television program *Chi L'ha Visto?* [Who Has Seen Him?]."

"No."

"It's one of the highest-rated programs on Italian television—a rip-off of your show *America's Most Wanted*. They've asked me to collaborate on a series of programs that would reconstruct the entire history of the Monster of Florence case, from the beginning to today."

Spezi wreathed himself in a triumphant cloud of blue smoke.

"*Fantastico!*" I said.

"And," he added, his eyes twinkling, "I've got a scoop for the show that nobody knows about, not even you!"

I sipped my coffee and waited.

"You remember when I spoke to you of the detective who told me the French tourists must have been killed on Saturday night, because they had larvae on them as big as cigarette butts? Well, I managed to get my hands on the photographs taken by the forensic team that Monday afternoon. Printed in the corner was the actual time the photographs were taken, around five o'clock, three hours after the bodies were discovered. Blowing them up you can see the larvae very well, and they are truly big. I did some research and discovered the top Italian expert on forensic entomology, internationally known, who with an American colleague ten years ago developed a technique for establishing the time of death based on the development of larvae. His name is Francesco Introna, director of the Istituto di Medicina Legale in Padova, director of the Laboratorio di Entomologia Forense at the Istituto di Medicina Legale of Bari, where he teaches; he's got three hundred scientific publications in medical journals and he's an expert consultant for the FBI! So I called him, sent him the photographs, and he gave me the results. Beautiful results. Here's the definitive proof we've always sought, Doug, that Pacciani was innocent, that Lotti and Pucci were liars, and that his picnicking friends had nothing to do with the killings!"

"Fabulous," I said. "But how does it work? What's the science behind it?"

"The professor explained it to me. The larvae are fundamentally important for arriving at the time of death. The *calliforidi*, the so-called blue flies, deposit on the cadaver a large number of eggs in a cluster. They lay eggs only during the day, because the flies don't fly at night. The eggs require between eighteen and twenty-four hours to hatch. And then they develop on a rigid schedule."

He pulled out the report. "Read it for yourself."

It was short and to the point. I parsed my way through the dense, scientific Italian. The larvae in the photographs of the French victim, the report stated, "had already passed the first phase of development and were in the second. . . . They could not have been deposited on the remains less than thirty-six hours previously. As a result, the theory that the homicide could have been committed the night of September 8 [Sunday night] and that the deposition of the eggs could have taken place at dawn on the ninth, with the photographs taken twelve hours later—at five o'clock in the afternoon—finds no support in the entomological data. The data places the time of death in the preceding day, at the minimum."

In other words, the French tourists *must* have been killed Saturday night.

"You understand what this means?" Spezi asked.

"It means the self-confessing eyewitnesses are damned liars—because they all claimed to have witnessed the killings on Sunday night!"

"And Lorenzo Nesi's testimony putting Pacciani near the scene of the crime Sunday night is irrelevant! If that's not enough, Pacciani had an alibi for his whereabouts Saturday night— the actual night of the murder. He had been at a country fair!"

This was absolutely decisive. The entomological evidence proved (as if more proof were needed) that Pacciani and his alleged accomplices had nothing to do with the Monster of

Florence killings. It also, therefore, demolished the satanic sect theory—which had been built entirely on the guilt of Pacciani, the false confession of Lotti, and the testimony of the other algebraic witnesses. They were exactly what Judge Ferri had called them in his book:"coarse and habitual liars."

This new evidence, Spezi said, would force investigators to reopen the Sardinian Trail. Somewhere in the murky depths of the Sardinian clan, the truth would be found and the Monster unmasked.

"This is incredible," I said."When this is broadcast, it'll cause one big beautiful uproar."

Spezi nodded silently. "And that's not all." He unwrapped the object on the table, to reveal a peculiar stone, carved in the shape of a truncated pyramid with polished sides, old and chipped, weighing perhaps five pounds.

"What is it?"

"According to Chief Inspector Giuttari, this is an esoteric object used to communicate between this world and the infernal regions. To everyone else it is a doorstop. I saw this one behind a door at the Villa Romana in Florence, now the German Cultural Institute. The director, Joachim Burmeister, is a friend of mine and he lent it to me. It looks almost identical to the stone collected in the Bartoline Fields near the scene of a Monster killing in 1981.

"*Chi L'ha Visto?*" Spezi went on, "will be shooting a segment in the Bartoline Fields, at the scene of the crime. I'll be standing at the very spot where the earlier doorstop was found, holding this one—proof that Giuttari's 'esoteric object' was merely a doorstop."

"Giuttari won't like it."

Spezi cracked a small, wicked smile. "I can't help that."

The program aired on May 14, 2004. Professor Introna appeared, presented his data, and explained the science of forensic entomology. Spezi appeared with his doorstop in the Bartoline Fields.

Instead of one fine, big, beautiful uproar, absolutely nothing happened. Neither the prosecutor's office nor the police showed a crumb of interest. Chief Inspector Giuttari dismissed out of hand Professor Introna's results. Police and prosecutors had no comment on the doorstop. As for the murder convictions of Lotti and Vanni, Pacciani's so-called picnicking friends, officials issued a bland statement that the Italian judicial system had reached verdicts in those cases and saw no need to revisit them. In general, officialdom carefully avoided commenting on the program. The press let them get away with it. The great majority of Italian newspapers ignored it completely. This was science—not another sexy story on satanic sects—and it wouldn't sell papers. The investigation into satanic sects, hidden masterminds, bodies exchanged in tombs, conspiracies among powerful people, and doorstops mistaken for esoteric objects continued unabated.

Spezi's appearance on television did have one definitive effect. It seemed to inspire Chief Inspector Giuttari's undying hatred.

On our last night in Florence before moving back to America, we joined Mario and Myriam with other friends for a farewell dinner in their apartment, on the terrazzo overlooking the Florentine hills. The date was June 24, 2004. Myriam had prepared an extraordinary dinner, starting with crostini with sweet peppers and anchovies served with a spumante from the Alto Adige; wild pheasant and partridge, shot by a friend the day before, wrapped in grape leaves; a Chianti classico from the Viticchio estate; wild field greens served with the spicy local olive oil and an intense twelve-year-old balsamico; fresh pecorino cheese from Mario's village of Sant'Angelo; and zuppa inglese.

The morning before, on June 23, Spezi had published an article in *La Nazione*, in which he had interviewed Vanni, the ex-postman of San Casciano, convicted of being Pacciani's accomplice. Spezi regaled us with the story of how he had encountered Vanni, by sheer chance, at a nursing home while pursuing an unrelated story. Nobody knew Vanni had been released from prison, for reasons of ill-health and advanced age. Spezi recognized him and seized the opportunity to interview him on the spot.

"I Will Die as the Monster But I Am Innocent," ran the headline. Spezi got the interview because, he said, he reminded Vanni of the "good old days" in San Casciano, when he and Vanni had briefly encountered each other during a festival, long before the poor postman became one of Pacciani's infamous picnicking friends. They had ridden around together in a car full of people, Vanni waving the Italian flag. Vanni remembered Spezi and waxed nostalgic—and that was how Spezi got him to talk.

The sun set over the Florentine hills as we

ate dinner, filling the landscape with a golden light. The bells of the nearby medieval church of Santa Margherita a Montici tolled out the hour, answered by the bells of other churches hidden in the hills around us. The air, warmed by the sinking rays of the sun, carried up the scent of honeysuckle. In the valley below, the crenellated towers of a large castle cast long shadows across its surrounding vineyards. As we watched, the hills sank from gold to purple and finally disappeared into the evening twilight.

The contrast between this magical landscape and the Monster that once stalked it struck me particularly hard at that moment.

Mario took the occasion to bring out a present for me. I unwrapped it to find a plastic Oscar statue, with a base that read, "The Monster of Florence."

"For when the film is made from our book," Mario said.

He also gave me a pencil drawing he had made many years earlier of Pietro Pacciani, sitting in the dock during his trial, on which he had written, "For Doug, in memory of a vile Florentine and our glorious labor together."

When we returned to the house we had built in Maine, I hung the drawing on the wall of my writing hut in the woods behind our house, along with a photograph of Spezi in his trench coat and fedora, Gauloise stuck in his mouth, standing in a butcher shop under a rack of hog jowls.

Spezi and I spoke frequently as we continued to work on the Monster book. I missed my life in Italy, but Maine was quiet, and with the frequent foul weather, fog, and cold, I found it a marvelous place to work. (I began to understand why Italy produced painters while England produced writers.) Our little town of Round Pond has five hundred and fifty residents and looks like something out of a Currier and Ives lithograph, with a white steepled church, a cluster of clapboard houses, a general store, and a harbor filled with lobster boats, surrounded by forests of oak and white pine. In the winter, the town is buried under a thick blanket of glittering snow and sea smoke rises from the ocean. The crime rate is almost nonexistent and few bother to lock their homes even when they go away on vacation. The annual bean supper at the local Grange is the front-page news in the paper. The "big town," twelve miles away, is Damariscotta, population 2,000.

The culture shock was considerable.

We continued to work on the book by e-mail and telephone. Spezi did most of the actual writing, while I read and commented on his work, adding some chapters in my miserable Italian, which Spezi had to rewrite. (I write Italian at what might generously be called a fifth grade level.) I wrote additional material in English, which was kindly translated by Andrea Carlo Cappi, the translator of my novels, who had become a good friend during our years in Italy. Spezi and I spoke on a regular basis and made excellent progress with the book.

On the morning of November 19, 2004, I went into my writing shack and checked my voice mail, to find an urgent message from Mario. Something shocking had happened.

CHAPTER
42

Polizia! *Perquisizione*! Police! This is a search!"

At 6:15 on the morning of November 18, 2004, Mario Spezi woke to the sound of his door buzzer and the raucous voice of a police detective demanding entrance.

Spezi's first clear thought, on rousing himself from bed, was to hide the floppy disk that contained the book we were writing together. He leapt out of bed and ran up the narrow staircase to his garret office, where he yanked open the plastic box containing the diskettes for his ancient computer, took the one with "Monster" written in English on the label, and shoved it down into his underwear.

He reached the front door just as the police came pouring in. There seemed to be no end to them, three ... four ... five. In the end Spezi counted seven. Most of them were fat and their big jackets of gray and brown leather bulked them up even more.

The oldest one was a commander from Giuttari's GIDES squad. The others were carabinieri and policemen. "Graybeard," the commander, wished Spezi a dry *"buongiorno"* and shoved a piece of paper at him.

"Procura della Repubblica presso il Tribunale di Perugia," read the letterhead—Office of the Public Prosecutor in the Tribunal of Perugia—and below that, "Search Warrant, Information and Guarantee to the Accused on the Right of Defense."

It had come straight out of the office of the public minister of Perugia, Giuliano Mignini.

"The person named above," the document read, "is hereby under official investigation for having committed the following crimes: A), B), C), D) ..." They were listed up to the letter R. Nineteen crimes, none of them specified.

"What are these crimes, A, B, C, etcetera?" Spezi asked Graybeard.

"It would take volumes to explain them" was the man's response. Spezi could not know what the crimes were—they were under a judicial order of secrecy.

Spezi read with incredulity the reason for the search. It said he had "evinced a peculiar and suspicious interest toward the Perugian branch of the investigation" and that Spezi "demonstrated a zealous effort in attempting to undermine the investigation through the medium of television." This, he figured, must refer to the *Chi L'ha Visto?* program of May 14, in which Professor Introna had completely cut the legs off the satanic sect investigation and Spezi had waved around the doorstop, making Chief Inspector Giuttari look like a fool.

The warrant authorized the search of the house but also of the "persons present or who may arrive" in search of any object that might have something to do with the Monster case, even peripherally. "There is sufficient reason to believe that such objects may be present in the premises of the person above indicated and on his own person."

Spezi went cold when he read this. It meant

they could search his body. He could feel the angular plastic case of the diskette digging into his flesh.

Meanwhile, Spezi's wife, Myriam, and twenty-year-old daughter, Eleonora, stood in the living room in their bathrobes, alarmed and confused.

"Tell me what you're interested in," Spezi said, "and I'll show you, so you won't trash my house."

"We want everything you have on the Monster," said Graybeard.

Which meant not only the entire archive Spezi had accumulated over a quarter of a century of researching and reporting on the case, but all the material that we were using to write the Monster book. Spezi was custodian of all the research; I had only copies of the most recent documents.

It suddenly occurred to him what this was about. They wanted to prevent publication of the book.

"Shit! When will you give it back to me?"

"As soon as we have checked through it," said Graybeard.

Spezi brought him up to his garret and showed him the masses of files that constituted his archive: packages of yellowed newspaper cuttings, mountains of photocopies of legal documents, ballistic analyses, ME reports, entire trial transcripts, interrogations, verdicts, photographs, books.

They began to load it all into big cardboard boxes.

Spezi called a friend of his at the news agency ANSA, the Italian equivalent to the Associated Press, and had the luck to catch him. "They're searching my house," he said. "They're taking away everything that I need to write my book with Douglas Preston on the Monster. I won't be able to write another word."

Fifteen minutes later the first story about the search broke on the computer screens of every newspaper and television station in Italy.

Meanwhile Spezi called the president of the Order of Journalists, the president of the Press Association, and the director of *La Nazione*. They were more scandalized than surprised. They told him they would raise hell with the story.

Spezi's cell phone began to ring like mad. One after another his colleagues called, even as the search plodded on. They all wanted to interview him. Spezi assured them that as soon as the search was over, he would meet with them.

The journalists began arriving under the house even while the search was still in progress.

The police didn't content themselves to taking only documents that Spezi had showed them. They began to rummage through drawers, pull books off the shelves, and open up CD holders. They went into his daughter's room and searched her closet, her files, her books, letters, diaries, scrapbooks, and photographs, scattering stuff on the floor and making a mess.

Spezi put his arm around Myriam. His wife was trembling. "Don't worry, this is just routine." Myriam was wearing a jacket and at the opportune moment he dove for the diskette, extracted it, and slid it into one of her pockets. He then gave her a kiss on the cheek as if to console her. "Hide it," he whispered.

Several minutes later, pretending to be upset, she sagged into a low ottoman that was coming apart at one of the seams. When the police had their backs turned she quickly slid the floppy disk into the ottoman.

After three hours of searching, they seemed to be finished. They strapped the loaded cartons onto luggage carriers and asked Spezi to follow them to the carabinieri barracks, where they would make an inventory, which he would be required to sign.

In the barracks, while he was seated on a brown Naugahyde chair waiting for the list to be ready, he received a telephone call on his cell phone. It was from Myriam, who was trying to put the house back in order, and who unwisely spoke to her husband in French. Spezi and his wife habitually spoke French in their home, as she was Belgian and they were a bilingual family. Their daughter had gone to French schools in Florence.

"Mario," she said in French, "don't worry, they didn't find what really interests you. But I can't find the documents about the scagliola." A scagliola is a type of antique table, and Spezi owned an extremely valuable one dating back to the seventeenth century, which they had just had restored and were thinking of selling.

It wasn't the most felicitous thing to say at that moment, in French, when it was obvious their cell phone was being tapped. He cut her off. "Myriam, this really isn't the time ... not now ..." Spezi flushed as he closed the phone. He knew his wife's comment was completely innocent, but that it could be interpreted in a sinister light, particularly since it had been spoken in French.

Not long after, Graybeard came in. "Spezi, we need you in here for a moment."

The journalist rose from the chair and followed them into the next room. Graybeard turned and stared at him, his face hostile. "Spezi, you're not cooperating. This isn't working at all."

"Not cooperating? What's that supposed to mean, cooperate? I left my entire house at your disposal so you could put your grubby hands wherever you pleased, what the hell more do you want?"

He stared at Spezi with his hard, marblelike eyes. "That's not what I'm talking about. Don't feign ignorance. It would be much better for you if you would only cooperate."

"Ah, now I understand . . . It's about what my wife said in French. You think she was trying to tell me something in code. But you see, that's my wife's language, and it's normal for her to speak French, we often speak French at home. As for the contents of what she said"—Spezi figured that Graybeard wasn't bilingual—"if you didn't understand it, she was referring to a document that you didn't see, which was my contract with the publishing house for my book on the Monster. She wanted to tell me that you hadn't taken it. That's all."

Graybeard continued to fix him with narrowed eyes, his expression unchanging. Spezi began to think that the problem might be with the word "scagliola." Not many Italians outside the antiquarian field knew what it meant.

"Is it the scagliola?" he asked. "Do you know what a scagliola is? Is that the problem?"

The policeman didn't respond, but it was clear that this was, in fact, the problem. Spezi tried to explain, to no avail. Graybeard was not interested in explanations.

"I regret to say, Spezi, that we're going to have to start all over again."

They turned around. The policemen and carabinieri got back into their vehicles, and they all drove back to the apartment with Spezi. For four more hours they turned the place upside down—and this time they trashed it for real.

They didn't miss anything, not even the space behind the books in the library. They took the computer, all the floppy disks (except the one still hidden in the ottoman), and even the menu of a Rotary Club dinner where Spezi had attended a conference on the Monster. They took his telephone book and all his letters.

They were not in a good humor.

Spezi was also beginning to lose his temper. When he passed through the door to the library, he gestured to the stone doorstop that he had borrowed from his German friend, the one he had waved about on the television show. It was sitting behind the door, doing what it was supposed to do—being a doorstop. "You see that?" he said sarcastically to the detective. "It's like the truncated pyramid found at the scene of one of the crimes which you insist on claiming is an 'esoteric object.' There it is, take a good look: can't you see it's only a doorstop?" He gave a mocking laugh. "You find them everywhere in Tuscan country houses."

It was an extremely serious mistake. The detective seized the doorstop and packed it away. And thus was added to the evidence against Spezi an object identical to the one that GIDES and Giuttari believed to be of prime importance to their investigation, something the *Corriere della Sera* had written about in a front-page story, calling it, without a trace of irony, "an object that served to put the earthly world in contact with the infernal regions."

In the report prepared by the police of the items taken from Spezi's house, the doorstop was described as a "truncated pyramid with a hexagonal base concealed behind a door," the wording implying that Spezi had made a special effort to hide it. The public minister of Perugia, Giuliano Mignini, justified the retention of the doorstop in a report that stated the object "connected the person under investigation [i.e., Spezi] directly with the series of double homicides."

In other words, because of that doorstop, Spezi was no longer suspected of merely obstructing or interfering with the Monster of Florence investigation. Now they believed that an object discovered in his house tied him directly with one of the crimes.

The *Chi L'ha Visto?* program and the June 23 article had fixed Giuttari's hatred and suspicion of Spezi. In a book Giuttari published about the case, *The Monster: Anatomy of an Investigation*, the chief inspector explained how his suspicions developed. It is an interesting look into the way his mind worked.

"On June 23," Giuttari wrote, "one of [Spezi's] articles came out in *La Nazione*, an 'exclusive' interview with the lifer Mario Vanni, entitled *I Will Die as the Monster but I Am Innocent*."

In the story, Spezi mentioned that he had encountered Vanni once, many years before the Monster killings, in San Casciano. This struck Giuttari as an important clue. "I was mildly surprised that the two had known each other since the days of their youth," he wrote. "But I was struck even more by the curious coincidence that the bitter public foe of the official investigation into the Monster case and the strenuous defender of the 'Sardinian Trail' had not only revealed himself as having excellent rapport with the indicted ex-pharmacist [Calamandrei] . . . but now stood revealed as a longtime friend of Mario Vanni."

Giuttari went on to say that Spezi had "participated in a television series" that attempted to focus attention back on the Sardinian Trail, "recycling the same old tired and unverified theories" that had been discredited long ago.

"Now," Giuttari wrote, Spezi's "interfering presence was beginning to look suspicious."

With the doorstop in hand, Giuttari and Mignini had the physical evidence they needed to connect Spezi to one of the actual crime scenes of the Monster.

When the policemen had left, Spezi slowly walked up the staircase to his garret, afraid of what he might find. It was even worse than he'd feared. He fell into the chair that I had given him upon my departure from Florence, in front of the empty space where his computer had been, and stared for a long time at the wreck all around him. In that moment, he thought back to that crystal-clear morning of Sunday, June 7, 1981—twenty-three years earlier—when his colleague had asked him to take the crime desk, assuring him that "nothing ever happens on a Sunday."

Never in a million years could he have imagined where it would end up.

He wanted to call me, he told me later, but by that time it was late at night in America. He couldn't write an e-mail—he didn't have a computer. He decided to leave the house, walk around the streets of Florence, and look for an Internet café where he could e-mail me.

Outside the apartment, a crowd of journalists and television cameras awaited. He said a few words, answered questions, and then got into his car and drove into town. In Via de' Benci, a few steps from Santa Croce, he went into an Internet café, full of pimply American students talking to their parents through VOIP. He seated himself in front of a machine. From somewhere, a little muted, came the sad trombone of Marc Johnson playing "Goodbye Pork Pie Hat" by

Charlie Mingus. Spezi connected to his mail server, entered the information for his mailbox, and saw that there was already a message from me, with an attachment.

While writing the Monster book, we had been exchanging e-mails on what we had corrected of each other's chapters. What he found was the last chapter of the book, which I had written, about the interview with Antonio. He sent me an e-mail telling me of the search of his home.

The next morning, after receiving the e-mail, I called and he related to me the story of the search. He asked for my help in publicizing the seizure of our research materials.

Among the documents taken by police were all the notes and drafts of the article we had written for *The New Yorker*, which had never been published. I called Dorothy Wickenden, the managing editor of the magazine, and she gave me a list of people who could help, while at the same time explaining that, since they hadn't actually published the article, the magazine did not feel it appropriate to intervene directly.

For days I called and wrote letters, but the response was minimal. The sad truth was that few in North America could get excited about an Italian journalist who had irritated the police and gotten his files taken away, at a time when journalists were being blown up in Iraq and murdered in Russia. "Now, if Spezi had been *imprisoned* ..." I heard many times, "well, then we could do something."

Finally, PEN intervened. On January 11, 2005, the Writers in Prison Committee of PEN International, in London, sent Giuttari a letter criticizing the search of Spezi's home and seizure of our papers. The letter stated that "International PEN is concerned that there has been a violation of Article 6.3 of the European Convention on Human Rights that guarantees the right of everyone charged with a criminal offence to be informed promptly 'and in detail of the nature and cause of the accusation against him.'"

Giuttari responded by ordering another search of Spezi's house, which took place on January 24. This time they took a broken computer and a walking stick that they suspected might contain a concealed electronic device.

But they never did get the diskette Spezi had stuffed down his undershorts, and we were able to resume working on the book. In succeeding months, the police eventually returned, in bits and pieces, most of Spezi's files, his archives, our notes, and his computer—but not the infamous doorstop. Giuttari and Mignini now knew exactly what was in the book, since they had captured all the drafts from Spezi's computer. And it seemed they did not like what they read.

One fine morning, Spezi opened his newspaper to read a headline that almost knocked him out of his chair.

NARDUCCI MURDER: JOURNALIST INVESTIGATED

Giuttari's suspicions had matured, like wine turning to vinegar in a poorly sealed cask. Spezi had gone from interfering journalist to murder suspect.

"When I read that," Spezi told me on the telephone, "I felt like I was inside a film of Kafka's *The Trial*, remade by Jerry Lewis and Dean Martin."

CHAPTER
43

For a year, from January 2005 to January 2006, Spezi's two lawyers tried and failed to learn what the specific charges were against him. The public minister of Perugia had sealed the accusations under an order of *segreto istruttorio*, a judicial secrecy order that makes it illegal to reveal anything about the charges. In Italy, an order of *segreto istruttorio* is often followed by selected leaks by prosecutors to their chosen reporters, who publish without fear of being charged. In this way, prosecutors allow their side of the story to be told while journalists are barred from publishing anything else. This is what seemed to happen now. Spezi was suspected of obstructing the inquiry into the Narducci murder, the newspapers claimed, which had aroused suspicions that he might be an accessory to the murder and the instigator of a cover-up. The implications of this were unclear.

In January of 2006, our book was finished and sent to the publishing house. The title was *Dolci Colline di Sangue*. A literal translation would be *Sweet Hills of Blood*, a play on the Italian phrase *dolci colline di Firenze*, the sweet hills of Florence. It was scheduled for publication in April 2006.

In early 2006, Spezi called me from a pay phone in Florence. He said that while working on a completely different story, unconnected with the Monster of Florence, he had met an ex-con named Luigi Ruocco, a petty criminal who, it turned out, was an old acquaintance of Antonio Vinci. This Ruocco told Spezi an extraordinary story—a story that would blow the case wide open. "This is the breakthrough I've been searching for for twenty years," Mario told me. "Doug, it's absolutely incredible. With this new information, the case will finally be solved. They're tapping my telephone and the e-mail is unsafe. So you have to come to Italy—and then

I'll tell you all about it. You'll be part of it, Doug. *Together we'll expose the Monster!*"

I flew to Italy with my family on February 13, 2006. Leaving them in a spectacular apartment on Via Ghibellina we had borrowed from a friend, owned by one of the Ferragamo heirs, I went up to Spezi's house to hear the incredible news.

Over dinner, Mario told me the story.

A few months back, he said, he had been researching an article about a woman who had been victimized by a doctor working for a pharmaceutical company. The doctor had used her, without her permission, as a test subject for a new psychopharmatropic drug. The case had been brought to his attention by Fernando Zaccaria, an ex–police detective who had once specialized in infiltrating drug trafficking rings, and who was now president of a private security firm in Florence. A crusader against injustice, Zaccaria had collected, pro bono, the evidence that helped convict the doctor for injuring the woman with his illegal experiments. He wanted Spezi to write the story.

One evening, when Spezi was at the injured woman's house with her mother and Zaccaria, he casually mentioned his work on the Monster of Florence case and took out a photograph he happened to be carrying of Antonio Vinci. The mother, who was pouring coffee, peered over at the photograph and suddenly exclaimed, "Why, Luigi knows that man there! And I knew him and all of them too, when I was a little girl. I remember they used to take me to their festivals in the country." The Luigi she referred to was Luigi Ruocco, her ex-husband.

"I've got to meet your husband," Spezi said.

They gathered the next evening around the same table: Zaccaria, Spezi, the woman, and Luigi Ruocco. Ruocco was the quintessential specimen of a small-time hood, taciturn, with a neck like a bull, a huge square face, and curly brown hair. He was dressed in gym clothes. There was, however, a cautious but open look in his blue eyes that Spezi liked. Ruocco looked at the photograph and confirmed that he knew Antonio and the other Sardinians very well.

Spezi quickly gave Ruocco a summary of the Monster of Florence case and his belief that Antonio might be the Monster. Ruocco listened with interest. In a few minutes Spezi got to the point: did Ruocco know of a secret house that Antonio may have used during the period of the killings? Spezi had often said to me that the Monster had probably used an abandoned house in the country, perhaps a ruin, as a place of retreat to use before and after a killing, where he hid his gun, knife, and other items. At the time of the killings the Tuscan countryside was dotted with such abandoned houses.

"I heard talk about it," Ruocco said. "I don't know where it is. But I know someone who does. 'Gnazio."

"Of course, Ignazio!" Zaccaria exclaimed. "He knows a whole bunch of Sardinians!"

Ruocco called Spezi a few days later. He had spoken to Ignazio and had the information on Antonio's safe house. Spezi and Ruocco met in front of a supermarket outside Florence. They retired to a café where Mario downed an espresso and Ruocco drank a Campari with a splash of Martini & Rossi. What Ruocco had to say was electrifying. Ignazio not only knew the safe house, but had actually been there only a month before with Antonio. He had observed an old armoire with a glass front in which he could see six locked metal boxes, lined up in a row. His eye fell on a drawer not fully closed below, in which he glimpsed two, possibly three pistols, one of which might have been a .22

Beretta. Ignazio asked the Sardinian what was in those metal boxes and the man had responded brusquely, "That's *my* stuff," slapping his chest.

Six metal boxes. Six female victims.

Spezi could hardly contain his excitement. "That's the detail that convinced me," he said over dinner. "Six. How could Ruocco know? Everyone talks about the seven or eight double killings of the Monster. But Ruocco said six boxes. Six: the number of female victims killed by the Monster, if you eliminate the 1968 killing, which he didn't do, and the time he mistakenly killed a gay couple."

"But he didn't mutilate all the victims."

"Yes, but the psychological experts said he would have taken souvenirs from each one. In almost every crime scene, the girl's purse was found lying on the ground, wide open."

I listened with fascination. If the Monster's Beretta, the most sought-after gun in Italian history, were in that armoire, along with items from the victims, it would be the scoop of a lifetime.

Spezi went on. "I asked Ruocco to go to the house, in order to tell me exactly where it was and describe it to me. He said he would. We met again a few days later. Ruocco told me that he had gone and looked inside, and could see the armoire through a window with the six metal boxes. He gave me directions to the house."

"Did you go?"

"I certainly did! Nando and I went together." The ruined house, Spezi said, was on the grounds of an enormous, thousand-acre estate west of Florence, called Villa Bibbiani, near the town of Capraia. "It's a spectacular villa," Spezi said, "with gardens, fountains, statues, and a stupendous park planted with rare trees."

He took out his cell phone and showed me a couple of pictures he had snapped of the villa. I gaped at the magnificence of it.

"How did you get in?"

"No problem! It's open to the public for sales of olive oil and wine, and they rent it out for weddings and such. The gates are wide open and there's even a public parking area. Nando and I walked around. Several hundred meters beyond the villa, a dirt road leads to two decrepit stone houses, one of which fit Ruocco's description. The houses can be reached by a separate road through the forest, very private."

"You didn't break in, did you?"

"No, no! I sure did think about it! Just to see if the armoire was really there. But that would be an insane thing to do. Not only would it be trespassing, but what would I do with the boxes and gun once I found them? No, Doug, we have to call the police and let them handle it—and hope to get the scoop afterwards."

"Have you called the police then?"

"Not yet. I was waiting for you." He leaned forward. "Think of it, Doug. In the next two weeks, the case of the Monster of Florence may be solved."

I then made a fateful request. "If the villa's open to the public, can I go see it?"

"Of course," said Spezi. "We'll go tomorrow."

CHAPTER
44

What the hell happened to your car?" It was the following morning, and we were standing in the parking area next to Spezi's apartment building. The door of his Renault Twingo had been ineptly forced open with what looked like a wrecking bar, ruining the door and much of the right side of the car.

"They stole my radio," Spezi said. "Can you believe it? With all these Mercedes, Porsches, and Alfa Romeos parked along here, they picked my Twingo!"

We drove to the security firm run by Zaccaria, a nondescript building in an industrial area on the outskirts of Florence. The ex-cop received us in his office. He looked every inch a movie detective, dressed in a pinstriped blue suit of the sharpest Florentine cut, his long gray hair almost to his shoulders, strikingly handsome, dashing, and animated. He spoke with a raffish Neapolitan accent, tossing in a bit of gangster-ish slang every once in a while to great effect, and speaking with his hands as only a Neapoli-tan can do.

Before going to the villa, we went to lunch. Zaccaria treated us to a repast at a local dive, and there, over a plate of *maltagliata al cing-hiale*, he regaled us with stories of his under-cover work infiltrating drug smuggling rings, some involving the American Mafia. I marveled that he had survived.

"Nando," Spezi said. "Tell Doug the story of Catapano."

"Ah, Catapano! Now there was a real Neapoli-tan!" He turned to me. "There was once a boss of the Neapolitan Camorra named Catapano. He was locked up in Poggioreale prison for mur-der. It just so happened that the murderer of his brother was in the same prison. Catapano vowed revenge. He said, *I will eat his heart.*"

Zaccaria took a moment to dig into his *malta-gliata* and take a swig of wine.

"Slow down," said Spezi, "and stop using so much dialect. Doug doesn't understand dialect."

"My apologies." He went on with the story. The prison authorities segregated the two men at opposite ends of the prison and made sure they would never encounter each other. But one day, Catapano heard that his nemesis was in the infirmary. He took two guards hostage with a spoon sharpened into a knife, used them to force his way to the infirmary, got the key, and entered, surprising three nurses and a doctor. He immediately set upon his enemy, cutting his throat and stabbing him to death while the doctor and nurses looked on in horror. Then he cried out, in a strangled voice, "Where's the heart? Where's the liver?" The doctor, under threat, gave Catapano a quick lesson in anatomy. With one enormous swipe of the knife Catapano opened the man up and ripped out the heart and liver, one in each hand, and then took a bite out of each in turn.

"Catapano," Zaccaria said, "became a legend among his people. In Naples, the heart is everything—courage, happiness, love. To rip it out of your enemy and bite it is to reduce your enemy to the level of meat, animal meat. It deprives him of what makes him human. And all the television coverage of it afterwards was useful in sending a signal to Catapano's enemies that he could administer justice with the most refined methods, even in prison. Catapano had proved his courage, his capacity for organization, his exquisite sense of theater, and he did it inside one of the highest-security prisons in Italy, under the horrified gaze of five witnesses!"

Lunch over, we set off for the Villa Bibbiani in an icy winter drizzle under skies the color of dead flesh. It was still raining when we arrived, entering the grounds through a pair of iron gates and up a long, curving driveway lined with massive umbrella pines. We parked in the parking area, got our umbrellas out, and walked to the salesroom. The wooden door was locked and barred. A woman leaned out the window and said the salesroom was closed for lunch. Zaccaria charmed her, asking where the gardener was, and she said we might find him around the back. We walked through an archway and entered a stupendous formal garden behind the villa, with sweeping marble steps, fountains, reflecting pools, statues, and hedges. The villa was originally built in the 1500s by the Frescobaldi family of Florence. The gardens were created a hundred years later by Count Cosimo Ridolfi; in the 1800s, thousands of rare botanical specimens and trees were added to the gardens and park by an Italian explorer and botanist who collected plants from the far ends of the earth. Even in the gray winter rain, the gardens and massive dripping trees retained a cold magnificence.

We moved past the villa to the far end of the park. A dirt road ran along the edge of the arboretum into a thick wood, where, in a clearing beyond, we could see a cluster of crumbling stone houses.

"That's it," murmured Spezi, pointing to one of the houses.

I gazed down the muddy road to the house that held the ultimate secret of the Monster of Florence. A chill mist drifted through the trees and the rain drummed on our umbrellas.

"Maybe we could just walk down there and take a look," I said.

Spezi shook his head. "Not a chance."

We returned to the car, shook out our umbrellas, and got in. It was a disappointing visit, at least to me. Ruocco's story seemed too perfect, and the setting struck me as an unlikely one for the secret hideout of the Monster of Florence.

As we drove back to Zaccaria's firm, Spezi explained the plan he and Zaccaria had worked out for communicating this information to the police. If they merely gave it to the police, and the police found the Monster's gun, the news would be all over Italy and Mario and I would lose the scoop. We also had to consider the physical danger to ourselves if Antonio knew we were the ones who had turned him in. Instead, Spezi and Zaccaria would approach a certain chief inspector of their acquaintance with what they claimed was an anonymous letter, which they were duly passing along as good citizens. That way, they would have the scoop but not the blame.

"If we pull this off," Zaccaria said, slapping Mario's knee, "they'll make me minister of justice!" We all laughed.

A few days after our visit to Villa Bibbiani, Spezi called me on my cell phone. "We did it," he said. "We did it all." He didn't go into details, but I knew what he meant: he had given the anonymous letter to the police. As I began to ask too many questions, Spezi cut me off, saying "*Il telefonino è brutto*," literally, "The cell phone is ugly," meaning he believed it was being tapped.

We arranged to meet in town, so he could tell me the full story.

We met at Caffè Cibreo. A strange thing happened, Spezi said, when they had approached the chief inspector. The inspector inexplicably refused to accept the letter, and brusquely told them to take it and their story to the head of the mobile squad instead, a special police unit that investigates homicides. He appeared anxious to have nothing to do with the whole affair and was decidedly unfriendly.

Why, Spezi asked me, would a chief inspector turn down out of hand what could be the most important coup in his career?

Zaccaria, a former inspector himself, had no answer.

CHAPTER
45

The morning of February 22, I headed out of the apartment into the streets of Florence to fetch espressos and pastries to carry back for breakfast. As I was crossing the street to a little café, my cell phone rang. A man speaking Italian informed me he was a police detective and wanted to see me—immediately.

"Come on," I said, laughing. "Who is this really?" I was impressed by the flawless, officious-sounding Italian, and I racked my brains as to who it might be.

"This is not a joke, Mr. Preston."

There was a long silence as it sank in that this was real.

"Excuse me—what's this about?"

"I cannot tell you. You must see us. It is *obbligatorio*."

"I'm very busy," I said, in a rising panic. "I don't have time. So sorry."

"You must *make* time, Mr. Preston," came the reply. "Where are you right now?"

"Florence."

"*Where?*"

Should I refuse to tell him or lie? That didn't seem a wise thing to do. "Via Ghibellina."

"Don't go anywhere—we're coming to you."

I looked around. It was a part of town I didn't know well, with narrow side streets and few tourists. This would not do. I wanted wit-nesses—American witnesses.

"Let's meet in the Piazza della Signoria," I countered, naming the most public square in Florence.

"Where? It's a big place."

"At the spot where Savonarola was burned. There's a plaque."

A silence. "I'm not familiar with that place. Let's meet instead at the entrance to the Palazzo Vecchio."

I called Christine. "I'm afraid I can't bring you coffee this morning."

I arrived early and walked around the piazza, thinking furiously. As an American, an author and journalist, I had always enjoyed a smug feeling of invulnerability. What could they possibly do to me? Now I wasn't feeling so untouchable.

At the appointed time I saw two men wending their way through the tourist masses, dressed casually in jeans, black shoes, and blue jackets, shades pushed up on their crew-cut heads. They were *in borghese*, in plainclothes, but even from a hundred yards away I could tell they were cops.

I went over. "I am Douglas Preston."

"Come this way."

The two detectives took me into the Palazzo Vecchio, where, in the magnificent Renaissance courtyard surrounded by Vasari's frescoes, they presented me with a legal summons to appear for an interrogation before the public minister of Perugia, Judge Giuliano Mignini. The detective politely explained that a no-show would be a serious crime; it would put them in the regrettable position of having to come and get me.

"Sign here to indicate you have received this piece of paper and understood what it says and what you must do."

"You still haven't told me what it's about."

"You'll find out in Perugia tomorrow."

"At least tell me this: is it about the Monster of Florence?" I asked.

"Bravo," said the detective. "Now sign."

I signed.

I called Spezi, and he was deeply shocked and concerned. "I never thought they'd act against you," he said. "Go to Perugia and answer the questions. Tell them just what they ask and no more—and for God's sake, don't lie."

CHAPTER
46

The next day I drove to Perugia with Christine and our two children, passing the shores of Lake Trasimeno on the way. Perugia, a beautiful and ancient city, occupies an irregular rocky hill in the upper Tiber valley, surrounded by a defensive wall that is still largely intact. Perugia has long been a center of learning in Italy, graced by a number of universities and schools, some of which date back five hundred years. Christine planned to sightsee with the kids and have lunch while I was interrogated. I had decided the whole interrogation was a bluff, a crude attempt at intimidation. I'd done nothing wrong and broken no law. I was a journalist and writer.

Italy was a civilized country. Or so I kept repeating to myself on the drive down.

The offices of the Procura, where the public minister worked, were in a modern travertine building just outside the ancient city walls. I was ushered into a pleasant room on a high floor. A couple of windows looked down to the beautiful Umbrian countryside, misty and green, wreathed in drizzle. I had dressed smartly and I carried a folded copy of the *International Herald Tribune* under my arm as a prop.

Present in the room were five people. I asked their names and wrote them down. One of the detectives who had summoned me was there, an Inspector Castelli, fashionably dressed for the important occasion in a black sports jacket and black shirt buttoned at the collar, wearing lots of hair gel. There was a small, extremely tense police captain named Mora with orange hair implants, who seemed determined to put on a good show for the public minister. There was a blonde female detective, who, at my request, wrote her name in my notebook in a scribble I have yet to decipher. A stenographer sat at a computer.

Behind a desk sat the public minister of Perugia himself, Judge Giuliano Mignini. He was a short man of indeterminate middle age, well groomed, his fleshy face carefully shaved and patted. He wore a blue suit and carried himself like a well-bred Italian, with a large sense of personal dignity, his movements smooth and precise, his voice calm and pleasant. Bestowing upon me the honorific of *dottore*, which in Italy denotes the highest respect, he addressed me with elaborate courtesy using the "*lei*" form. I had the right to an interpreter, he explained, but that finding one might take many hours, during which I would be inconveniently detained. In his opinion I spoke Italian fluently. I asked if I needed a lawyer and he said that, although it was of course my right, it wasn't necessary, as they merely wanted to ask a few questions of a routine nature.

I had already decided not to assert journalistic privilege. It's one thing to fight for your rights in your own country, but I had no intention of going to prison on principle in a foreign land.

His questions were gentle, and posed almost diffidently. The secretary typed the questions and my answers into the computer. Sometimes Mignini rephrased my answers in better Italian, checking solicitously if that was what I really meant to say. At first he rarely, if ever, looked at me, keeping his eyes down to his notes and his papers, occasionally looking over the shoulder of the stenographer to see what she was typing on the screen.

At the end of the interrogation, I would be refused both a transcript of the interrogation and a copy of the "statement" I was required to sign. My account of the interrogation appearing here is taken from notes I jotted down immediately after the interrogation and a much fuller account I wrote up two days later from memory.

Mignini asked many questions about Spezi, always listening with respectful interest to the answers. He wanted to know what our theories were involving the Monster case. He questioned me closely about one of Spezi's two lawyers, Alessandro Traversi. Did I know who he was? Had I met him? Had Spezi ever discussed with me Traversi's legal strategies? If so, what were those legal strategies? On this latter point he was particularly insistent, probing deeply for what I might know of Spezi's legal defense. I truthfully claimed ignorance. He reeled off lists of names and asked if I had ever heard them. Most of the names were unfamiliar. Others, such as Calamandrei, Pacciani, and Zaccaria, I knew.

The questions went on like this for an hour,

and I was starting to feel reassured. I even had a glimmer of hope that I might get out of there in time to join my wife and children for lunch.

Mignini then asked me if I had ever heard the name Antonio Vinci. I felt a faint chill. Yes, I said, I knew that name. How did I know it and what did I know of him? I said we had interviewed him, and under further questioning described the circumstances. The questioning turned to the Monster's gun. Had Spezi mentioned the gun? What were his theories? I told him our belief that the gun had always remained within the circle of Sardinians, and that one of them had gone on to become the Monster.

At this, Mignini dropped the genteel tone and his voice became edged with anger. "You say that you and Spezi persist in this belief, even though the Sardinian Trail was closed in 1988 by Judge Rotella, and the Sardinians were officially absolved of any connection in the case?"

I said yes, that we both persisted in this belief.

Mignini steered the questions toward our visit to the villa. Now the tone of his voice became darker, accusatory. What did we do there? Where did we walk? What did we talk about? Were Spezi and Zaccaria always within sight of me? Was there any moment, even briefly, when they were out of my sight? Was there talk of a gun? Of boxes of iron? Was my back ever to Spezi? When we spoke, how far were we from one another? Did we see anyone there? Who? What was said? What was Zaccaria doing there? What was his role? Did he speak about his desire to be appointed minister of justice?

I answered as truthfully as I could, trying to suppress a damnable habit of overexplanation.

Why did we go there? Mignini finally asked.

I said that it was a public place and we went there in our capacity as journalists—

At the mention of the world "journalist" Mignini interrupted me in a loud voice, overriding me before I had finished. He made an angry speech that this had nothing to do with freedom of the press, that we were free to report on whatever we wanted, and that he didn't care a whit what we wrote. This, he said, was a *criminal* matter.

I said it did matter, because we were journalists—

Again he interrupted me, drowning me out with a lecture that freedom of the press was irrelevant to this inquiry and that I should not bring up the subject again. He asked me in a sarcastic tone if I thought that, just because Spezi and I were journalists, did that mean we could not *also* be criminals? I had the distinct feeling he was trying to prevent anything I might say about press freedom or journalistic privilege from reaching the tape recording that was surely being made of the interrogation.

I began to sweat. The public minister began repeating the same questions over and over again, phrased in different ways and in different forms. His face flushed as his frustration mounted. He frequently instructed his secretary to read back my earlier answers. "You said *that*, and now you say *this*? Which is true, Dr. Preston? *Which is true?*"

I began to stumble over my words. If the truth be known, I am far from fluent in Italian, especially with legal and criminological terms. With a growing sense of dismay, I could hear from my own stammering, hesitant voice that I was sounding like a liar.

Mignini asked, sarcastically, if I at least remembered speaking by telephone to Spezi on February 18. Flustered, I said I couldn't remember a particular conversation on that exact date, but that I had talked to him almost every day.

Mignini said, "Listen to this." He nodded to the stenographer, who pressed a button on the computer. Through the set of speakers attached to the computer, I could hear the ringing of a phone, and then my voice answering:

"*Pronto*."

"*Ciao, sono Mario*."

They had wiretapped our phone calls.

Mario and I chatted for a moment while I listened in amazement to my own voice, clearer on the intercept than in the original call on my lousy cell phone. Mignini played it once, then again, and yet again. He stopped at the point where Mario said, "We did it all." He fixed his glittering eyes on me: "What exactly did you do, Dr. Preston?"

I explained Spezi was referring to delivering the information to the police.

"No, Dr. Preston." He played the recording again and again, asking over and over, "What is this thing you did? *What did you do*?" He seized on Spezi's other comment, in which he had said, "The cell phone is ugly."

"What does this mean, 'The cell phone is ugly'?"

"It meant he thought the phone was tapped."

Mignini sat back and swelled with triumph. "And why is it, Dr. Preston, that you were concerned about the telephone being tapped *if you weren't engaged in illegal activity*?"

"Because it isn't nice to have your phone tapped," I answered feebly. "We're journalists. We keep our work secret."

"That is *not* an answer, Dr. Preston."

Mignini played the recording again, and again. He kept stopping at several other words, repeatedly demanding to know what I or Spezi meant, as if we were speaking in code, a common Mafia ploy. He asked me if Spezi had a gun in the car with us. He asked me if Spezi had carried a gun during our visit to the villa. He wanted to know exactly what we had done there and where we had walked, minute by minute. Mignini brushed all my answers aside. "There is so much more behind this conversation than you are telling us, Dr. Preston. You know much more than you are letting on." He demanded to know what kind of evidence the Sardinians might have hidden in the villa, in the boxes, and I said I didn't know. Take a guess, he said. I replied perhaps arms or other evidence—jewelry from the victims, maybe pieces of the corpses.

"Pieces from the *corpses*?" the judge exclaimed incredulously, looking at me as if I were a lunatic for even thinking of such a vile thing. "But the killings took place twenty years ago!"

"But the FBI report said—"

"Listen again, Dr. Preston!" And he pressed the button to play the call again.

This time the police captain jumped in, speaking for the first time, his voice as tense and shrill as a cat's.

"I find it very strange that Spezi laughs at that point. Why does he laugh? The Monster of Florence case is one of the most tragic in the history of the Italian republic, and it is no laughing matter. So why does Spezi laugh? *What is so funny?*"

I refrained from answering the question, since it hadn't been addressed to me. But the indefatigable man wanted an answer, and he turned and repeated the question to me directly.

"I am not a psychologist," I answered as coldly as I could, the desired effect ruined when I mispronounced the word *psicologo* and had to be corrected.

The captain stared at me, his eyes narrowing, then turned to Mignini and with the expression on his face of a man who refuses to allow himself to be fooled. "This is something I note for the record," he shrilled. "It is *very* strange that he laughs at that point. It is not psychologically normal, no, *not normal at all.*"

I remember at this point looking at Mignini, and finding his gaze on me. His face was flushed with a look of contempt—and triumph. I suddenly knew why: he had expected me to lie, and now I had met his expectation. I was proving to his satisfaction that I was guilty.

But of what?

I stammered out a question: did they think we had committed a crime at the villa?

Mignini straightened up in his chair and with a note of triumph in his voice said, "Yes."

"What?"

He thundered out, "You and Spezi either planted, or were planning to plant, a gun or other false evidence at that villa in an attempt to frame an innocent man for being the Monster of Florence, to derail this investigation, and to deflect suspicion from Spezi himself. *That* is what you were doing. This comment: 'We did it all'—that's what he meant. And then you tried to call the police. But we had warned them ahead of time—and they would have nothing to do with the deception!"

I was floored. I stammered that this was just a theory, but Mignini interrupted me and said,

"These are not theories! These are facts! And you, Dr. Preston, you know a great deal more about this business than you are letting on. Do you realize the utmost seriousness, the enormous gravity, of these crimes? You well know that Spezi is being investigated for the murder of Narducci, and I think you know a great deal about it. That makes you an accessory. Yes, Dr. Preston, I can hear it in your voice on that telephone call, I can hear the tone of knowledge, of deep familiarity with these events. Just listen again." His voice rose with restrained exultation. "Listen to yourself!"

And for maybe the tenth time he replayed the conversation.

"Perhaps you have been duped," he went on, "but I don't think so. *You know*. And now, Dr. Preston you have one last chance—*one last chance*—to tell us what you know—or I will charge you with perjury. I don't care, I will do it, even if the news goes around the world tomorrow."

I felt sick and I had the sudden urge to relieve myself. I asked for the way to the bathroom. I returned a few minutes later, having failed to muster much composure. I was terrified. As soon as the interrogation ended, I would be arrested and taken off to jail, never to see my wife and children again. Planting false evidence, perjury, accessory to murder . . . Not just any murder, but one connected to the Monster of Florence . . . I could easily spend the rest of my life in an Italian prison.

"I've told you the truth," I managed to croak. "What more can I say?"

Mignini waved his hand and was handed a legal tome that he placed on his desk with the utmost delicacy, then opened to the requisite page. In a voice worthy of a funeral oration, he began to read the text of the law. I heard that I was now *indagato* (indicted) for the crime of reticence and making false statements.[1] He announced that the investigation would be suspended to allow me to leave Italy, but that it would be reinstated when the investigation of Spezi had concluded.

In other words, I was to get out of Italy and not come back.

[1] Here and elsewhere I have translated the word *indagato* as "charged" or "indicted." To be more precise, to be *indagato* is to be formally named as the official suspect of a crime, your name recorded in a book along with the reasons why. It is one step short of an actual indictment in the American sense, although in Italy it amounts to much the same thing, especially in terms of public opinion and the effect it has on the person's reputation.

The secretary printed out a transcript. The two-and-a-half-hour interrogation had been boiled down to two pages of questions and answers, which I corrected and signed.

"May I keep this?"

"No. It is under *segreto istruttorio*."

Very stiffly, I picked up my *International Herald Tribune*, folded it under my arm, and turned to leave.

"If you ever decide to talk, Dr. Preston, we are here."

On rubbery legs I descended to the street and into a wintry drizzle.

CHAPTER
47

We drove back to Florence in the pouring rain. Along the way, I called the American embassy in Rome on my cell phone. An official in the legal department explained they could do nothing for me since I had not been arrested. "Americans who get into trouble in Italy," he said, "need to hire a lawyer. The American embassy can't intervene in a local criminal investigation."

"I'm not some American who did something stupid and got involved in a local criminal investigation!" I cried. "They're harassing me because I'm a journalist. This is a freedom-of-press issue!"

That did not impress the embassy official. "Re-

gardless of what you think, this is a local criminal matter. You're in Italy," he said, "not America.
We can't intervene in criminal investigations."

"Can you at least recommend a lawyer?"

"We're not in the business of rating Italian lawyers. We'll send you a list of the lawyers known
to the embassy."

"Thanks."

Above all, I had to speak to Mario. Something
big was coming—my interrogation was only a
shot across the bow. Even for a man as powerful
as the public minister of Perugia, it was a brazen
step to take into custody an American journalist and subject him to the third degree. If they
were willing to do that to me, at the risk of bad
publicity (which I fully intended to bring down
upon their heads like a ton of bricks), what
would they do to Spezi? He was the man they
were really after.

I couldn't call Spezi on my cell phone. When
I got back to Florence, I arranged a meeting
through borrowed cell phones and calls from
phone booths. At close to midnight, Spezi, Zaccaria, and Myriam showed up at our apartment
in Via Ghibellina.

Spezi, Gauloise stuck in his mouth, paced the
elegant living room, trailing clouds of smoke.

"I never would have thought they would take this step. Are you *sure* they charged you with perjury?"

"I'm sure. I'm a *persona indagata*."

"Did they serve you with an *avviso di garanzia*?"

"They said they would mail it to my address in Maine."

I related to them as much as I could remember of the interrogation. When I got to the point where Mignini accused us of planting a gun at the villa to incriminate an innocent man and to deflect suspicion from Spezi himself, Spezi stopped me.

"He said that? 'To deflect suspicion' from me?"

"That's what he said."

Spezi shook his head. "*Porca miseria*! Those two, Giuttari and Mignini, don't just think me guilty of some journalistic shenanigans, planting a gun for a scoop. They think I was directly involved in the Monster's murders—or at least in the murder of Narducci!"

"In a crazy way," I said, "their fantasy fits the facts. Look at it from their point of view. For years we've been insisting Antonio is the Monster. Nobody's paid any attention. So we go to the villa, we walk around, then a few days later we call the police and say Antonio hid evidence at the villa, come and get it. I hate to say it, Mario, but it's a believable theory that we might have planted something."

"Come now!" Spezi cried. "It's a theory not only lacking all investigative logic, but all logic entirely! A moment's thought would discredit it. If I was behind the murder of Narducci, to 'deflect suspicion' from myself, would I really enlist in my plot an ex-con I didn't know, a policeman who had been one of the finest detectives in the Florentine mobile squad, and a famous American writer? Who could possibly think that you, Doug, would come to Italy and sneak around like a crook planting evidence for the police to find? You're a best-selling author here already! You don't need a scoop! And Nando, he's president of an important security company. Why would he risk everything for a sordid scoop? It doesn't make any sense at all!"

He paced, scattering ashes.

"Doug, you have to ask yourself: why are Giuttari and Mignini working so hard to attack us now? Is it perhaps because in just two months we'll publish a book on this same subject, questioning their investigation? Might this be an effort to discredit our book before publication? They know what's in the book already—they've read it."

He took a turn around the room.

"The worst thing for me, Doug, is the accusation that I did this to *deflect suspicion from myself*. Suspicion of what? That I'm one of the instigators of the Narducci killing! The newspapers have all been writing the same thing, a strong indication that they have been using the same source, well informed, and certainly official. What does that make me?"

Pace, turn.

"Doug, do you realize what they really think? I'm not just an accessory or someone involved in the Narducci killing. I'm one of the *masterminds* behind the Monster killings. *They think I'm the Monster!*"

"Give me a cigarette," I said. I didn't normally smoke but now I needed it.

Spezi gave me a cigarette and lit another one for himself.

Myriam began to cry. Zaccaria sat on the edge of the sofa, his long hair disheveled, his once crisp suit limp and wrinkled.

"Consider this," Spezi said. "I'm supposed to have planted the Monster's gun at the villa to incriminate an innocent man. Where did I get the Monster's gun, if I'm not the Monster myself?"

The ash hung in a curl from the end of his cigarette.

"Where's the damn ashtray?"

I fetched Spezi and myself a plate from the kitchen. Spezi stubbed out his half-smoked cigarette with violence and lit another. "I'll tell you where Mignini gets these ideas. It's that woman from Rome, Gabriella Carlizzi, the one who said the cult of the Red Rose was behind the 9/11 attacks. Have you read her website? This is the woman the public minister of Perugia listens to!"

Spezi had gone full circle, from Monstrologer to Monster.

I left Italy the next morning. When I returned to my house in Maine, which stands on a bluff overlooking the gray Atlantic, and I listened to the rhythmic breakers on the rocks below and the seagulls wheeling above, I was so glad to be free, so happy not to be rotting in some Italian jail, that I felt the tears trickling down my face.

Count Niccolò called me the day after my return. "So, Douglas! I see you have been making trouble in Italy! Good show!"

"How did you know?"

"They say in the papers this morning that you're now an official suspect in the Monster of Florence case."

"It's in the papers?"

"Everywhere." He laughed quietly. "Don't be concerned."

"Niccolò, for God's sake, they accused me of being an accessory to murder, they said I planted a gun at that villa, they've indicted me for making false statements and obstruction of justice! They threatened me if I ever return to Italy. And you tell me I shouldn't be concerned?"

"My dear Douglas, anyone who is anybody in Italy is *indagato*. I offer you my congratulations on becoming a genuine Italian." His voice lost its cynical drawl and became serious. "It is our mutual friend Spezi who should be concerned. *Very* concerned."

CHAPTER
48

I began to make calls to the press as soon as I got home. I was terrified for Mario; he was obviously their real target. I hoped that if I could make a big enough stink in America, it might provide Spezi with some protection against an arbitrary and capricious arrest.

When Spezi had had his house searched, the American press could not have cared less about an Italian journalist who had his papers taken away. But now, because an American was the target, the press picked it up. "Trapped in His Own Thriller" ran the front-page headline in the *Boston Globe*. "Life was fine for Douglas Preston as he worked on his latest book. Then he became part of the story." The *Washington Post* ran a piece: "Best-selling thriller author Douglas Preston entangled in probe of Tuscan serial killings." Stories went out on the AP wire, and news items appeared on CNN and ABC News.

Back in Italy, the papers were also full of my interrogation. A headline in the *Corriere della Sera* read:

MONSTER CASE:
DUEL BETWEEN PUBLIC MINISTER AND AMERICAN WRITER
Serial killings of Florence. Thriller writer indicted for perjury. His colleagues mobilize.

A report went out over ANSA, the Italian news agency: "The prosecutor's office of Perugia interrogated the American writer Douglas Preston as a material witness, and then indicted him for perjury. Preston and Mario Spezi have written a book on the case, which will be published in April, entitled *Dolci Colline di Sangue*, which Spezi has called a kind of counterinvestigation to the official one. Two years ago, Spezi was investigated for being an accessory to the murder of Narducci, and subsequently he was accused of participating in the murder." Other articles contained information that appeared to have been leaked from Mignini's office, claiming that Spezi and I had tried to plant the infamous .22 Beretta—the Monster's pistol—at the villa, in order to frame an innocent man.

But the bright light of press scrutiny and publicity, if anything, seemed to make Giuttari and Mignini more aggressive. On February 25, two days after I left Italy, the police raided Spezi's apartment yet again. He was placed under intense police surveillance, followed whenever he left his house and secretly videotaped. His phones were tapped and he assumed his apartment had also been bugged and his e-mail was being intercepted.

In order to communicate, Spezi and I arranged for the use of various e-mail addresses and borrowed phones. Spezi managed to send an e-mail to me from an Internet café after losing his police tail. In it he proposed a system: when he sent me an e-mail from his regular account saying *"salutami a Christine"* ("say hi to Christine for me"), it meant he wanted me to call him on a borrowed telephone number the following day at a certain time.

Niccolò regularly sent me news stories about the case, and we spoke often by telephone.

On March 1, Spezi finally took his car to a neighborhood mechanic to fix the broken door and put in a new radio. The mechanic emerged from the car holding a fistful of sophisticated electronic equipment from which dangled red and black wires. It consisted of a black box the size of a cigarette package, with a piece of tape covering the LCDs indicating "On" and "Off," wired to a second mysterious device, two inches by five, which had been connected to the old radio's power supply wires.

"I don't know a lot," said the mechanic, "but this looks like a microphone and recorder to me."

He went around and opened the hood. "And that," he said, pointing to another black cigarette pack tucked in a corner, "must be the GPS."

Spezi called *La Nazione*, and they sent a photographer to take pictures of the journalist holding up the electronic equipment in both hands, like a pair of prize fish.

That very day Spezi went to the prosecutor's office in Florence and filed a legal complaint against persons unknown, seeking damages for the wrecking of his car. He presented himself to a prosecutor in Florence, a man he knew, with the complaint in hand. The man didn't want to touch it. "This business, Dr. Spezi, is far too delicate," he said. "Present your complaint in person to the head prosecutor." So Spezi carried it into the office of the head prosecutor, where, after having to wait, a policeman came and took the complaint, saying the prosecutor would accept it. Spezi heard nothing more about it.

On March 15, 2006, Spezi received a call from his local carabinieri post, inviting him down to the barracks. He was received in a tiny room by an officer who seemed strangely embarrassed. "We're giving you back your car radio," the man explained.

Spezi was flabbergasted. "You're . . . *admitting* you took it and wrecked my car doing it?"

"No, not us!" He fiddled nervously with his papers. "We were given the job of returning it by the prosecutor's office of Perugia, by Judge Mignini, who gave the orders to Chief Inspector Giuttari of GIDES to return your radio."

Spezi with difficulty tried to stifle a laugh. "That's incredible! You mean they actually put it in an official document that they wrecked my car to steal my radio?"

The carabinieri officer shifted uncomfortably. "Sign here, please."

"Well," Spezi said triumphantly, "what if they

broke it? I can't possibly take it back without knowing!"

"Spezi, will you just sign, please?"

Spezi quickly filed a second complaint for damages, this time against Mignini and Giuttari, now that they had (unaccountably) provided him with the very proof he needed.

In that same month, March 2006, Giuttari's new book on the Monster of Florence was published by RCS Libri, *The Monster: Anatomy of an Investigation*, and it became a huge bestseller. In the book, Giuttari took several shots at Spezi, accusing him of being an accessory to Narducci's murder and darkly hinting that he was involved in some way in the Monster killings.

Spezi promptly filed a civil lawsuit against the chief inspector for libeling him in the book and for violating the laws of judicial secrecy relating to the Monster case. The lawsuit was filed in Milan, where Giuttari's book was published by Rizzoli, another imprint of our publisher, RCS Libri. (In Italy libel suits must be filed in the place of publication.) It asked for the seizure and destruction of all copies of Giuttari's book. "It is no pleasure for a writer to call for the seizure of a book," Spezi wrote, "but this is the only remedy that will limit the damage to my reputation."

Spezi wrote most of the lawsuit himself, every word perfectly pitched to infuriate his foe:

> *For more than a year, I have been the victim not just of half-baked police work, but of what could be said to be authentic violations of civil rights. This phenomenon—which pertains not just to me, but to many others—brings to mind the most dysfunctional societies, such as one might expect to find in Asia or Africa.*
>
> *Mr. Michele Giuttari, a functionary of the State Police, is the inventor and indefatigable promoter of a theory, according to which the crimes of the so-called Monster of Florence are the work of a mysterious satanic, esoteric, and magical sect, an organized "group" of upper-middle-class professionals (bureaucrats, police and carabinieri, magistrates—and in their service, writers and journalists) who commissioned individuals from the very poorest*

levels of society to commit serial killings of pairs of lovers, paying handsomely to gain possession of female anatomical parts with the goal of using them in certain inscrutable, undetermined, and otherwise improbable "rites."

According to the fantastic conjectures of this self-described brilliant and diligent investigator, this criminal assembly of seemingly upstanding persons dedicated itself to orgies, sadomasochism, pedophilia, and other vile abominations.

Spezi then proceeded to deliver an uppercut to Giuttari's soft underbelly—his literary talent. In the lawsuit, Spezi quoted extract after extract from Giuttari's book, savaging his logic, ridiculing his theories, and mocking his writing ability.

The suit was dated March 23 and filed a week later, on March 30, 2006.

CHAPTER
49

Back in America, I watched the gathering storm from afar. Spezi and I had received a curt e-mail from our editor at RCS Libri, who was seriously alarmed at what was happening. She was terrified that the publishing house would be dragged into a legal mess, and she was particularly incensed that I had given her telephone number to the reporter for the *Boston Globe*, who had called and asked her to comment. "I must tell you," she wrote me and Mario, "that this call seriously annoyed me.... Right or wrong, personal disputes have nothing to do with me nor do they interest me.... I pray both of you to keep RCS out of any

461

eventual legal disputes connected to your personal business."

Meanwhile, curious to find out more about this Gabriella Carlizzi and her website, on a whim I went online and checked it out. What I read infuriated me. Carlizzi had posted pages of personal information on me. With the diligence of a rat collecting its winter store of seeds, she had gathered bits and pieces of information about me from all over the Web, managed to find someone to translate it all into Italian (she herself was monolingual), and had mixed it all together with out-of-context excerpts from my novels—usually descriptions of people being murdered. She managed to dig up public remarks I had made in Italy that I had no idea were even being taped, and she made particular use of a lame joke I had told at a book presentation, that had Mario Spezi decided not to write about crime, he would have made a marvelous criminal himself. To this brew she added her own sinister insinuations, creepy asides, and animadversions. The end result was a toxic portrait of me as a mentally disturbed person who wrote novels full of gratuitous violence that toadied to the basest human instincts.

That was bad enough. But what really enraged

me the most was to see my wife's and children's names, taken from my biography, posted next to pictures of the serial killer Jeffrey Dahmer and the burning Twin Towers.

I fired off an outraged e-mail to Carlizzi, demanding that my wife's and children's names be removed from her website.

Her response to my e-mail was unexpectedly mild, even ingratiating. She apologized and promised to take down the names, which she promptly did.

My e-mail had achieved the results I'd hoped, but now Carlizzi had my e-mail address. She wrote me back: "Even if brief, our little exchange of ideas, touching as they do upon spheres both delicate and in a certain sense intimate, it seems silly to address each other formally using 'lei.' Souls, when they speak from the heart, speak to each other using 'tu.' Would it displease you, Douglas, if we used the 'tu' form with each other?"

I should have known better than to reply to that one. But I did.

A flood of e-mails from Carlizzi followed, each one running to many pages, written in an Italian so contorted, so full of smarmy confidences and loopy conspiracy logic that they were almost impossible to decipher. Decipher them I did.

Gabriella Carlizzi knew the truth about the Monster of Florence, and she desperately wanted to share it with me.

Hi Douglas, did you get my long e-mail? Are you perhaps frightened of the fact that I asked you to reserve the front page of *The New Yorker* to reveal the name and the face of the Monster of Florence? . . . I will write on my website a piece, declaring my invitation to you to reserve this prestigious page, and I will notify *The New Yorker* as well . . .

Re: I PRAY YOU . . . YOU MUST BELIEVE ME . . . IF ONLY YOU AND YOUR WIFE COULD LOOK INTO MY EYES . . .
Dearest Douglas,
. . . Know that even while I write you, I am thinking that I am speaking not just to you, but also to your wife, and to those you love and that I know well how much they mean to your life as a man, beyond that of a journalist and a writer, but simply a man, a friend, a father. . . . I have embarked on this battle, this search for the truth, I do it only to maintain a promise I made to the Good Lord and to my Spiritual Father, a famous Exorcist, Father Gabriele . . . I made this

promise, Douglas, as a way of thanking the Lord for the miracle of my own son Fulvio, who after only a quarter of a day of life died, and while in the hospital, when they were dressing him for his coffin, I telephoned to Father Gabriele for a blessing, and the Father answered me, "Don't pay it any mind my daughter, your son will live longer than Methuselah." After a few instants, a hundred doctors in the hospital of San Giovanni in Rome cried out, "But it is a miracle, the baby is revived." Back then I didn't have the Faith I have now, but with regard to the gift God gave to me, in some way, sooner or later, I would have to pay him back. . . . Dear Douglas, I have the photographs of every crime, when the victims became aware of the Monster, and screamed, their scream was photographed by a minicamera given by the secret service. . . .

. . . And I found, dear Douglas, in Japan, a document that I think is useful, which would prevent the Monster from killing someone close to you. I am undertaking investigations of this document. . . .

Look at the article I have published on my site, where I have written that truly I invite you to come to see me, and to prepare the first page of *The New*

Yorker . . . I wrote that only to convince you that I am not joking.

Alarmed by these references to *The New Yorker* and this business of the Monster killing "someone close" to me, which would appear from the creepy references to be my wife, I went back to Carlizzi's site and discovered she had added a page, in which she reproduced the cover of my novel *Brimstone* next to the cover of a novel Spezi had written, *Il Passo Dell'Orco*.

Gabriella [read the website] *has not wasted any time and has invited Preston to come visit her and gaze with his own eyes on the Monster and his victims. She puts it in black and white and responds to the e-mail of Preston: "Save the front page of* The New Yorker *and come to me, I will give you the scoop that you've been waiting for for a long time." How will Douglas react? Will he accept the invitation or suffer the prohibition of an Italian friend? Certainly* The New Yorker *will not let this scoop slip away. . . .*

And above all—she continues—I want to serenely ask Douglas Preston: "You, what would happen to you if one day proof comes in that 'your' Monster is a blunder, while the real Monster is another. . . . You would discover that he is very close to you, that you worked with him, you became friends with him, you held him in esteem as a professional, and that never did you perceive that inside such a person so cultivated, so sensitive, so full of goodwill, there was a labyrinth in which the Beast had hidden itself since completing its Great Work of Death . . . a Monster who is respected, who knows how to fool everyone. . . . Wouldn't that be for you, dear Preston, the most upsetting experience of your life? Then you surely could write the most unique thriller in the world, and perhaps, with the royalties you receive, even buy The New Yorker.

So that was it. Spezi was the Monster. The flood of crazy e-mails came in like the tide at full moon, hitting my inbox multiple times during the course of each day. In them Carlizzi elaborated on her theories and urged and begged me to come to Florence. She hinted that she had a special relationship with the public minister, and that if I came to Italy she could guarantee I would not be arrested. She would, in fact, see to it that the charges against me were dropped.

. . . Florence has always been under orders to protect the true Monster, and these orders come from on high, because the Monster could at any time reveal horrible things regarding the pedophilia of illustrious magistrates, who because of this threat of blackmail will never capture him. Dear Douglas, you, unknowingly, are being used, in Italy, by the Monster, who uses as a cover illustrious names. . . . I pray you, Douglas, come to me immediately even with your wife, or give me your telephone number, I have sent you mine, we will consult with each other . . . don't say anything to Spezi. . . . I will explain all. . . . I pray to God that you and your wife will believe me . . . I can show you everything. . . .

•

One day, if you would care to write my biography, you will realize that you can leap beyond fantasy and fiction, with a true story.

•

You can well imagine that the investigation marches along even at night and on holidays. For this I pray you CONTACT ME WITH THE GREATEST URGENCY! . . . Remember: this is to be treated with the maximum secrecy.

•

Dear Douglas, I still haven't received a response to my e-mails: is there a problem? I pray you, let me know, I am worried and I want to understand what to do to bring clarity.

I soon stopped reading all but the subject lines:

Re: WHERE ARE YOU?

Re: LET US PRAY FOR MARIO SPEZI.

Re: NOW DO YOU BELIEVE ME?

Re: URGENTISSIMO URGENTISSIMO

And finally, forty-one e-mails later:

Re: BUT WHAT IN THE WORLD HAS HAPPENED TO YOU?

The e-mail barrage left me reeling, not from the sheer madness of it, but from the fact that the public minister of Perugia and a chief inspector of police took a person like this seriously. And yet, as Carlizzi herself claimed, and as Spezi's later investigative work would show, this woman was the key witness who had convinced Judge Mignini and Chief Inspector Giuttari that the death of Narducci was connected—through a satanic sect—to the crimes of the Monster of

Florence. It was Carlizzi who directed the public minister's suspicions to Spezi and who first claimed he was involved in the so-called murder of Narducci. (Spezi was later able to show that entire paragraphs in legal documents produced by the public minister's office closely paralleled the paranoid ramblings that Carlizzi had earlier posted at her website. Carlizzi, it might seem, had a Rasputin-like influence over Mignini.)

Even more incredibly, Gabriella Carlizzi had somehow managed to become an "expert" in the Monster case. Around the same time she was filling my inbox with e-mails, she was much sought after by magazines and newspapers in Italy to comment on the Monster investigation, and quoted at length as a reliable expert. She appeared on some of the most noted talk shows in Italy, where she was treated as a serious and thoughtful person.

In the middle of this bombardment, I mentioned to Mario that I'd been exchanging e-mails with Carlizzi. He chided me. "Doug, you may find it amusing, but you're playing with fire. She can do great harm. For God's sake, stay away from her."

Carlizzi, for all her craziness, seemed to have excellent sources of information. I had been shocked at what she'd managed to dig up on me. Sometimes, she seemed almost prescient in her predications about the case, so much so that Spezi and I wondered if she might not have an inside source in the public minister's office.

At the end of March, Carlizzi had some special news to announce on her site: the arrest of Mario Spezi was imminent.

CHAPTER
50

The call came on Friday, April 7, 2006. Count Niccolò's voice boomed over the transatlantic line. "They've just arrested Spezi," he said. "Giuttari's men came to his house, lured him outside, and bundled him in a car. I don't know any more than that. The news is just breaking."

I could hardly speak. I never really believed it would go this far. I croaked out a stupid question. "Arrested? What for?"

"You know very well what for. For several years now, he has made Giuttari, a Sicilian, look like an arrant fool in front of the entire nation. No Italian could tolerate that! And I have to say, dear Douglas, that Mario has a wickedly sharp

472

pen. It's all about *face*, something you Anglo-Saxons will never understand."

"What's going to happen?"

Niccolò drew a long breath. "This time they have gone too far. Giuttari and Mignini have stepped over the line. This is too much. Italy will be embarrassed before the world, and that cannot be allowed to happen. Giuttari will take the fall. As for Mignini, the judiciary will close ranks and wash their dirty linen behind closed doors. Giuttari's comeuppance may very well come at him from an entirely different direction, but he is going down—mark my words."

"But what will happen to Mario?"

"He will, unfortunately, spend some time in prison."

"I hope to God it won't be long."

"I will find out all I can and call you back."

I had a sudden thought. "Niccolò, you should be careful. You're the perfect candidate for this satanic sect yourself . . . a count from one of the oldest families of Florence."

Niccolò laughed heartily. "The idea has already crossed my mind." He broke out in a singsong Italian, as if reciting a nursery rhyme, speaking not to me, but to a hypothetical person wiretapping our telephone conversation.

Brigadiere Cuccurullo,
Mi raccomando, segni tutto!

Brigadier Cuccurullo,
Be sure to record everything!

"I always feel so dreadfully sorry for the poor fellow who has to listen to these calls. *Mi sente, Brigadiere Gennaro Cuccurullo? Mi dispiace per lei! Segni tutto!*" ("Are you listening, Brigadier Gennaro Cuccurullo? I am sorry for you! Record everything!")

"Do you really think your phone is being tapped?" I asked.

"Bah! This is Italy. They're probably tapping the pope's telephones."

There was no answer at Spezi's house. I went online to look for news. The story was just breaking on ANSA, the Italian news agency, and Reuters:

MONSTER OF FLORENCE: JOURNALIST SPEZI ARRESTED FOR OBSTRUCTION OF JUSTICE

Our book was to be published in twelve days. I was seized with fear that this was a prelude to stopping publication of the book, or that our publisher would get cold feet and withdraw it. I called our editor at Sonzogno. She was already in a meeting about the situation and unavailable, but I spoke to her later. She was rattled by Spezi's arrest—it isn't often that one of your best-selling authors orders the arrest of another one—and she was angry at me and Spezi. Her view was that Spezi, in pursuing a "personal" vendetta against Giuttari, had unnecessarily provoked the chief inspector, possibly dragging RCS Libri into an ugly legal mess. I rather hotly pointed out that Spezi and I were pursuing our legitimate rights as journalists seeking the truth, and that we had broken no laws nor done anything unethical. She seemed, to my surprise, to be somewhat skeptical of that last assertion. It was an attitude I would find all too prevalent among Italians.

News from the meeting, at least, was encouraging. RCS Libri had made a decision to forge ahead with publication of our book. More than that, the house would push the book's distribution up by a week to get it into the bookstores quickly. As part of this effort, RCS had ordered the release of the book from their warehouses as soon as possible. Once out of the warehouse, it would be far more difficult for the police to seize the print run, since the books would be scattered across Italy in thousands of bookstores.

I finally got hold of Myriam Spezi. She was holding up, but barely. "They tricked him into coming down to the gate," she said. "He was in slippers, he had nothing with him, not even his wallet. They refused to show a warrant. They threatened him and forced him in a car and took him away." They drove him first to GIDES's headquarters in the Il Magnifico building for an interrogation and then spirited him away, sirens blaring, to the grim Capanne prison in Perugia.

The evening news in Italy carried the story. Flashing pictures of Spezi, the Monster's murder scenes, the victims, and pictures of Giuttari and Mignini, the announcer intoned, "Mario Spezi, the writer and longtime chronicler of the Monster of Florence case, was arrested with the ex-convict Luigi Ruocco, accused of having obstructed the investigation into the murder of Francesco Narducci . . . in order to cover up the doctor's role in the Monster of Florence murders. The public minister of Perugia . . . hypothesizes that the two tried to plant false evidence at Villa Bibbiani in Capraia, including objects and documents, as a way to force the reopening of the Sardinian investigation, closed in the nineties. Their motive was to divert attention from the investigations linking Mario Spezi and the pharmacist of San Casciano, Francesco Calamandrei, with the murder of Francesco Narducci . . ."

And then a video of me appeared on the television, taken as I walked out of Mignini's office after the interrogation.

"For the same alleged crime," the announcer said, "two other people are under investigation, an ex-inspector of police and the American writer Douglas Preston, who with Mario Spezi has just written a book on the Monster of Florence."

Among the many calls I received, one came from the State Department. A pleasant woman informed me that the American embassy in Rome had made inquiries about my status to the public minister of Perugia. The embassy could confirm that I was indeed *indagato*—that is, a person officially suspected of committing a crime.

"Did you ask what the *evidence* was against me?"

"We don't get into the details of cases. All we can do is clarify your status."

"My status was already clear to me, thank you very much, it's in every paper in Italy!"

The woman cleared her throat and asked if I had engaged a lawyer in Italy.

"Lawyers cost money," I muttered.

"Mr. Preston," she said, in a not unkindly tone of voice, "this is a very serious matter. It isn't going to go away. It's only going to get worse, and even with a lawyer it could drag on for years. You can't let it fester. You've got to spend the money and hire a lawyer. I'll have our embassy in Rome e-mail you their list. We can't recommend any particular one, unfortunately, because—"

"I know," I said. "You're not in the business of rating Italian lawyers."

At the end of the conversation, she asked, tentatively, "You aren't, by any chance, planning a return to Italy in the near future?"

"Are you kidding?"

"I'm *so* glad to hear that." The relief in her voice was palpable. "We certainly wouldn't want the, ah, problem of dealing with your arrest."

The list arrived. It was mostly lawyers who dealt in child custody cases, real estate transactions, and contract law. Only a handful dealt in criminal matters.

I called a lawyer on the list at random and spoke to him in Rome. He'd been reading the papers and already knew of the case. He was very glad to hear from me. I had reached the right person. He would interrupt his important work to take the case, and enlist as a partner one of the preeminent lawyers in Italy, whose name would be well known and respected by the public minister of Perugia. The very hiring of such an important man would go halfway toward settling my case—that was how things worked in Italy. By hiring him, I would show the public minister that I was a *uomo serio*, a man not to be trifled with. When I timidly inquired about the fee, he said it would take a mere twenty-five thousand euros, as a retainer, to get the ball rolling—and that low, *low* fee (practically pro bono) was only possible because of the high profile of the case and its implications for freedom of the press. He would be glad to e-mail me the fund-wiring instructions, but I had to act *that very day* because this most-important-lawyer-in-Italy's schedule was filling up . . .

I went to the next lawyer on the list, and then the next. I finally found one who would take my case for about six thousand euros and who actually sounded like a lawyer, not a used-car salesman.

Before Mario's arrest, we would later learn,

Villa Bibbiani in Capraia and its grounds were searched by the men of GIDES, looking for the gun, objects, boxes, or documents we were supposed to have planted. Nothing was found. To the ever resourceful Giuttari, this was not at all a problem. He had acted so promptly, he said, that we hadn't time to carry out our nefarious plot—he had stopped it dead in its tracks.

CHAPTER
51

On April 7, the day of his arrest, Spezi finally arrived at Capanne prison, twenty kilometers outside Perugia. He was hustled into the prison grounds and brought to a room with nothing but a blanket spread on the cement floor, a table, a chair, and a cardboard box.

His guards told him to empty his pockets. Spezi did so. They told him to take off his watch and the crucifix he wore around his neck. Then one of them yelled at him to strip.

Spezi took off his sweater, shirt, and undershirt, and shoes. And waited.

"Everything. If your feet are cold, stand on the blanket."

Spezi stripped until he was completely naked.

"Bend over three times," the head guard ordered him.

Spezi wasn't sure what he meant.

"Do like this," said another, demonstrating a crouch. "All the way to the ground. Three times. And push."

After a degrading search, he was told to dress himself in the prison garb he would find in the cardboard box. The guards allowed him a single pack of cigarettes. They filled out some forms and ushered him to a cold cell. One of the guards opened the door and Spezi went in. Behind him, he heard the four loud clashings of steel as the cell door was slammed shut and barred, and the lock turned.

His dinner that night was bread and water.

The next morning, April 8, Spezi was allowed to meet with one of his lawyers, who had arrived at the prison early. Later, he would supposedly be allowed a short visit with his wife. The guards escorted him into a room where he found his lawyer seated at a table, a stack of files in front of him. They had barely exchanged greetings when a new guard rushed in with a big smile on his pockmarked face.

"This meeting is canceled. Orders of the prosecutor's office. Counsel, if you don't mind—?"

Spezi barely had the time to tell his lawyer to reassure his wife that he was well, before he was hauled back and locked up in isolation.

For five days, Spezi wouldn't know why he had been suddenly denied a lawyer and placed in isolation. The rest of Italy learned the next morning. The day of Spezi's arrest, Public Minister Mignini had asked the examining magistrate in Spezi's case, Judge Marina De Robertis, to invoke a law normally used only against dangerous terrorists and Mafia kingpins who pose an imminent threat to the state. Spezi would be denied access to his lawyers and kept in isolation. The purpose of the law was to prevent a violent criminal from ordering the killing or intimidation of witnesses through his lawyers or visitors. Now it was applied against the extremely dangerous journalist Mario Spezi. The press noted that Spezi's treatment in prison was even harsher than that meted out to Bernardo Provenzano, the Mafia boss of bosses, captured near Corleone, Sicily, four days after Spezi was arrested.

For five days, nobody had any idea of what had happened to Spezi, where he was, or what they might be doing to him. His judicial disappearance caused exquisite psychological anguish to all of his friends and family. The authorities refused to release any information about him, his state of health, or the conditions of his imprisonment. Spezi simply vanished into the black maw of Capanne prison.

CHAPTER
52

Back in America, I recalled Niccolò's words—that Italy would be ashamed before the world. I was determined to make that happen. I hoped to cause an uproar in America that would embarrass the Italian state and force it to remedy this miscarriage of justice.

I called every organization I knew that was concerned with freedom of the press. I wrote an appeal and broadcast it on the Web. It concluded, "I ask all of you, please, for the love of truth and freedom of the press, come to Spezi's aid. This should not be happening in the beautiful and civilized country that I love, the country that gave the world the Renaissance."

The appeal included the names, addresses, and e-mail addresses of the prime minister of Italy, Silvio Berlusconi, the minister of the interior, and the minister of justice. The appeal was picked up and published at many websites, translated into Italian and Japanese, and written about by various bloggers.

The Boston branch of PEN organized an effective letter-writing campaign. A novelist friend of mine, David Morrell (the creator of Rambo), wrote a letter of protest to the Italian government, as did many other well-known writers who belonged to International Thriller Writers (ITW), an organization I helped found. Many of these writers were best-selling authors in Italy, too, and their names carried weight. I received an assignment from the *Atlantic Monthly* to write a story about the Monster case and Spezi's arrest.

The worst was not knowing. Spezi's disappearance created a void filled with grim speculations and terrible rumors. Spezi was at the mercy of the public minister of Perugia, a man of great power, and Chief Inspector Giuttari, whom the newspapers had dubbed *il superpoliziotto*, the supercop, because he operated with an apparent lack of oversight. For those five silent days I woke up thinking of Spezi in prison, not knowing what they might be doing to him, and it drove me crazy. We all have a psychological breaking point and I wondered whether they would find Spezi's—because breaking him was surely their plan.

Every morning I would sit in my hut in the Maine woods, having made every call I could think of, shaking with frustration, feeling powerless while waiting for return phone calls, waiting for the organizations I had contacted to take some kind of action.

The managing editor of *The New Yorker* had put me in touch with Ann Cooper, executive director of the Committee to Protect Journalists (CPJ), a New York–based organization. This organization, above all others, understood the urgency of the situation and leapt into action. CPJ immediately launched an independent investigation of the Spezi case in Italy, directed by Nina Ognianova, program coordinator for Europe, interviewing journalists, police, judges, and colleagues of Spezi.

In the early days following Spezi's arrest, most of the major daily newspapers in Italy—especially in Tuscany and Umbria, and particularly Mario's home paper, *La Nazione*—shied away from covering the full story. They reported Spezi's arrest and the charges against him, but they treated it as a simple crime story. Most remained silent on the larger questions of freedom of the press raised by the arrest. There were almost no protests. Few journalists commented on one of the most insidious charges against Spezi, that of "obstructing an official investigation by means of the press." (Inside *La Nazione*, we would learn later, a number of Spezi colleagues were fighting with the paper's management over the newspaper's lily-livered coverage.)

In my conversations with Italian friends and journalists, I was surprised to discover that quite a few suspected that at least some of the accusations were true. Perhaps, some of my Italian colleagues demurred, I didn't understand Italy well after all, as this was the sort of thing Italian journalists did all the time. They viewed my outrage as naïve and a bit gauche. To be outraged is to be earnest, to be sincere—and to be a dupe. Some Italians were quick to strike the pose of the world-weary cynic who takes nothing at face value and who is far too clever to be taken in by Spezi's and my protestations of innocence.

"Ah!" said Count Niccolò in one of our frequent

conversations. "*Of course* Spezi and you were up to no good at that villa! *Dietrologia* insists that it be so. Only a naïf would believe that you two journalists went to the villa 'just to have a look.' The police wouldn't have arrested Spezi for no reason! You see, Douglas, an Italian must always appear to be *furbo*. You don't have an English equivalent for that marvelous word. It means a person who is wily and cunning, who knows which way the wind is blowing, who can fool you but never be fooled himself. Everyone in Italy wants to believe the worst of others so they don't end up looking gullible. Above all, they want to be seen as *furbo*."

I had trouble, as an American, appreciating the climate of fear and intimidation in Italy surrounding the issue. True freedom of the press does not exist in Italy, especially since any public official can ask that criminal charges be lodged against a journalist for "*diffamazione a mezzo stampa*"—defamation by means of the press.

The intimidation of the press was particularly evident in the refusal of our book publisher, RCS Libri, part of one of the largest publishing conglomerates in the world, to make a statement of support for Spezi. Indeed, our editor assiduously avoided the press except when tracked down by a reporter from the *Boston Globe*. "Journalist Spezi and the main police investigator hate each other," she told the *Globe*. "Why? I don't know. . . . If they [Preston and Spezi] think they have discovered something useful to police and law, they should say something without insulting police and judges."

Meanwhile, from the Capanne prison near Perugia, there was no word on the fate of Mario Spezi.

CHAPTER
53

On April 12, the five-day blackout was lifted, and Spezi was finally allowed to meet with his lawyers. On that day, his case would be reviewed by the examining magistrate, Marina De Robertis, in the Italian equivalent of a habeas corpus hearing. Its purpose was to determine if Spezi's arrest and incarceration were justified.

On that day, for the hearing, Spezi was for the first time given a change of clothes, a bar of soap, and a chance to shave and take a bath. The public minister, Guiliano Mignini, appeared before Judge De Robertis to argue why Spezi was a danger to society.

"The journalist," Mignini wrote in his brief,

"accused of obstructing the investigation of the Monster of Florence is at the center of a genuine disinformation campaign, not unlike that which might be undertaken by a deviant secret service." This disinformation operation, Mignini explained, was an attempt to derail the investigation into the "group of notable people" who had been the masterminds behind the killings of the Monster of Florence. Among these notables was Narducci, who had hired and directed Pacciani and his picnicking friends to kill young lovers and take their body parts. Spezi and his fellow criminal masterminds had a strategy: to keep the blame for the Monster of Florence murders restricted to Pacciani and his picnicking friends. When that strategy failed, and the investigation began to strike closer to home—with the reopening of Narducci's death—Spezi had desperately tried to redirect the investigation back to the Sardinian Trail, because "in that case there wouldn't be even the minimum danger that the investigation might touch the world of the notables and the masterminds."

The statement included not a shred of solid forensic evidence—just a cockamamie conspiracy theory spun out to fantastic lengths.

Dietrologia at its purest.

At the hearing, Spezi protested the conditions in which he was being held. He insisted he was merely conducting legitimate research as a journalist, not running a "disinformation campaign of a deviant secret service."

Judge Marina De Robertis looked at Spezi and asked a single question: the only question she would ask during the entire hearing.

"Have you ever belonged to a satanic sect?"

At first Spezi wasn't sure he had heard correctly. His lawyer nudged him in the side and hissed, "Don't laugh!"

A simple no to the question seemed insufficient. Dryly, Spezi said, "The only order I'm a member of is the Order of Journalists."

With that, the hearing was over.

The judge took four leisurely days making up her mind. On Saturday, Spezi met with his lawyer to hear the verdict.

"I have good news and bad news," said Traversi. "Which do you want to hear first?"

"The bad news."

Judge De Robertis had ruled he must remain in preventive detention, because of the danger he posed to society.

"And the good news?"

Traversi had seen, in the window of a book-store in Florence, a bunch of copies of *Dolci Colline di Sangue* for sale.The book was finally out.

CHAPTER
54

Meanwhile, Chief Inspector Giuttari forged ahead with the investigation, "toscano" cigar clamped between his determined teeth. For some time, the lack of a second body in the so-called Narducci murder had been an embarrassment, two corpses being necessary to make the double switch with Narducci's. Giuttari finally found a suitable body in that of a South American, bashed on the head, which had been left unclaimed in the morgue of Perugia since 1982, kept under refrigeration. The man seemed, at least to some, to resemble the dead body of Narducci in the photograph taken on the dock after he had been fished out of the water. After

Narducci had been murdered, the body of this previously dead South American had been stolen from the morgue and dumped in the lake in its stead, Narducci's body had been hidden, perhaps in the morgue, perhaps somewhere else. Then, many years later, when the exhumation of Narducci looked imminent, the bodies were switched again, Narducci's being put back in his coffin and the South American's spirited away and parked back in the refrigerator.

With Spezi in prison, Giuttari spoke to *La Nazione* about the excellent progress he was making in the Narducci case: "Yes, we're working on the death of this man which occurred in '82, and there are elements that are quite interesting and which may lead us to something concrete. . . . I believe that it is now beyond doubt that the body recovered from Lake Trasimeno was not Narducci's. . . . And now, in light of these new facts, the situation may become clearer." But something must have gone wrong with this particular theory, since the dead South American was never mentioned by Giuttari again and the facts surrounding the alleged double body switch remained—and still remain—as murky as ever.

Spezi's lawyers began working to obtain a

hearing before the Tribunal of Reexamination, an appeals court for those ordered imprisoned before trial, similar to a bail hearing in the United States, to determine whether there were grounds to hold Spezi in "preventive detention" until the time of his trial, or to release him under house arrest or other conditions. Italian law has no provisions for monetary bail, and the judgment is made on the basis of how dangerous the accused is and whether there is a likelihood he will flee the country.

A date was set for Spezi's hearing: April 28. The review would take place before three other judges from Perugia, close colleagues of the public minister and of the examining magistrate. The Tribunal of Reexamination was not known for reversing its colleagues, especially in a highly visible case like this one, on which the public minister had placed all his credibility as a prosecutor.

On April 18, twelve days after Spezi's arrest, the Committee to Protect Journalists had finished its investigation into Spezi's case. The next day, Ann Cooper, the executive director, faxed a letter to the prime minister of Italy. It said, in part:

Journalists should not be fearful to conduct their own investigations into sensitive matters or to speak openly and criticize officials. In a democratic country such as your own, one that is an integral part of the European Union, such fear is unacceptable. We call on you to make sure that Italian authorities clarify the serious charges against our colleague Mario Spezi and make public all available evidence supporting those charges, or release him immediately.

The persecution of Mario Spezi and his U.S. colleague Douglas Preston, who is afraid to travel to Italy for fear of prosecution, sends a dangerous message to Italian journalists that sensitive stories such as the Tuscany killings should be avoided. Government efforts to promote this climate of self-censorship are anathema to democracy.

Copies of the letter went to Public Minister Mignini, the U.S. ambassador to Italy, the Italian ambassador to the United States, Amnesty International, Freedom Forum, Human Rights Watch, and a dozen other international organizations.

This letter, along with protests from other international organizations, including Reporters sans Frontières in Paris, seemed to turn the tide in Italy. The Italian press found its courage— with a vengeance.

"The Jailing of Spezi Is an Infamy," cried an editorial in *Libero*, written by the vice director of the magazine. *Corriere della Sera* ran a major editorial on the front page entitled "Justice without Evidence," calling Spezi's arrest a "monstrosity." The Italian press finally took up the question of what Spezi's arrest meant for freedom of the press and Italy's international image. A flood of articles followed. Spezi's colleagues at *La Nazione* signed an appeal, and the paper issued a statement. Many journalists began to recognize that Spezi's arrest was an attack on a journalist for the "crime" of disagreeing with an official investigation—in other words, the criminalization of journalism itself. Protests mounted in Italy from press organizations and newspapers. A group of eminent journalists and writers signed an appeal, which said in part, "Frankly, we did not think that in Italy the strenuous search for the truth could be misunderstood as illegally favoring and assisting the guilty."

"The case of Spezi and Preston casts a heavy

weight on the international image of our country," the president of Italy's Information Safety and Freedom organization told the *Guardian* newspaper of London, "and risks relegating us to the bottom of any list defining press freedom and democracy."

I was besieged with calls from the Italian press and I gave a number of interviews. My lawyer in Italy was not pleased to see me quoted so liberally. She had had a meeting with the public minister of Perugia, Giuliano Mignini, to discuss my case and to try to find out what the charges were against me, which had been sealed, naturally, in *segreto istruttorio*. She wrote me a letter saying that she sensed a "certain disapproval" from the public minister of statements I had made to the press after my interrogation. She added, dryly, "The Public Minister must not have welcomed the raising of the issue to the international diplomatic level. . . . It is not helpful to your case to make personal statements against the Public Minister . . . and it would be opportune that, after having reexamined some of the statements made by you at that time (which must have had a negative impact on Dr. Mignini), you would mitigate their effects by distancing yourself from them."

She confirmed that the charges against me were for making false statements to the public minister, for the crime of "calumny" in attempting to frame an innocent person for a crime, defamation by means of the press, and interference with an essential public service. I was not being charged, as I had feared, with being an accessory to the murder of Narducci.

I wrote back, saying that I was sorry that I could not distance myself from the statements I had made, and that there was nothing I could do to mitigate the discomfort Mignini might be feeling about the case being raised to the "international diplomatic level."

In the midst of this, I received another long e-mail from Gabriella Carlizzi, who had, it seemed, been one of the very first purchasers of our book, *Dolci Colline di Sangue*.

Here I am, dear Douglas. . . . Yesterday evening I came back from Perugia very late, in this last week I have been to the magistrate's office three times, because you know, since Mario Spezi has been imprisoned, many people who were living for years in terror have contacted me, and each one has wanted to tell of his experiences with Mario's actions. . . .

You might ask: why did these people not speak before?

For fear of Mario Spezi and those they suspect, very strongly, of having an interest in "covering up for him."

And so we turn to you.

As I have been deposed in these recent days, it has given me the opportunity to make it understood to Dr. Mignini how you couldn't possibly be involved, and I repeat to you Douglas, as far as you are concerned the magistrate is convinced and serene. . . .

Meanwhile I renew my invitation for you to come to Italy, and you will see that all will become cleared up with the magistrate, who if you wish you can meet even in Perugia, you and your lawyer, I hope different from Spezi's lawyers, and you will be completely absolved of any accusations.

I read the book, *Dolci Colline di Sangue*: I say to you right away that it would have been much better had your name not been on that book. The book has been obtained by the prosecutor's office and I think there will be judicial consequences. . . . Unfortunately, Douglas, you signed the contents of this book. This is a very serious business, that has nothing to do with the work of Mignini, but is by now under the eye of the Criminal Justice System, and it risks blemishing your career as a writer. . . . Spezi, leaning on the prestige of your name, has involved you in a situation that if you come to Italy, I will help you mitigate your responsibility, and I repeat, it is urgent that we see each other, believe me. . . . On this book, *porca miseria*, there is your name! Excuse me but it makes me furious when I think of the diabolicalness of this Spezi. . . .

I await your news and I warmly embrace you and your family.

Gabriella

One other thing: Since I think it is right that *The New Yorker* should also "dissociate" itself from Spezi and his actions, if you wish, I can explain certain things in an interview, getting you out of the situation into which Spezi has pulled you, that is to say I can demonstrate to the American press your lack of involvement in the "fraud."

I read the e-mail with disbelief, and finally, for the first time in weeks, I found myself laughing

at the absurdity of it all. Could any novelist, even a writer with the *coglioni* of, say, Norman Mailer, have dared invent a character like this woman? I think not.

April 28, the day of Spezi's appearance before the Tribunal of Reexamination, approached. I spoke to Myriam on April 27. She was extremely fearful of what might happen at the hearing, and she told me Spezi's lawyers shared her pessimism. If the judges kept Spezi in preventive detention, he would remain in prison for at least another three months before the next judicial review could take place, and a reversal of his imprisonment would be even more unlikely. The Italian judicial system moves at a glacial pace; the ugly truth was that Spezi could remain in prison for years before his case finally came to trial.

Spezi's lawyers had learned that Mignini was preparing a full-court press at the hearing to make absolutely sure Spezi wasn't released. This had become the most visible case the public minister had undertaken in his career. The criticism of him in the national and worldwide press had been scorching and was rising daily. His reputation depended on winning this hearing.

I called Niccolò and asked if he had any predictions on what Mario's fate would be. He was guarded and pessimistic. "Judges in Italy protect their own" was all he would say.

CHAPTER
55

On the appointed day, April 28, 2006, a van arrived at Capanne prison to take Spezi and the other prisoners with hearings that day to the Tribunale of Perugia. Spezi's guards brought him out and he was herded into a cage in the back of the van with the others.

The Tribunale, one of the famous edifices in the medieval heart of Perugia, rises from Piazza Matteotti like an airy Gothic castle of white marble. It is listed in the guidebooks and admired by thousands of tourists every year. Designed by two famous Renaissance architects, it was built on the foundations of a twelfth-century wall that once surrounded Perugia, itself laid upon a three-thousand-year-old Etruscan foundation of massive stone blocks that had once been part of the wall enclosing the ancient city of Perusia. Above the building's grand entrance stands a statue of a woman in robes, sword clasped in her hands, beaming an enigmatic smile at all who enter; the inscription below identifies her as IUSTITIAE VIRTUTUM DOMINA, Ruler of the Virtue of Justice. She is flanked by two griffins, symbols of Perugia, grasping in their claws a calf and a sheep.

The van parked in the piazza outside the Tribunale, where a crowd of journalists and television reporters awaited Spezi's arrival. Because of them, tourists began to gather, curious to see the infamous criminal who merited such attention.

The other prisoners were taken out, one by one, for their hearings. The hearing for each prisoner lasted twenty to forty minutes. They were closed to everyone: journalists, the public, even spouses. Myriam had arrived in Perugia by car and had seated herself on a wooden bench in the corridor outside the courtroom, awaiting news.

At ten-thirty, Spezi's turn came. He was taken out of the cage and brought up to the courtroom.

He had a chance to smile at Myriam from a distance as he was led in, giving her a thumbs-up for courage.

The three judges sat behind the long table. They were three women, wearing traditional robes. Spezi was seated in the middle of the room, before the judges, in a hard wooden chair with no arms or table in front. At a table to his right sat the public minister, Mignini, and his assistants; to the left, Spezi's lawyers, of which he now had four.

Instead of taking twenty to forty minutes, the hearing would last seven and a half hours.

Later, Spezi would write about the hearing, "I don't have a complete memory of all seven and a half hours, only snippets. . . . I remember the passionate words of my lawyer, Nino Filastò, one who knew like no one else the entire history of the Monster of Florence case and the monstrousness of the investigations, a man who possessed a fiery sense of righteousness. I remember the red face of Mignini, bending over his papers, while the voice of Nino thundered. I remember the wide eyes of the young court reporter, perhaps stunned by the ardor of a lawyer who did not care to bandy about euphemisms. I heard Filastò mention the name of Carlizzi. . . . I heard Mignini say that I denied being involved in the murder of Narducci and in the Monster of Florence case, but little did I know that he, Mignini, had in his possession 'extremely delicate and sensitive material' that proved my guilt. I heard Mignini shouting ... that in my house they had found 'hidden behind a door, a satanic stone that the accused persists in calling a doorstop.'"

Spezi remembered Mignini pointing a shaking finger at him and railing about "the inexplicable rancor that Spezi has demonstrated toward the investigation." But most of all he remembered Mignini speaking of the "extremely dangerous manipulation of information and the mass-media chorus that the subject succeeded in raising" against his arrest. He remembered Mignini shouting, "The accusations brought before this Tribunal today are only the tip of an iceberg of horrifying dimensions."

What surprised Spezi most of all was the many parallels between Mignini's arguments before the Tribunal and the accusations made by Gabriella Carlizzi on her conspiracy website months before. Sometimes even the wordings were similar, if not identical.

The three judges in robes listened impassively, taking notes.

After a break for lunch, the hearing resumed. At one point Mignini rose and went into the corridor. And there, outside the courtroom, Myriam had been waiting. When she saw the public minister walking alone in the corridor, she rose in a fury and, like an avenging angel, pointed an accusing finger at the man. "I know you are a believer," she cried out in a voice full of fire. "God will punish you for what you have done. *God will punish you!*"

Mignini's face flushed a deep red, and without saying a word he walked stiffly down the corridor and disappeared around a corner.

Later, Myriam said to her husband that she couldn't be silent when "I heard Mignini shouting inside the courtroom, saying terrible things about you, that you were a criminal."

When Mignini returned to the courtroom, he resumed his brief, and it began to sound more like an inquisition than a judicial proceeding. He spoke of Spezi's "high intelligence, which renders even more dangerous his great criminal capacity." He concluded his speech with "The reasons for Spezi to remain in prison have become even more urgent. Because he has now demonstrated his enormous dangerousness by succeeding, even when locked up in a prison cell, in organizing a mass-media campaign in his favor!"

Spezi remembered that moment. "A pen fell from the hand of the president of the Tribunal and made a little *click* on the table . . . from that moment on, she took no more notes." She had clearly come to some kind of conclusion.

At the end, after everyone else had spoken, it was Spezi's turn.

I had long admired Spezi's abilities as a public speaker—his witty turn of phrase, his light and impromptu delivery, the logical organization of his information, the facts presented one after another like the paragraphs of a perfectly written news story, neat, concise, and clear. Now he turned those considerable gifts on the court. Facing Mignini directly, Spezi began to speak. Mignini refused to meet his eyes. Those who were there said he demolished Mignini's accusations, one after another, with an edge of quiet contempt in his voice, bulldozing his rickety conspiracy logic and pointing out that Mignini lacked any physical evidence at all to back up his theories.

As he spoke, Spezi told me later, he could see his words were having a visible effect on the judges.

Spezi thanked the public minister for praising his intelligence and memory, and he pointed out, word for word, the phrases in Mignini's brief that were identical to those posted, months before, by Gabriella Carlizzi on her website. He asked if Mignini could explain this singular coincidence between his words now and her words then. He asked if it was not a fact that Carlizzi had already been convicted of defamation, having written ten years before that the writer Alberto Bevilacqua was the Monster of Florence? And was it not also a fact that this same Carlizzi was currently on trial for fraud against incapacitated persons?

Then Spezi turned to the president of the Tribunal. "I am only a journalist who tries his best to do what is right in his work, and I am a good person."

He was finished.

The hearing was over. Two guards in the courtroom escorted Spezi down the elevators, into the ancient basements of the medieval palace, where they locked him in a tiny, barren cell that had probably been holding prisoners for centuries. He leaned his back against the stone wall and slid to the ground, utterly exhausted, his mind empty.

After a while, he heard a sound and opened his eyes. It was one of his guards, standing with a cup of hot espresso that he had purchased with his own money. "Spezi, take it. You look like you need it."

CHAPTER
56

That night they loaded Mario Spezi into the van and carried him back to his cell in Capanne prison. The next day was Saturday, and the Tribunal closed at one o'clock. The judges would issue their decision before that time.

That Saturday, as one o'clock neared, Spezi waited in his cell. His fellow prisoners in his cellblock—who had come to know him even if they couldn't see him—were also waiting to hear the verdict. One o'clock passed, and then one-thirty. As two o'clock neared, Spezi began to resign himself to the fact that the verdict had gone against him. And then a cheer went up among his fellow prisoners at the far end of the row of cells. Someone had heard something on an unseen television blaring somewhere. "Uncle! You're free! Uncle! You can go! Uncle, they've let you go without conditions!"

Myriam, waiting in a café for the news, received a call from a colleague of Mario's at the paper. "Fantastic news! Congratulations! We won! Won! On every single point!"

"After twenty-three days in prison," RAI, the national television station of Italy reported, "journalist Mario Spezi, accused of obstruction of justice in the serial killings of Florence, has been set free. Such is the decision of the Tribunal of Reexamination." The three judges hadn't even attached conditions to his release, as was normal—no house arrest, no passport confiscation. He was absolutely and unconditionally freed.

It was an enormous rebuke to the public minister of Perugia.

A guard came to Spezi's cell holding a big black garbage bag. "Hurry up. Put all your stuff in here. Let's go."

Spezi threw it all in and turned to leave, to find the door blocked by the guard. One more indignity remained. "Before you leave," the guard said, "you have to clean your cell."

Spezi thought he must be kidding. "I never asked to come here," he said, "and I was put here illegally. If you want it clean, clean it yourself."

The guard narrowed his eyes, yanked the metal door from Spezi's hands, and slammed it shut. He turned the key and said, "If you like it so much, go ahead and stay!" He began to walk off.

Spezi could hardly believe it. He seized the bars. "Listen, you cretin. I know your name, and if you don't let me out immediately, I'll denounce you for false imprisonment. You understand? I'll report you."

The guard paused, took a few more steps toward his post, then turned slowly and came back, as if graciously conceding the point, and unlocked the door. Spezi was passed off to another stone-faced guard, who escorted him to a waiting room.

"Why aren't you letting me out?" Spezi asked.

"There's some paperwork. And . . ." The guard hesitated. "Then there's the problem of keeping public order outside."

Spezi finally emerged from Capanne prison,

holding the big black garbage bag, and was greeted by a roar from the waiting crowd of journalists and onlookers.

Niccolò was the first to call me. "Extraordinary news!" he cried. "Spezi is free!"

CHAPTER
57

Spezi and I had a long conversation that day, and he said he was going off with Myriam to the sea, just the two of them. But only for a few days. "Mignini," he said, "is hauling me back to Perugia for another interrogation. On May 4."

"About what?" I asked, aghast.

"He's preparing new charges against me."

Mignini had not even waited for the written opinion of the Tribunal of Reexamination to be issued. He had appealed Spezi's release to the Supreme Court.

I asked a question I had been wanting to ask for weeks. "Why did Ruocco do it? Why did he make up that story about the iron boxes?"

"Ruocco really knew Antonio Vinci," he said. "He said it was Ignazio who told him about the iron boxes. Ignazio is a kind of *padrino* to the Sardinians . . . I haven't spoken to Ruocco since our arrest, so I don't know if it was Ruocco who made up the story, or if Ignazio was involved in some way. Ruocco might have done it for money—from time to time I gave him a few euros to cover his expenses, buy gas for his car. But it never amounted to much. And he paid a heavy price—he was jailed too as my 'accomplice.' Who knows? Maybe the story is true."

"Why the Villa Bibbiani?"

"Sheer chance, perhaps. Or perhaps the Sardinians really did use the old farmhouses at some time."

Spezi called me on May 4, immediately after the interrogation. To my great surprise, he was in an expansive mood. "Doug," he said, cackling with laughter, "the interrogation was beautiful, just beautiful. It was one of the finest little moments of my life."

"Tell me."

"That morning," Spezi said, "my lawyer picked me up in his car and we stopped by the newsstand for the paper. I could hardly believe my eyes when I saw the headline. I have it here. I'll read it to you."

There was a dramatic pause.

"'Chief of GIDES Giuttari Indicted for Falsifying Evidence.' *Bello*, eh?"

I laughed gleefully. "*Fantastico*! What did he do?"

"It had nothing to do with me. They say he doctored a tape recording of a conversation with some other person in the Monster case— an important person, a judge. But that's not even the best part. I folded the newspaper so that the headline was displayed and carried it into Mignini's office for the interrogation. When I sat down, I placed the paper on my knees, so that the headline was turned toward Mignini."

"What did he do when he saw it?"

"He never saw it! Mignini never once looked at me, he kept his eyes averted the whole time. The interrogation didn't last long—I invoked my right not to answer questions and that was it. Five minutes. The funny thing was, the *stenographer* did see the headline. I watched the man as he arched his neck like a turtle to read it, and then the poor fellow tried frantically to signal Mignini's attention! No luck. Not a second after I left the office, when I was still in the hall, the door to Mignini's office flew open and a carabinieri officer went hurtling down the stairs toward the door, without a doubt heading to the nearest newsstand." He laughed wickedly. "Apparently, Mignini hadn't read the papers that morning! He knew nothing about it!"

Back outside the public minister's office, following the brief interrogation, a crowd of journalists awaited. While the cameras whirred and clicked, Spezi held up the paper and opened it to the headline. "This is all the comment I need to make today."

"Is it not as I said?" Count Niccolò told me the next day. "Giuttari is taking the fall. With your campaign, you have *sputtanato* [cast aspersions on] the Italian judiciary in front of the whole world, with the risk of making them an international laughingstock. They don't give a damn about Spezi and his rights. They just wanted to get it over with as quickly as possible. All they care about is preserving face. *La faccia, la faccia*! The only surprise to me is that it happened a great deal sooner than I expected. My dear Douglas, this is the beginning of the end for Giuttari. How swiftly does the pendulum swing!"

That very same day, our book, *Dolci Colline di Sangue*, hit best-seller lists in Italy.

The pendulum indeed had swung in our direction, and it swung hard. The Supreme Court of Italy summarily rejected Mignini's appeal with a curt opinion that it was "inadmissible," and dismissed all the proceedings against Spezi. There would be no trial and no more investigations of him. "An enormous load has been lifted," Spezi said. "I am a free man."

A few months later, Giuttari's and Mignini's offices were raided by the police, who carried away boxes of files. They discovered that Mignini had been invoking a special antiterrorist law to order wiretaps of journalists who had written critically about his Monster of Florence investigation—wiretaps carried out by Giuttari and GIDES. In addition to wiretapping journalists, Giuttari had also been taping telephone calls and conversations with a number of Florentine judges and investigators, including his counterpart in Florence, the public minister Paolo Canessa. It seemed that Mignini suspected them of being part of a vast Florentine conspiracy working against his investigation into the masterminds behind the Monster killings.

In the summer of 2006, both Giuttari and Mignini were indicted for abuse of office. GIDES was disbanded, and questions were immediately raised that indicated it had never been officially authorized in the first place. Giuttari lost his staff and the Monster of Florence case was taken away from him. He became a chief inspector *a dispozione*, that is, with no portfolio and no permanent assignment.

Mignini so far has retained his position of public minister of Perugia, but two more prosecutors were added to his staff, allegedly to help him with his workload; their real assignment, everyone knew, was to keep him out of trouble. Both Mignini and Giuttari will have to stand trial for abuse of office and other crimes.

On November 3, 2006, Spezi was awarded the most coveted journalistic prize in Italy for *Dolci Colline di Sangue* and named Writer of the Year for Freedom of the Press.

CHAPTER
58

The article in the *Atlantic Monthly* was published in July. A few weeks later the magazine received a letter on old-fashioned stationery, hand-typed on a manual typewriter. It was an extraordinary letter, written by Niccolò's father, Count Neri Capponi, the head of one of Italy's most ancient and illustrious noble families.

When I first met Niccolò, he had mentioned the reason for his family's long success in Florence: they had never thrust themselves into controversy, remained discreet and circumspect in all their dealings, and never tried to be first. For eight hundred years the Capponi family had prospered by avoiding being "the nail that sticks out," as Niccolò had put it in his drafty palace seven years earlier.

But now, Count Neri had broken with family tradition. He had written a letter to the editor. This was no ordinary letter, but a ripping indictment of the Italian criminal justice system from a man who was himself a judge and a lawyer. Count Neri knew whereof he spoke, and he spoke plainly.

THE
COUNT CAPPONI

Sir

The travesty of justice undergone by Douglas Preston and Mario Spezi is the tip of the iceberg. The Italian judiciary (which includes the public prosecutors) is a branch of the civil service. This particular branch chooses its members, is self ruling and is accountable to no one: a state within a state! This body of bureaucrats can be roughly divided into three sections: a large minority, corrupt and affiliated with the former communist party, a large section of honest people who are too frightened to stand up to the political minority (who controls the office of the judiciary), and a minority of brave and honest men with little influence. Political and dishonest judges have an infallible method of silencing or discrediting opponents, political or otherwise. A bogus, secret indictment, the tapping of telephones, the conversations (often doctored) fed to the press who starts a smear campaign which raises the sales, a spectacular arrest, prolonged preventive detention under the worst possible conditions, third degree interrogations, and finally a trial that lasts many years ending in the acquittal of a ruined man. Spezi was lucky because the powerful Florentine public prosecutor is no friend of the Perugia one and, I am told, "suggested" that Spezi be freed: the Perugia court, I am told, accepted the "suggestion".

It may be of interest to know that miscarriages of justice in Italy (excluding acquittals with a ruined defendant) amount to four million and a half in fifty years.

Yours
sincerely,
Neri Capponi

P.S. If possible I would ask you to withhold my signature or reduce it to initials because I fear reprisals on myself and my family. If withholding my signature is not possible, then go ahead, God will look after me! The truth must out.

The *Atlantic* printed the letter, with his name.

The British newspaper the *Guardian* also ran an article on the case and interviewed Chief Inspector Giuttari. He said I had lied when I claimed to have been threatened with arrest if I returned to Italy, and he insisted that Spezi and I were still guilty of planting false evidence at the villa. "Preston did not tell the truth," he said. "Our recordings will prove this. Spezi," he insisted, "will be prosecuted."

The *Atlantic* article attracted the attention of a producer at *Dateline NBC*, who asked Mario and me to participate in a program on the Monster of Florence. I returned to Italy in September 2006 with some trepidation, traveling with the *Dateline NBC* film crew. My Italian lawyer had informed me that given Giuttari's and Mignini's legal troubles, it was probably safe to return, and NBC promised to raise hell if I were arrested at the airport. Just in case, an NBC television crew met me at the airport ready to capture my arrest on tape. I was glad to deprive them of that scoop.

Spezi and I took Stone Phillips, the show's anchor, to the scenes of the crimes, where we were filmed discussing the murders and our own brush with Italian law. Stone Phillips interviewed Giuttari, who continued to insist that Spezi and I had planted evidence at the villa. He also criticized our book. "Evidently, Mr. Preston did not do the least bit of fact-checking ... In 1983, when the two young Germans were killed, this person [Antonio Vinci] was in prison for another crime unrelated to the monster crimes." Phillips managed a brief interview with Antonio Vinci, off camera. Vinci confirmed what Giuttari said, that he had been in prison during one of the Monster's killings. Perhaps Giuttari and Vinci didn't expect NBC to check the facts. In the show, Stone Phillips said, "We later checked his record and found that [Antonio] had never been in jail during any of the Monster killings. He and Giuttari were either mistaken or lying about that."

Vinci was far more incensed about being accused of impotence than of being the Monster of Florence. "If Spezi's wife were younger and prettier," he told Phillips, "I'd show them who isn't impotent—I'd show you right here, right now, on this table."

At the very end of the program, Phillips asked Antonio Vinci a question: "Are you the Monster of Florence?"

"He locked eyes," said Phillips, "gripped my hand, and said one word. *Innocente.*"

CHAPTER
59

While filming with *Dateline NBC*, Spezi and I
had one experience in Italy that never made it
on camera. Stone Phillips wanted to interview
Winnie Rontini, the mother of Pia Rontini, one of
the Monster's victims, murdered at La Boschetta
near Vicchio on June 29, 1984. While the crew
waited by the parked vans in the town square,
in the shadow of the statue of Giotto, Spezi and
I walked down the street to the old Rontini villa
to see if she was willing to be interviewed.

We gazed at the house in silent dismay. The rusty
iron gate hung from a single hinge. Skeletonized
shrubbery in the garden rattled in the wind, and
dead leaves had piled up in the corners. The shut-

ters were closed, the slats broken and hanging. A half dozen crows lined the roof peak, like so many black rags.

Mario punched the gate buzzer but no sound came. It was dead. We looked at each other.

"It doesn't look like anyone lives here," Mario said.

"Let's knock on the door."

We pushed open the broken gate with a groan of rust and stepped into the dead garden, our footfalls crunching dried leaves and twigs. The door to the villa was locked tight, its green paint cracked and peeling up in tiny rolls, the wood underneath splitting. The house buzzer was gone, leaving a hole with a frayed wire sticking out.

"Signora Rontini?" Mario called out. "Is anybody home?"

The wind whispered and chuckled about the deserted house. Mario pounded on the door, the sound of his blows echoing, in a muffled way, through the empty rooms within. With a flapping of wings, the birds took off, rising into the sky, their irritated cries like fingernails on a blackboard.

We stood in the garden, looking up at the abandoned house. The crows circled above, cawing and cawing. Mario shook his head. "In town they'll know what happened to her."

In the piazza, a man told us the bank had finally foreclosed on the house and Signora Rontini now lived on public assistance in housing for indigents near the lake. He gave us the address.

With a feeling of dread we searched for the housing project, finding it tucked behind the local Casa del Popolo. It was unlike anything an American might imagine as public housing, a cheerful building, stuccoed a pale cream, neat as a pin, with flowers on the windowsills and pretty views of the lake. We walked around to the back and knocked on the door to her apartment. She met us and showed us in, offering us seats in a tiny kitchen-dining area. Her apartment was the reverse of the dark, cadaverous house; bright and cheerful, it was filled with plants, knickknacks, and photographs. The sun streamed in the windows and warblers chirped and flitted about in the sycamore trees outside. The room smelled of fresh laundry and soap.

"No," she said with a sad smile in response to our question, "I won't be interviewed again. Never again." She was dressed in a sparkling yellow dress, her dyed red hair carefully coiffed, her voice mild.

"We still hope to find the truth," said Mario. "One never knows ... this could help."

"I know it might help. But I'm not interested in the truth anymore. What difference will it make? It won't bring Pia or Claudio back. For a long time I thought knowing the truth would somehow make everything better. My husband died searching for the truth. But now I know it doesn't matter and that it won't help me. I had to let it go."

She fell silent, her small, plump hands folded in her lap, her ankles crossed, a faint smile hovering about her face.

We chatted some more and she told us matter-of-factly how she had lost the house and all she owned to bankruptcy. Mario asked her about some of the photographs on the walls. She rose and plucked one off, passing it to Mario, who then passed it to me. "That was the last photograph taken of Pia," she said. "It was for her driver's license a few months before." She moved on to the next one. "This is Pia with Claudio." It was a black-and-white photo of them smiling, arms about each other's neck, utterly innocent and happy, she giving a thumbs-up to the camera.

She moved to the far wall. "This is Pia at fifteen. She was a pretty girl, wasn't she?" The hand moved along the wall. "My late husband, Renzo." She unhooked a black-and-white photograph, gazed at it awhile, and handed it to us. We passed it around. It was a portrait of a vigorous, happy man, in the prime of life.

She lifted a hand and gestured toward the photographs, turning her blue eyes on me. "Just the other day," she said, "I walked in here and realized that I was surrounded by the dead." She smiled sadly. "I'm going to take these photographs down and put them away. I don't want to be surrounded by death anymore. I'd forgotten something—that I'm still alive."

We rose. At the door she took Mario's hand. "You're welcome to keep searching for the truth, Mario. I hope you find it. But please don't ask me to help you. I'm going to try to live my last years without that burden—I hope you understand."

"I understand," said Mario.

We walked out into the sunlight, the bees droning in the flowers, the bright sun throwing a shimmering trail on the surface of the lake, the light spilling over the red-tiled roofs of Vicchio and flinging streamers of gold through the vineyards and olive groves beyond the town.

The *vendemmia*, the grape harvest, was in progress, the fields full of people and carts. The air carried up from the vineyards the perfume of bruised grapes and fermenting must.

Another flawless afternoon in the immortal hills of Tuscany.

CHAPTER
60

The trial of Francesco Calamandrei, for being one of the instigators behind the Monster killings, began on September 27, 2007.

Mario Spezi attended the first day of the trial, and he sent me a report by e-mail a few days later. This is what he wrote:

The morning of September 27 dawned unexpectedly cold after a month of dry heat. The real news that morning was the absence of spectators at the trial of a man alleged to be a mastermind behind the Monster. In the courtroom, where more than ten years before Pacciani had first been convicted and then acquitted, nobody was seated in the space reserved for the public. Only the benches reserved for journalists were occupied. I had trouble understanding the indifference of Florentines toward a person who, according to the accusation, was almost the very incarnation of Evil. Skepticism, incredulity, or disbelief of the official version must have kept spectators away.

The accused entered the courtroom taking hesitant little steps. He looked meek, even resigned, his dark eyes lost in unknowable thoughts, carrying with him the air of a retired gentleman, wearing an elegant blue overcoat and gray fedora, his obese body swelled with unhappiness and psychopharmacological drugs. He was half-supported by his lawyer, Gabriele Zanobini, and his daughter Francesca. The pharmacist of San Casciano, Francesco Calamandrei, seated himself on the front bench, indifferent to the flashes of the news photographers and the television cameras that swung his way.

A journalist asked him how he felt. He answered: "Like someone who has fallen into a film, knowing nothing of the plot or characters."

The prosecutor's office of Florence had

accused Calamandrei of masterminding five of the Monster's killings. They claim he paid Pacciani, Lotti, and Vanni to commit the crimes and take away the sex organs of the female victims so that he could use them for horrendous, but unspecified, esoteric rites. He stands accused of actually participating in the killings of the two French tourists at the Scopeti clearing in 1985. He is also charged with having ordered the killings in Vicchio in 1984, those of September 1983 in which the two Germans were killed, and those of June 1982 in Montespertoli. The prosecution is silent on the vexing question of who might have committed the other Monster killings.

The evidence against Calamandrei is risible. It consists of the delirious ravings of his schizophrenic wife, so desperately ill that her doctors have forbidden her to give testimony in the courtroom, and the same "coarse and habitual liars" known as Alpha, Beta, Gamma, and Delta, who testified against Pacciani and his picnicking friends ten years before. Notably, all four of these algebraic witnesses are now dead. Only the serial witness Lorenzo Nesi remains alive, ready to remember whatever might be required.

Also arrayed against Calamandrei is a mountain of paper: twenty-eight thousand pages of the trial against Pacciani; nineteen thousand pages of the investigation of his picnicking friends; and nine thousand pages collected on Calamandrei himself: fifty-five thousand pages in all, more than the Bible, *Das Kapital* of Marx, Kant's *Critique of Pure Reason*, the *Iliad*, the *Odyssey*, and *Don Quixote* all put together.

In front of the accused, mounted high behind an imposing bar, was seated Judge De Luca in the place of the usual two magistrates and the nine members of the popular jury who comprise the Court of Assizes, the Tribunal reserved for judging the most serious crimes. In a surprise move, Calamandrei's lawyer had asked for a so-called abbreviated trial, usually only requested by those who have admitted guilt in order to obtain a reduced sentence. Zanobini and Calamandrei asked for it for another reason entirely: "In order that the trial be conducted as rapidly as possible," Zanobini said, "seeing that we have nothing to fear from the result."

To the left of the pharmacist, on another bench in the front row, sat the public minister of Florence, Paolo Canessa, with another prosecutor. The two smiled and joked in low voices, perhaps to give an outward show of confidence, or perhaps to needle the defense.

Before the end of the day, Zanobini would wipe the smiles off their faces.

Zanobini launched into his case with fire, pointing out a technical but very embarrassing legal oversight by Canessa. He then attacked the Perugian branch of the Monster investigation, conducted by Public Minister Mignini, which had linked Calamandrei to the death of Narducci. "Almost all the results of the Perugian investigation are like so much wastepaper," he said. "Allow me to give you an example." He raised a sheaf of papers, which he said constituted a statement taken by Public Minister Mignini and kept under seal until now. "How is it possible that a magistrate would take seriously and believe a document like the one I will read to you now?"

As Zanobini began to read, the cameras swung from Calamandrei to . . . me. I couldn't believe it, Doug, but I was the star of the document! This document was the so-called spontaneous statement of a woman who had been in contact with Gabriella Carlizzi. She repeated many of Carlizzi's theories to Judge Mignini, claiming she had heard them years ago from a long-deceased Sardinian aunt who knew all the people involved. Mignini had it all written down, recorded, sworn, and signed. Despite the clear absurdity and lack of proof of the woman's allegations, Judge Mignini had then slapped a seal of secrecy on the document, "given the gravity and sensitivity" of the accusations.

As Zanobini read the document in the gray courtroom of the Tribunale, I heard, along with everyone else, that I wasn't really the son of my father. My real father—or so this woman claimed in her statement—was a famous musician of sick and perverse habits who had committed the first two killings of 1968; I heard that my mother had conceived me on a Sardinian farm in Tuscany; I heard that upon discovering the truth about my real father, I had carried on his diabolical work as a family tradition, becoming the "real Monster of Florence." This crazy aunt claimed we were all conspiring together: me, the Vinci brothers, Pacciani and his picnicking friends, Narducci, and Calamandrei. From our diabolical association, she told Mignini, "each derives his own benefit: the voyeurs enjoyed their particular activities, the cultists used the anatomical parts taken from the victims for their rites, the fetishists conserved the pieces taken from the victims, and SPEZI, my aunt always told me, mutilated the victims with a tool known as a cobbler's knife. . . . Certain fellow citizens of Villacidro told me, recently, that the writer Douglas Preston, Spezi's friend, is connected to the American Secret Service."

She explained to Mignini, "I hadn't spoken of this up until now because I am afraid of Mario SPEZI and his friends. . . . When Spezi was arrested by you I gathered up my courage and decided to speak about it with Carlizzi, because I trusted her and I knew she sought the truth. . . ."

It was absurd stuff and I had to smile as Zanobini read the statement. But I felt no mirth; I couldn't forget that I had ended up in prison partly because of Carlizzi's black-hearted accusations.

The first day of Calamandrei's trial ended with a clear win for the defense. Judge De Luca fixed the next three trial days for November 27, 28, and 29. Breaks of this length in trials are, unfortunately, the norm in Italy.

That was the end of the e-mail.

I called up Mario. "So I'm in the American Secret Service? Damn."

"It was all reported in the press the next day."

"What are you going to do about these absurd accusations?"

"I've already brought suit against the woman for defamation."

"Mario," I said, "the world is full of crazy people. How is it that in Italy, the statements of such people are taken down by a public minister as serious evidence?"

"Because Mignini and Giuttari will never give up. This is clear evidence they're still out to get me, one way or another."

As of this writing, Calamandrei's trial continues, with an acquittal nearly certain, leaving the old pharmacist to live out what is left of his ruined life—one more victim of the Monster of Florence.

The Monster investigation grinds on with no end in sight. Spezi's complaint against Giuttari for defamation was rejected by the Tribunal. He has heard nothing about his suit against Giuttari and Mignini for damages relating to the wrecking of his car. The Supreme Court ruling in Spezi's favor allowed him to ask for damages for his illegal detention. Spezi asked for compensation in the amount of three hundred thousand euros; the lawyers for the state countered with forty-five hundred euros. Mignini is dragging his heels officially closing the investigation against Spezi, while at the same time claiming that Spezi cannot ask for any damages at all because the investigation is still open.

In November 2007, Mignini became involved in another sensational case, that of the brutal murder of a British student, Meredith Kercher, in Perugia. Mignini quickly ordered the arrest of an American student, Amanda Knox, whom he suspected of involvement in the murder. As of this writing, Knox is in Capanne prison, awaiting the outcome of Mignini's investigation. It appears from press leaks that Mignini is spinning an improbable theory about Knox and two alleged co-conspirators in a dark plan of extreme sex, violence, and rape.

As if on cue, Perugian prosecutors were reported to be looking into a potential satanic sect angle, because the crime had occurred the day before the traditional Italian Day of the Dead. "I will give you ten to one odds," said Niccolò, "that they will eventually drag the Monster of Florence into this." I declined the wager.

Within a week of the murder, Gabriella Carl-izzi had weighed in at her website:

> Meredith Kercher: a brutal murder . . . Perhaps
> connected to the Narducci case and the Monster
> of Florence, to ask Satan for protection in
> exchange for a human sacrifice? For what purpose?
> In the end to save those under investigation in
> the Narducci case who are responsible for his
> homicide.

Giuttari was acquitted for falsifying evidence in the Monster case, but is now serving a suspended sentence after he was convicted of making false statements in an unrelated case.

On January 16, 2008, the first pretrial hearing took place for Giuttari and Mignini, accused of abuse of office and, in Mignini's case, conflict of interest in favor of Giuttari. The public minister of Florence, Luca Turco, shocked the court with his blunt language. The two accused, he said, were "two diametrically different people." Mignini was "on a crusade in thrall to a sort of delirium," a person "ready to go to any extreme defending himself against anyone who criticized his investigation." Giuttari exploited this form of delirium, Turco said, "for his own personal, vindictive interests beyond the bounds of his professional responsibilities."

As Mignini left the courtroom after the hearing, he cried out to the waiting press, "I contest this!"

I remain a *persona indagata* in Italy for a series of crimes that are still, more or less, under judicial seal and secret. Not long ago I received a registered letter from Italy to my little post office in Round Pond, informing me that I had been denounced before the Tribunal of Lecco, a city in the north of Italy, for *diffamazione a mezzo stampa*, defamation through means of the press, a criminal offense. Curiously, the person or persons asking for the state to bring charges against me, and for what article or interview, were omitted from the document. To even know the name of my accuser and the crime I am supposed to have committed, I will have to pay thousands more euros to my Italian lawyer.

The question I am most often asked is this: Will the Monster of Florence ever be found? I once believed fervently that Spezi and I would unmask him. Now I'm not so sure. It may be that truth can disappear from the world completely, forever unrecoverable. History is replete with questions that will never be answered—among them, perhaps, the identity of the Monster of Florence.

As a thriller writer, I know that a crime novel, to be successful, must contain certain elements. There must be a killer who has a comprehensible motive. There must be evidence. There must be a process of discovery that leads, one way or another, to the truth. And all novels, even *Crime and Punishment*, must have an ending.

The fatal mistake that Spezi and I made was in assuming that the Monster of Florence case would follow this pattern. Instead, these were murders without motive, theories without evidence, and a story with no end. The process of discovery has led investigators so far into a wilderness of conspiracy theory that I doubt they will ever find their way out. Without solid physical evidence and reliable witnesses, any hypothesis about the Monster case will remain like a speech by Hercule Poirot at the end of an Agatha Christie novel, a beautiful story awaiting a confession. Only this is not a novel, and there won't be a confession. Without one, the Monster will never be found.

Perhaps it was inevitable that the investigation would end up in a bizarre and futile search for a satanic sect dating back to the Middle Ages. The Monster's crimes were so horrific that a mere man could not possibly have committed them. Satan, in the end, had to be invoked.

After all, this is Italy.

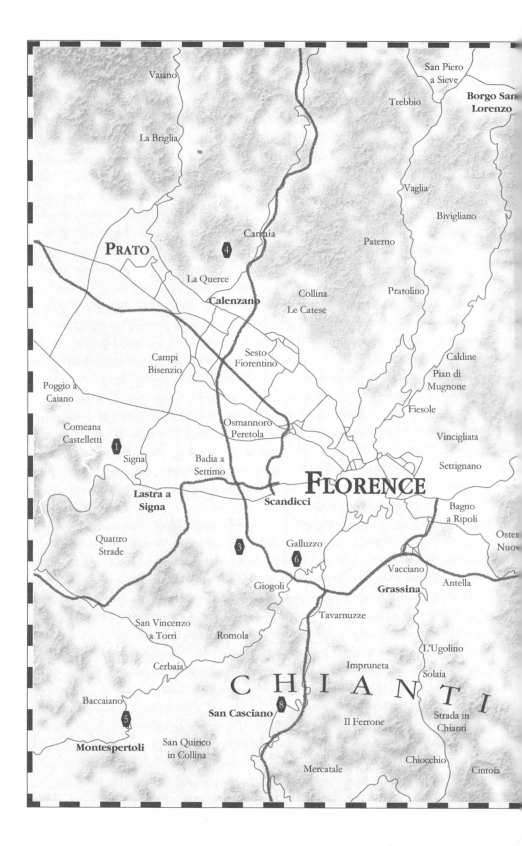